Midwest Studies in Philosophy
Volume XXXVII

MIDWEST STUDIES IN PHILOSOPHY

EDITED BY
PETER A. FRENCH
HOWARD K. WETTSTEIN

ASSISTANT EDITOR:
MEGAN HENRICKS STOTTS (UNIVERSITY OF CALIFORNIA, RIVERSIDE)

EDITORIAL ADVISORY BOARD:
ROBERT AUDI (UNIVERSITY OF NEBRASKA)
PANAYOT BUTCHVAROV (UNIVERSITY OF IOWA)
FRED I. DRETSKE (DUKE UNIVERSITY)
JOHN MARTIN FISCHER (UNIVERSITY OF CALIFORNIA, RIVERSIDE)
GILBERT HARMON (PRINCETON UNIVERSITY)
MICHAEL J. LOUX (UNIVERSITY OF NOTRE DAME)
ALASDAIR MACINTYRE (UNIVERSITY OF NOTRE DAME)
RUTH BARCAN MARCUS (YALE UNIVERSITY)
JOHN R. PERRY (STANFORD UNIVERSITY)
ALVIN PLANTINGA (UNIVERSITY OF NOTRE DAME)
DAVID ROSENTHAL (CITY UNIVERSITY OF NEW YORK GRADUATE CENTER)
STEPHEN SCHIFFER (NEW YORK UNIVERSITY)

Many papers in MIDWEST STUDIES IN PHILOSOPHY are invited and all are previously unpublished. The editors will consider unsolicited manuscripts that are received by January of the year preceding the appearance of a volume. All manuscripts must be pertinent to the topic area of the volume for which they are submitted. Address manuscripts to MIDWEST STUDIES IN PHILOSOPHY, Department of Philosophy, University of California, Riverside, CA 92521.

The articles in MIDWEST STUDIES IN PHILOSOPHY are indexed in THE PHILOSOPHER'S INDEX.

Midwest Studies in Philosophy Volume XXXVII
The New Atheism and Its Critics

Editors

Peter A. French
Arizona State University

Howard K. Wettstein
University of California, Riverside

WILEY PERIODICALS, INC. • BOSTON, MA & OXFORD, UK

Midwest Studies in Philosophy (ISSN 0363-6550 print; ISSN 1475-4975 online) is published annually as a supplement to the *Journal of Social Philosophy* (Spring, Summer, Fall and Winter) by Wiley Subscription Services, Inc., a Wiley Company, 111 River St., Hoboken, NJ 07030-5774. Periodical postage paid at Hoboken, NJ and additional offices. Postmaster: Send all address changes to MIDWEST STUDIES IN PHILOSOPHY, Journal Customer Services, John Wiley & Sons Inc., 350 Main St., Malden, MA 02148-5020.

INFORMATION FOR SUBSCRIBERS *Midwest Studies in Philosophy* is published annually as a supplement to the *Journal of Social Philosophy* (Spring, Summer, Fall and Winter).
Institutional subscription prices for 2013 are: Print & Online: US$636 (The Americas), US$985 (Rest of the World), €639 (Europe), £503(UK). Prices are exclusive of tax. Asia Pacific GST, Canadian GST and European VAT will be applied at the appropriate rates. For more information on current tax rates, please go to wileyonlinelibrary.com/tax-vat. The prices includes online access to the current and online back files to January 1st 1998, where available. For other pricing options, including access information and terms and conditions, please visit wileyonlinelibrary.com/access www.wileyonlinelibrary.com/access

DELIVERY TERMS AND LEGAL TITLE Prices include delivery of print journals to the recipient's address. Delivery terms are Delivered Duty Unpaid (DDU); the recipient is responsible for paying any import duty or taxes. Legal title passes to the customer on despatch by our distributors.

PUBLISHER *Midwest Studies in Philosophy* is published by Wiley Periodicals, Inc., Commerce Place, 350 Main Street, Malden, MA 02148; Telephone: 781 388 8200; Fax: 781 388 8210. Wiley Periodicals, Inc. is now part of John Wiley & Sons.

JOURNAL CUSTOMER SERVICES For ordering information, claims and any enquiry concerning your journal subscription please go to wileyonlinelibrary.com/support or contact your nearest office.
Americas: Email: cs-journals@wiley.com; Tel: + 1 781 388 8598 or +1 1800 835 6770 (Toll free in the USA & Canada)
Europe, Middle East and Africa: Email: cs-journals@wiley.com; Tel: +44 (0) 1865 778315
Asia Pacific: Email: cs-journals@wiley.com; Tel: +65 6511 8000
Japan: For Japanese speaking support, Email: cs-japan@wiley.com; Tel: +65 6511 8010 or Tel (Toll-free) 005 316 50 480
Visit our Online Customer Self Help available in 7 languages at http://onlinelibrary.custhelp.com

PRODUCTION EDITOR Nurzarifah Hassan (email: MISP@wiley.com)

This journal is available online at Wiley Online Library. Visit wileyonlinelibrary.com to search the articles and register for table of contents e-mail alerts.

BACK ISSUES Single issues from current and recent volumes are available at the current single issue price from customerservices@blackwellpublishing.com. Earlier issues may be obtained from Periodicals Service Company, 11 Main Street, Germantown, NY 12526, USA. Tel: +1 518 537 4700, Fax: +1 518 537 5899, Email: psc@periodicals.com.

MICROFILM The journal is available on Microfilm. For microfilm service, address inquiries to University Microfilms International, 300 North Zeeb Road, Ann Arbor, MI 48106-1346, USA.

COPYRIGHT AND PHOTOCOPYING Midwest Studies in Philosophy © 2013 Wiley Periodicals, Inc. All rights reserved. No part of this publication may be reproduced, stored or transmitted in any form or by any means without the prior permission in writing from the copyright holder. Authorization to photocopy items for internal and personal use is granted by the copyright holder for libraries and other users registered with their local Reproduction Rights Organisation (RRO), e.g. Copyright Clearance Center (CCC), 222 Rosewood Drive, Danvers, MA 01923, USA (www.copyright.com), provided the appropriate fee is paid directly to the RRO. This consent does not extend to other kinds of copying such as copying for general distribution, for advertising and promotional purposes, for creating new collective works or for resale. Special requests should be addressed to: permissionsUK@wiley.com

ABSTRACTING AND INDEXING The journal is indexed by the Arts & Humanities Citation Index; CatchWord; Ingenta; Online Computer Library Center FirstSearch Electronic Collections Online; Philosopher's Index; and POIESIS: Philosophy Online Serials.

DISCLAIMER The Publisher and Editors cannot be held responsible for errors or any consequences arising from the use of information contained in this journal; the views and opinions expressed do not necessarily reflect those of the Publisher and Editors, neither does the publication of advertisements constitute any endorsement by the Publisher and Editors of the products advertised.

ISSN 0363-6550 (Print)
ISSN 1475-4975 (Online)

For submission instructions, subscription and all other information visit: wileyonlinelibrary.com

Printed in USA by The Sheridan Press.

MIDWEST STUDIES IN PHILOSOPHY
Volume XXXVII
The New Atheism and Its Critics

Varieties of Sense-Making	A. W. Moore	1
Making Room for Faith: Does Science Exclude Religion?	Michael Ruse	11
So What Else Is Neo? Theism and Epistemic Recalcitrance	David Shatz	25
Religious Agnosticism	Gary Gutting	51
How to Vanquish the Lingering Shadow of the Long-Dead God	Kenneth A. Taylor	68
Limited Belief	Andrew Winer	87
Epistemic Toleration and the New Atheism	Richard Fumerton	97
Affective Theism and People of Faith	Jonathan L. Kvanvig	109
Discreditable Origins and the Significance of Natural Theology	Gregg Ten Elshof	129
New Atheism and the Scientistic Turn in the Atheism Movement	Massimo Pigliucci	142
The New Atheists and the Cosmological Argument	Edward Feser	154
Evidence, Theory, and Interpretation: The "New Atheism" and the Philosophy of Science	Alister E. McGrath	178

Midwest Studies in Philosophy
Volume XXXVII

Varieties of Sense-Making

A. W. MOORE

Is there more than one way to make sense of things? This question is far too loose as it stands to have much philosophical purchase. But I take it that there are ways of tightening the question whereby there is room for genuine uncertainty concerning what to say, inasmuch as a philosophically substantive case can be mounted for each of the answers yes and no. And I further take it that at least one strand in the new atheism rests, in part, on a version of the view that the answer is no: the extreme naturalistic view that the only way to make sense of things is the way of natural science. For if we accept this view; if we accept that theism is an attempt to make sense of things; and if we accept that the methods and resources of the natural sciences cannot possibly vindicate theism: then we are bound to conclude that theism is, in its own terms, a failure, in which case we should either reject it in favor of atheism or dismiss the very choice between theism and atheism as one that lacks any genuine significance.

Interestingly, those who are often invoked as being among the fiercest critics of theism, namely logical positivists, were not naturalists in this extreme sense. And although their own revolt against theism might be thought to be a paradigmatic example of this second approach—the approach of dismissing the very choice between theism and atheism as one that lacks any genuine significance—it was not *straightforwardly* an example of this approach at all.

Logical positivists were always among the first to insist that there are varieties of sense-making. They were even prepared to acknowledge that the question that was of primary concern to them, namely, what it is for an utterance of a declarative sentence to be meaningful (which itself hardly exhausts the question of what it is for an attempt to make sense of things to be successful), could be interpreted in more than one way. When they insisted that there was a whole class of utterances of declarative sentences that lacked meaning, what they meant was that these utterances lacked what they sometimes called "literal" meaning: such utterances were not candidates for truth or falsity. But they could still have meaning of other kinds. They could still express feelings, prescriptions, or proscriptions, for example. This left open the possibility that utterances of declarative sentences involving religious vocabulary could express a distinctively religious way of making sense of things to which the methods and resources of the natural sciences were simply irrelevant.

It is instructive in this connection to consider the following passage from A. J. Ayer's *Language, Truth and Logic*:

> According to the account that we have given of religious assertions, there is no logical ground for antagonism between religion and natural science. As far as the question of truth or falsehood is concerned, there is no opposition between the natural scientist and the theist who believes in a transcendent god. For since the religious utterances of the theist are not genuine propositions at all [*i.e.* they lack literal meaning], they cannot stand in any logical relation to the propositions of science ...
>
> An interesting feature of this conclusion is that it accords with what many theists are accustomed to say themselves (Ayer 1971, 154–56).

Rudolf Carnap likewise recognized different ways of making sense of things. Even in his famous assault on the work of traditional metaphysicians, he acknowledged that they might defend themselves by denying that their work was an attempt to discover and state truths. They could, he admitted, insist that their work was an attempt to convey meaning of some other kind; and that it was less a scientific exercise than an artistic exercise. Carnap's complaint about any such defense of traditional metaphysics was not that there was anything wrong with it per se. His complaint was rather that, insofar as traditional metaphysics was an artistic exercise, it was a third-rate artistic exercise. "Metaphysicians," he wrote, "are musicians without musical ability" (Carnap 1959, 80).

Be the artistic merits of traditional metaphysics as they may, it is unsurprising that many theists have reacted to the new atheism by protesting that, in effect, it inappropriately acknowledges only one way to make sense of things, the way of natural science. The protest has a familiar pedigree. Earlier versions of it include Wittgenstein's remarks on Frazer's *Golden Bough* (Wittgenstein 1987) and indeed that old crude saw that science is concerned with "How?" questions while religion is concerned with "Why?" questions.[1] Not that the protest can amount to much without a robust individuation of ways of making sense of things. It is no more than an opening move in the discussion. Even so, the idea that there are ways of making sense of things that are nonscientific without being unscientific does have clear

---

1. See also Wittgenstein (1980), 30 ff.

potential to undermine at least some of the thinking behind at least some of the new atheism.

An indication of what I have mind is provided by the following three quotations by Richard Dawkins. The first is taken from a 1992 debate with John Habgood at the Edinburgh Science Festival. The remaining two are taken from his book *The God Delusion*.

> You can't escape the scientific implications of religion. A universe with a God would look quite different from a universe without one. A physics, a biology where there is a God is bound to look different. So the most basic claims of religion *are* scientific. Religion *is* a scientific theory. (Quoted in Johnston 2009, 46, emphasis in original)
>
> Either [God] exists or he doesn't. It is a scientific question; one day we may know the answer, and meanwhile we can say something pretty strong about the probability. (Dawkins 2007, 70)
>
> God's existence or non-existence is a scientific fact about the universe, discoverable in principle if not in practice. If he existed and chose to reveal it, God himself could clinch the argument, noisily and unequivocally, in his favour. (Dawkins 2007, 73)

It is interesting to speculate in what way Dawkins thinks that God could "clinch" the argument. What sequence of events does Dawkins think would leave us with no alternative but to acknowledge that God exists? It is not obvious to me what he has in mind. But that is largely because I do not believe that the question whether God exists is a scientific question and it is not obvious to me what other, scientific question Dawkins has confused it with. For now, this is less significant than his sheer deafness, or what appears to be his sheer deafness, to the possibility that we ought not to think about an issue of this kind in scientific terms at all, perhaps not even in terms of truth or falsity. Dawkins does concede that there may be "some genuinely profound and meaningful questions that are forever beyond the reach of science" (Dawkins 2007, 80) adding that "maybe quantum theory is already knocking on the door of the unfathomable" (ibid.). But he does not have in mind non-scientific questions. He has in mind scientific questions that are simply too hard for us to answer.

Naturalism of the extreme kind that is of concern here seems to me to be subject to a damning criticism, quite apart from its relation to religion. It is not true that the only way to make sense of things is the way of natural science, because that is not the way, in particular, to make sense of that way of making sense of things: natural science is unsuited to providing a satisfactory account of how natural science itself is possible. W. V. Quine, who famously defends something like this extreme form of naturalism, equally famously attempts to forestall this very objection. He argues that we can provide a satisfactory account, in broadly natural-scientific terms, of how we make natural-scientific sense of things: such is the project of what he calls "naturalized epistemology" (Quine 1969). The story that we are required to tell, on Quine's view, is a story about "how we, physical denizens of the physical world, can have projected our scientific theory of that world from our meagre contacts with it: from the mere impacts of rays and particles on our surfaces and a few odds and ends such as the strain of walking uphill" (Quine 1995, 16). He believes that we can tell such a story by drawing on the relevant branches of natural science such as optics and neurophysiology. The problem with this, as many commentators have observed, is that the impacts of rays and particles on our surfaces, the strain of walking uphill, and suchlike, which are indeed well suited to appear in such a story, are unable, for that very reason, to stand in any but causal relations with what we subsequently do and say. They cannot stand in logical or rational relations with anything. They cannot act as *evidence*. So no story of this kind can do justice to the elementary way in which our natural-scientific sense-making is grounded in how things appear to us to be.[2]

There is a further point. This grounding is not a deductive consequence relation. Theory is underdetermined by evidence. To arrive at a theory from evidence we need, among other things, to draw conclusions about the unobserved from premises about the observed. Making sense of how we make natural-scientific sense of things must therefore include some account of this process and of the normativity that attaches to it. In particular, it must include some account of how the process manages to be so successful. This is another reason why it cannot itself be a simple exercise in making natural-scientific sense of things. It is not just that a simple exercise in making natural-scientific sense of things cannot adequately reckon with the normative, though that is certainly true. Also pertinent is the fact that, insofar as our conclusions concern that which cannot possibly have affected us, for instance because it lies in the future, the *truth* of those conclusions cannot be part of any natural-scientific account of how we arrive at them. In natural-scientific terms the inferences involved cannot help looking like exercises of unjustified faith, as it may be faith in the uniformity of nature. In the present context this is doubly pertinent: it means that some of what is liable to appear to a naturalist as unjustified faith is a staple of the very form of sense-making that extreme naturalism proclaims is the only one there is.

Ralph Walker has fastened on this fact in an attempt not only to remove some of the stigma from what appears to the naturalist as unjustified faith, but also to urge a case for theism. "The world," he writes, "*keeps on* meeting our expectations, from moment to moment and from year to year. Does this not need explanation? Does it not suggest that things have been arranged in our interest, with the independent world on the one hand, and our system of beliefs in [sic] the other, in a harmony continually and benevolently sustained?" (Walker 1989, emphasis in original). For Walker, it is not just that the naturalist needs to acknowledge the propriety of our drawing conclusions that strictly go beyond the evidence. He also takes the success that we enjoy in drawing these conclusions to be the basis of an argument for the existence of a benevolent designer.

I make no comment here on the appeal of this argument. I simply note that to subscribe to it is to take an extra step. The first and less controversial step is just

---

2. See, for example, Stroud (1984), chap. 6, esp. 250–54; and McDowell (1996), Afterword, part I, §3. One of the signal features of the phenomenological tradition is its recoil from such naturalism on such grounds; see, for example, Husserl (1981).

to usher the extreme naturalist out of his or her naturalism. Once this has been accomplished, the simple argument against a theistic attempt to make sense of things—that it lacks any natural-scientific vindication—lapses. But something more is clearly required (something of the sort that Walker himself provides) if theism is to be reinstated. The sheer fact that there are different ways to make sense of things, a fact that has in any case still not been properly explicated, does not sanction anyone's making theistic sense of anything.

Indeed, in acknowledging that there are different ways to make sense of things, the theist incurs certain risks. One principal risk, which is incurred by nontheists, too, if they do not subscribe to the extreme naturalism that we have been considering, is that of thinking—what is surely false—that a religious way of making sense of things can be somehow self-contained, impervious to any other way of making sense of things. Consider the following quotation from Stephen Jay Gould:

> The net, or magisterium, of science covers the empirical realm: what is the universe made of (fact) and why does it work this way (theory). The magisterium of religion extends over questions of ultimate meaning and moral value. These two magisteria do not overlap. . . . (Gould 1999, 6)

Gould certainly seems to have fallen victim to the risk that I have in mind. Another casualty may be Peter Winch. He refers at one point to "those forms of life called 'science,' 'art,' etc." (Winch 1958, 41)—a reference that brings to mind Hilary Putnam's famous complaint about the "fondness [of Wittgensteinians] for the expression 'form of life'," namely that it "appears to be directly proportional to its degree of preposterousness in a given context" (Putnam 1970, 60). At any rate, to distinguish two or more ways of making sense of things falls some way short of claiming that they are cleanly separable, a claim which, in the case of a religious way of making sense of things and a broadly scientific way of making sense of things, would surely be utterly implausible.[3]

Bernard Williams warns of the danger, to the (Christian) theist, of trying to effect a clean separation between "talk about God" and other talk, in the following terms:

> If all talk about God were talk only about God, and all talk about the world talk only about the world, how could it be that God was the God of the Christian believer, who is a toiler in the world of men? Would not the views about the nature of God retire more and more away from the world of men[?] . . . And if that happened, it could not be of much concern whether he were there or not. (Williams 2006, 14, emphasis removed)

Not that Williams is concerned to defend talk about God. On the contrary, having issued this warning, he straightway issues a second warning, this time of the opposite danger to the theist of allowing talk about God and talk about the world to mix. He writes:

---

3. Cf. McGrath (2007): 17–18. See also note 7 below.

> Although we must have some statement which says something about both God and the world, when we have it we find that we have something that we cannot properly say.... [For] when we come to a statement that is about both God and temporal events, it must be unsatisfactory; for if it were not, we should have adequately described the relation of the temporal events to God in terms appropriate only to the temporal events [which are the only terms we understand]: and this would mean either that we had described only the temporal events, and left God out, or had described God as a temporal being, which he is not. (ibid., 14–15)

Williams sees a dilemma for the theist, then.

This dilemma might be thought not to be a dilemma about mixing talk of God with other talk at all, but rather a dilemma simply about talk of God: the dilemma, namely, that we need to have some basic understanding of such talk for it to count as *talk* of God, whereas we need to lack any basic understanding of it for it to count as talk of *God*.[4] In a way this is right. But the considerations about mixing such talk with other talk survive; for our having some basic understanding of such talk would consist partly in its being satisfactorily mixable with other talk that we understand, while our lacking any basic understanding if it would consist partly in its not being.

Certainly a theist who insists that there is a distinctively theistic way of making sense of things needs to tread very carefully: it cannot be too distinctive or it will no longer count as a way of making sense of things; but it had better be distinctive enough for the point of insisting on its distinctiveness not to be compromised.

As far as the point of insisting on its distinctiveness is concerned, I have so far focused only on the inadequacy of an atheism founded on the extreme naturalistic conviction that the only way to make sense of things is the way of natural science. But that is by no means the only reason we might have for insisting that there is a distinctively theistic way of making sense of things. Equally important is the bearing of this issue on what seems to me a much more reasonable atheism fueled by the classic problem of suffering: atheism, in other words, founded on the conviction that the existence of a being that is both omnipotent and perfectly benevolent is incompatible with the existence of suffering. There is of course a huge amount to be said about this problem, indeed a huge amount that has been said about it, and the problem is not about to go away. Still, I think it is worthwhile, in this context, to make the following point: even if the existence of a being that is both omnipotent and perfectly benevolent is indeed incompatible with the existence of suffering, this only means that one cannot consistently accept that there is suffering and believe that there is such a being. It does not mean that one cannot consistently accept that there is suffering and be a theist. Nor do I have in mind here the simple point that our definition of God may not include omnipotence and

---

4. A similar dilemma afflicted Descartes. He needed to have some basic grasp of his idea of God for it to count as a genuine idea; he needed to lack any basic grasp of it for it to be the kind of idea that he took it to be, an idea of something so great that only something that great could explain how he had come by it. See Williams (1978), 143–45.

perfect benevolence (though the simple point deserves to be made, too). Rather, I have in mind the point that theism may be part of a distinctive way of making sense of things that does not consist in holding any particular truth-evaluable belief. This would mean that one could *consistently* be a theist no matter what one accepted. It is a further question, of course, whether one could *reasonably* be a theist no matter what one accepted, and to address that question we should need to provide some positive account of what exactly theism is. But there is at any rate not the direct route that there appeared to be from suffering to atheism.

Very well; but what positive account of theism can we provide that distances it from the holding of any truth-evaluable belief? Well, people sometimes distinguish between belief *in God* and belief *that God exists*.[5] Perhaps we could equate theism with belief in God.—Yes, but what would be meant by belief in God?—One way of drawing the distinction between belief in God and belief that God exists would be on the model of the distinction between belief in justice and belief that justice exists. Someone can believe in justice in a given context, in the sense that he or she can believe that it is important for justice to prevail there, even while recognizing that it does not (yet). On this model belief in God would be, roughly, belief that it is important to promote and cherish whatever bespeaks God; belief that God exists would be belief that whatever bespeaks God speaks truly. One might even have the former belief alongside a compelling argument that whatever bespeaks God cannot be understood as speaking truly (or indeed, cannot be understood as making any sense at all). Here a quotation from Iris Murdoch is pertinent:

> No existing thing could be what we have meant by God. Any existing God would be less than God. An existent God would be an idol or demon. . . . God does not and cannot exist. But what led us to conceive of him does exist and is *constantly* experienced and pictured . . . [It is] incarnate in knowledge and work and love. . . . We *experience* both the reality of perfection and its distance away, and this leads us to place our idea of it outside the world of existent being as something of a different unique and special sort. Such experience of the reality of good . . . is a discovery of something independent of us. . . . If we read these images aright they are not only enlightening and profound but amount to a statement of a belief that most people unreflectively hold. (Murdoch 1993, 508, emphasis in original)

But would this distance theism from the holding of any truth-evaluable beliefs? Not obviously. Belief that it is important to promote and cherish whatever bespeaks God certainly *seems* to be truth-evaluable. What it might do is to help with the problem of suffering, inasmuch as belief that it is important to promote and cherish whatever bespeaks God, even if truth-evaluable, is not obviously incompatible with belief that there is suffering. But for a way of extricating theism from the classic (intellectual) problem of suffering altogether we require something more radical.

---

5. For example, Price (1965).

For this we can perhaps turn to Kant, and in particular to Kant's notion of a regulative principle. By a regulative principle Kant means a rule directing us to act in accord with some given supposition (Kant 1998, A508–15/B536–43 and A669/B697 ff.). We can construe belief in God as the embracing of such a rule. To believe in God, on this construal, is to live one's life *as if* God exists.

But how can one live one's life as if God exists if one has a compelling argument that God does not exist? For that matter, what about the lesson, or the apparent lesson, of the quotations from both Bernard Williams and Iris Murdoch, namely that we can have no understanding of what it would even *be* for God to exist? If we can have no understanding of what it would even be for God to exist—if the very idea that God exists is shot through with incoherence—then surely we have no prospect of living our lives as if God exists?

This conclusion seems to me too precipitate. This in turn is for reasons that I have tried to advance elsewhere and that I shall take the liberty of sketching here. To live one's life as if some given supposition holds is to exercise a kind of knowledge. But such knowledge is not knowledge that anything is the case. In fact it is not even expressible. It is knowledge of how to cope with situations in a certain way. It involves making a certain nontruth-evaluable sense of things. What then makes the exercise of it the living of one's life as if *that* supposition holds? The fact that, if one were to attempt (unsuccessfully) to put the knowledge into words, then what one would do is to give voice to that supposition. In the current case, which I take to be a case in point, one would say that God exists. (It follows that the claim that God exists, without being an expression of the relevant knowledge, could, if made in the right way in the right context, help to celebrate, nurture, proclaim, or even impart that knowledge.) But this does not require that the idea that God exists should actually be credible. It does not even require that the idea that God exists should be intelligible. It requires only that the sentence "God exists" should conjure up all sorts of relevant images and have all sorts of relevant associations and connotations.[6] These images, associations, and connotations may include notions of *constancy*, for example, where these in turn may correspond to certain hopes that can sustain us in our commitment to making this particular sense of things; hopes that can reinforce our confidence that the contingencies that enable us to make such sense are in some way necessary, just as the contingencies that enable the earth to carry on spinning on its axis are in some sense necessary: utterly steadfast, utterly to be relied upon. We saw earlier that Walker thought that he could argue from these contingencies to the existence of God. I do not myself believe that any such argument can be successful. But I do acknowledge the way in which these contingencies can put us in mind of God, and the way in which talk of God can put us in mind of them. In the present context, this is as much as is required of them.

The relevance of belief in God to the problem of suffering may lie not in the capacity of the latter to refute the former, then, but in the capacity of the former to help cope with the latter. And indeed it is noteworthy how frequently extremes of

---

6. For a full defense of these ideas, see Moore (1997), esp. chaps 7–9; chap. 10, §5; and 277–278. See also Moore (2003).

suffering draw people into a belief in God rather than away from it. This is not just a matter of the consolations that such a belief affords. It is a matter of the conceptual shape that it helps people to impose on their suffering: the sense that it helps them to make of it. As Nietzsche insisted, it is not suffering that people find unbearable, but senseless suffering (Nietzsche 1967, Second Essay, §7, and Third Essay, §28). A quotation from Wittgenstein is also relevant:

> Life can educate one to a belief in God. And *experiences* too are what bring this about; but I don't mean visions and other forms of sense experience which show us the "existence of this being", but, e.g., sufferings of various sorts. These neither show us God in the way a sense impression shows us an object, nor do they give rise to *conjectures* about him. Experiences, thoughts,—life can force this *concept* on us. (Wittgenstein 1980, 86, first two emphases in original, third added)

It is a common complaint that the belief that God exists, construed as a truth-evaluable belief, receives no vindication from considerations of this kind. Dawkins in particular has voiced this complaint. "Religion's power to console," he writes, "doesn't make it true" (Dawkins 2007, 394). Indeed it does not. But that is uncontentious common territory in this particular discussion. It merely reinforces what I hope this essay as a whole has gone some way toward showing: that there are grounds for a powerful response to the new atheism in a due acknowledgement of the varieties of sense-making.[7]

REFERENCES

Ayer, A. J. 1971. *Language, Truth and Logic*, 2nd ed. Harmondsworth, UK: Penguin.
Carnap, Rudolf. 1959. "The Elimination of Metaphysics Through Logical Analysis of Language," trans. Arthur Pap. In *Logical Positivism*, ed. A. J. Ayer, 60–81. Glencoe, IL: Free Press.
Citron, Gabriel. 2012. " 'What's Ragged Should Be Left Ragged': A Wittgensteinian Investigation into the Messiness of Religious Beliefs and Utterances" (unpublished D.Phil. dissertation, Oxford University).
Dawkins, Richard. 2007. *The God Delusion*. London: Black Swan.
Gould, Stephen Jay. 1999. *Rock of Ages: Science and Religion in the Fullness of Life*. New York: Ballantine Books.
Husserl, Edmund. 1981. "Phenomenology," an article for *Encyclopedia Britannica* (1927), revised trans. Richard E. Palmer, reprinted in *Husserl: Shorter Works*, ed. Peter McCormick and Frederick A. Elliston. Notre Dame, IN: University of Notre Dame Press.
Johnston, Mark. 2009. *Saving God: Religion After Idolatry*. Princeton, NJ: Princeton University Press.
Kant, Immanuel. 1998. *Critique of Pure Reason*, trans. and ed. Paul Guyer and Allen W. Wood. Cambridge: Cambridge University Press.

---

7. I should like to take this opportunity to commend Gabriel Citron's outstanding doctoral thesis (Citron 2012), in which he argues that not only are varieties of sense-making important to the philosophy of religion, but so, too, is what he calls their "messiness." This allows for the various different kinds of sense-making exhibited in religious beliefs sometimes to mix with one another in indeterminate and fluid ways. It seems to me that due acknowledgement of this point makes the response to the new atheism toward which I have been gesturing all the more powerful.

McDowell, John. 1996. *Mind and World*, 2nd ed. Cambridge, MA: Harvard University Press.
McGrath, Alister, with Joanna Collicutt McGrath. 2007. *The Dawkins Delusion? Atheist Fundamentalism and the Denial of the Divine*. London: SPCK.
Moore, A. W. 1997. *Points of View*. Oxford: Oxford University Press.
———. 2003. "Ineffability and Religion." *European Journal of Philosophy* 11: 161–76.
Murdoch, Iris. 1993. *Metaphysics as a Guide to Morals*. Harmondsworth, UK: Penguin.
Nietzsche, Friedrich. 1967. *On the Genealogy of Morals: A Polemic*, trans. Walter Kaufmann and Reginald J. Hollingdale, in *On the Genealogy of Morals and Ecce Homo*. New York: Random House.
Price, Henry H. 1965. "Belief 'In' and Belief 'That'." *Religious Studies* 1(1): 5–28.
Putnam, Hilary. 1970. "Is Semantics Possible?" In *Language, Belief, and Metaphysics*, ed. Howard E. Kiefer and Milton K. Munitz, 50–63. Albany: State University of New York Press.
Quine, W. V. O. 1969. "Epistemology Naturalized." In W. V. O. Quine, *Ontological Relativity and Other Essays*. New York: Columbia University Press.
———. 1995. *From Stimulus to Science*. Cambridge, MA: Harvard University Press.
Stroud, Barry. 1984. *The Significance of Philosophical Scepticism*. Oxford: Oxford University Press
Walker, Ralph. 1989. *The Coherence Theory of Truth: Realism, Anti-Realism, Idealism*. London: Routledge.
Williams, Bernard. 1978. *Descartes: The Project of Pure Enquiry*. Harmondsworth, UK: Penguin.
———. 2006. "Tertullian's Paradox." In *Philosophy as Humanistic Discipline*, ed. A. W. Moore, 3–21. Princeton, NJ: Princeton University Press.
Winch, Peter. 1958. *The Idea of a Social Science and its Relation to Philosophy*. London: Routledge & Kegan Paul.
Wittgenstein, Ludwig. 1980. *Culture and Value*, ed. Georg H. von Wright and Heikki Nyman and trans. Peter Winch. Oxford: Blackwell.
Wittgenstein, Ludwig. 1987. *Remarks on Frazer's* Golden Bough, ed. Rush Rhees and trans. A. C. Miles and Rush Rhees. Doncaster, UK: Brynmill.

Making Room for Faith: Does Science Exclude Religion?

MICHAEL RUSE

The so-called New Atheists and fellow travelers are quite convinced that science has solved the God question. In the light of modern science, God does not exist. Hence religion is based on a false foundation. Teaching it is immoral and practicing it is foolish and probably dangerous. Using Charles Darwin's theory of evolution through natural selection as a springboard, Richard Dawkins (1995) has plunged right in:

> In a universe of blind physical forces and genetic replication, some people are going to get hurt, other people are going to get lucky, and you won't find any rhyme or reason in it, nor any justice. The universe we observe has precisely the properties we should expect if there is, at bottom, no design, no purpose, no evil and no good, nothing but blind, pitiless indifference. As that unhappy poet A. E. Housman put it:
>
> > For Nature, heartless, witless Nature
> > Will neither know nor care.
>
> DNA neither knows nor cares. DNA just is. And we dance to its music. (1995, 133)

The Nobel laureate for physics, Steven Weinberg says: "Religion is an insult to human dignity. Without it you would have good people doing good things and evil people doing evil things. But for good people to do evil things, that takes religion."[1] Speaking as a scientist, he tells us: "This is one of the great social functions of science—to free people from superstition" (1977, 231). He is unambiguous: the greatest superstition of them all is religion. And it is here that science has its great debunking role. "It's a consequence of the experience of science. As you learn more and more about the universe, you find you can understand more and more without any reference to supernatural intervention, so you lose interest in that possibility. Most scientists I know don't care enough about religion even to call themselves atheists. And that, I think, is one of the great things about science—that it has made it possible for people not to be religious."[2] Science does not stop at refuting religion. It makes it boring!

Philosopher Philip Kitcher (2007) concurs.

> A large number of Christians, not merely those who maintain that virtually all of the Bible must be read literally, are providentialists. For they believe that the universe has been created by a Being who has a great design, a Being who cares for his creatures, who observes the fall of every sparrow and who is especially concerned with humanity. Yet the story of a wise and loving Creator, who has planned life on earth, letting it unfold over four billion years by the processes envisaged in evolutionary theory, is hard to sustain when you think about the details. (122–23)

Like a sinner at a moral rearmament meeting, Kitcher tells of earlier beliefs that one could hold to Darwinism while being a Christian, and now insists that he alone should be held responsible for "the earlier errors that I recant here" (2007, 180).

Let me say at once that there is much here with which I agree entirely. I share the rather bleak vision of Dawkins. I do not think there is any meaning to the universe. I agree with Weinberg about the dangers of religion and how too often it leads people astray. I think for instance that many of the troubles of the Catholic Church with respect to sexual abuse of the young are a direct function of the unnatural constraints put upon its clergy and, while I do not think that Islam is quite the evil force supposed by some New Atheists, I do not think it blameless with respect to some of the attacks of the past decade or so. And I agree with Kitcher that it is not only the biblical literalists who have troubles with the evils and troubles of this world. Having said this, however, I am not convinced that there is quite the direct connection between science and nonbelief that is supposed by these and many other of today's critics of religion.

I am not denying that there are connections between science and nonbelief. You cannot hold to a universal flood some few thousand years ago and to modern geology. In the light of modern astronomy, you cannot believe that God created the sun and the moon on the Fourth Day. You must reject a literal Adam and Eve if you are to accept findings in paleoanthropology, the study of human origins. But

---

1. Address at the Conference on Cosmic Design, American Association for the Advancement of Science, Washington, DC (April 1999).
2. Quoted in Natalie Angier, "Confessions of a Lonely Atheist," *New York Times Magazine*, January 14, 2001.

whether science as such makes impossible the central beliefs of religion—meaning now the theism of the Abrahamic religions (Judaism, Christianity, Islam)—is another matter. I am not sure that science as such refutes a Creator God, one who is a necessary being and cause of himself. I am not sure that science as such refutes us humans as having a special place in this creation, as conscious beings with intelligence and a moral sense. I am not sure that science as such refutes a meaning to it all, with the possibility of some kind of eternal existence with the deity. As I say, I do not believe any of this. But I am not sure that science as such leads to my nonbelief. I reject theism because I have troubles with the very notion of God, of a necessary being. I reject theism because I don't think I need God to have morality or to be moral. I reject theism above all because I cannot reconcile the God of the believers with the fact of evil. For me, God died with Anne Frank in Bergen-Belsen and I regard it as obscene to suggest that on balance the free will of Adolf Hitler and Heinrich Himmler and the other Nazi leaders made things better than otherwise. These are reasons enough without bringing in science.

METAPHOR

How am I to make my case? I want to stress that I see little point in making the case if I am going to rely on premises and arguments that would generally be rejected. That would rather defeat the purpose of what I am about. I do not expect or seek total unanimity about my starting points, but I want them to be reasonable and accepted by many if not most. This said, let me cut to the quick and talk about metaphor. It is generally agreed that metaphor—using concepts from one area of understanding to explore another area of potential understanding—is an important method of thinking. Literally no doubt metaphors are false. "A mighty fortress is our God." God is not literally a fortress. But we use the idea of a fortress to explore the nature of God—strong, protective, perhaps a little stern and forbidding. The important point for this discussion is that nowhere is metaphor more important than in science (Hesse 1966). Every area of science reeks (metaphor!) with metaphor. Physics: force, attraction, work, flavor (as in quarks), charm (of quarks), Big Bang (there was no air, so there was no sound). Biology: natural selection, genetic code, adaptive landscape, arms race (between predator and prey). Social science: Oedipus complex, public sphere, emotional landscape, division of labor.

Whether or not metaphors are absolutely essential has been debated since Aristotle. Some, like Thomas Hobbes, would say not. Others, like the leading linguist George Lakoff, would say yes (Lakoff and Johnson 1980). We can sidestep this issue by simply saying that metaphors are awfully important and while (to adapt Richard Braithwaite [1953] who spoke of models) the price of the use of metaphor is eternal vigilance, no serious scientist would ever think of removing them. Apart from anything else, they have prodigious heuristic value. As soon as people started to think of the sub-molecules along the DNA polymer as a "code," the race was on to "crack" it and before long there was success and an absolutely vital piece of information had been added to the molecular picture. Now, as students of metaphor have pointed out, not all metaphors are equal. Some are more fundamental than others. To take one of Lakoff's examples: argument as warfare. We have the overall metaphor of battle. Then things fit into this. I caught him out. He beat me down. We tried a different strategy. Some metaphors are really basic, what Stephen Pepper (1942) called "root" metaphors. These are the ones that give you a whole perspective on reality, what the Germans call *Weltanschauugen*.

FROM ORGANISM TO MACHINE

Moving now from philosophy to history, but I trust still remaining at a fairly uncontentious level, I want to suggest that the history of Western science saw—at the time of the so-called Scientific Revolution in the sixteenth and seventeenth centuries—a change in root metaphors. This was the really big event and informed and directed everything else. Before Copernicus and Kepler and Galileo and Descartes and Newton the world was seen organically. Plato actually thought the world was an organism. Aristotle did not go that far but he, too, thought that organisms are the key to understanding. We look for various kinds of proximate causes but as important we look for final causes. As with organisms, when we ask what is the end or purpose of the eye, so Aristotle instructed us to ask such questions of everything when we are exploring the empirical world. The stone falls in order to find its proper place in the universe, just as the heart beats (as we now know) in order to circulate the blood. Then in the Scientific Revolution the metaphor switched. No longer was the world organic. It was now mechanical. The new metaphor was that of the machine (Ruse 2013).

The chemist and philosopher Robert Boyle (1996) is the point man here. He refers to a magnificent clock in Strasbourg cathedral built (between 1571 and 1574) by the Swiss mathematician Cunradus Dasypodius. Planets circle, moons wax and wane, and a host of other wonderful things happen on the hour, every hour.

> And those things which the school philosophers ascribe to the agency of nature interposing according to emergencies, I ascribe to the wisdom of God in the first fabric of the universe; which he so admirably contrived that, if he but continue his ordinary and general concourse, there will be no necessity of extraordinary interpositions, which may reduce him to seem as if it were to play after-games—all those exigencies, upon whose account philosophers and physicians seem to have devised what they call nature, being foreseen and provided for in the first fabric of the world; so that mere matter, so ordered, shall in such and such conjunctures of circumstances, do all that philosophers ascribe on such occasions to their omniscient nature, without any knowledge of what it does, or acting otherwise than according to the catholic laws of motion. And methinks the different between their opinion of God's agency in the world, and that which I would propose, may be somewhat adumbrated by saying that they seem to imagine the world to be after the nature of a puppet, whose contrivance indeed may be very artificial, but yet is such that almost every particular motion the artificer is fain (by drawing sometimes one wire or string, sometimes another) to guide, and

oftentimes overrule, the actions of the engine, whereas, according to us, it is like a rare clock, such as may be that at Strasbourg, where all things are so skillfully contrived that the engine being once set a-moving, all things proceed according to the artificer's first design, and the motions of the little statues that as such hours perform these or those motions do not require (like those of puppets) the peculiar interposing of the artificer or any intelligent agent employed by him, but perform their functions on particular occasions by virtue of the general and primitive contrivance of the whole engine. (12–13)

It is all just matter in motion, governed by unbending eternal laws. There is no place for final-cause thinking. Francis Bacon called them vestal virgins—decorative but sterile. Descartes was even more contemptuous. By what right do we discern God's purposes?

Yet surely this was premature? Isn't the whole point of machines that they have ends, purposes? The automobile is for traveling. The electric chair is for killing. Soon, however, people found that the only part of the metaphor that was of use was that of the machine going on endlessly, without intervention from outside, according to unbroken law. God was not denied but He got pushed out of science. In the words of one of the great historians of the Scientific Revolution, God became a "retired engineer" (Dijksterhuis 1961, 491). Which was all very well, but what about organisms? Surely we cannot do without final-cause thinking here? Hands are for grasping. Eyes are for seeing. A hundred years after Boyle we find Immanuel Kant (1951) worrying about this problem and in the *Third Critique* he goes as far as to say that in the life sciences there will always be a case for ends, for purposes. For this reason, because the life sciences can never aspire to be at one with the physical sciences, "there will never be a Newton of the blade of grass" (270).

As we now know, a hundred and fifty years after the publication of the *Origin of Species*, Charles Darwin (1859) changed all of that. He showed how organisms can be explained as the result of development from primitive forms—evolution—and he also showed how to explain final-cause-like effects in terms of proximate causes. There is no need of such end-directed thinking—at least there is no need of such end-directed thinking as something that takes you beyond the machine metaphor, the mechanical vision. Natural selection not only explains change, it explains change as producing those very features (known as "adaptations") as apparently in need of final-cause explanation. Hands and eyes do seem to serve ends but only because in the past those organisms with hands and eyes did better to survive and reproduce than those that did not. Dawkins (1976) puts it nicely.

> We are survival machines, but 'we' does not mean just people. It embraces all animals, plants, bacteria, and viruses. The total number of survival machines on earth is very difficult to count and even the total number of species is unknown. Taking just insects alone, the number of living species has been estimated at around three million, and the number of living insects may be a million, million, million.

> Different sorts of survival machines appear very varied on the outside and in their internal organs. An octopus is nothing like a mouse, and both are quite different from an oak tree. Yet in their fundamental chemistry they are rather uniform, and, in particular, the replicators which they bear, the genes, are basically the same kind of molecule in all of us—from bacteria to elephants. We are all survival machines for the same kind of replicator—molecules called DNA—but there are many different ways of making a living in the world, and the replicators have built a vast range of machines to exploit them. A monkey is a machine which preserves genes up trees, a fish is a machine which preserves genes in the water; there is even a small worm which preserves genes in German beer mats. DNA works in mysterious ways. (22)

Finally, in recent years there has been an assault on that bastion that even Descartes thought beyond the machine metaphor—the mind. Thanks to so-called cognitive science we are now taught to regard the mind as a machine, namely as a computer. The philosopher Andy Clark (2000) writes:

> The computer scientist, Marvin Minsky once described the human brain as a meat machine—no more, no less. It is, to be sure, an ugly phrase. But it is also a striking image, a compact expression of both the genuine scientific excitement and the rather gung-ho materialism that has tended to characterize the early years of cognitive science research. Mindware—our thoughts, feelings, hopes, fears, beliefs, and intellect—is cast as nothing but the operation of the biological brain, the meat machine in our head (1).

I am not saying that all of this is unproblematic, and indeed I shall have some questioning things to say about it shortly. My point simply is that modern science embraces one all-powerful root metaphor, namely the world as a machine. Note that I am not in any sense suggesting that it is silly or irrational to do this. On the contrary, I take it that the aim of empirical science is to understand the physical world (including the world of behavior and thought even) and that this means explanation and prediction and so forth—digging down into the often unseen causes of things and showing connections that are not obvious and the like. There is nothing wrong with the organic model or metaphor per se. It lasted for a couple of thousand years. It is just that it is not as good at achieving the aims of science as is the mechanical model or metaphor. Metaphors do not have some divine status, some kind of compelling internal necessity. Ultimately it is all a matter of pragmatics. Which one works better? And the answer seems to be the mechanical metaphor. Obviously this has not come about without some pushing and shoving and trimming and altering. Who would have thought that a machine could cover electricity and the like? But it did. Who would have thought that a machine could cover the antics of sub-atomic particles? But here we are with quantum mechanics. So to use a metaphor of the philosopher Max Black (1962), we see the world through the lens of a machine. It is not literally a machine. But we regard it as being one.

METAPHORS AS CONSTRICTING

Switching back to philosophy again, later in life after he had achieved stunning success with *The Structure of Scientific Revolutions* (1962), Thomas Kuhn was much given to stressing the inherently metaphorical nature of his key notion of a "paradigm" (Kuhn 1993). Not so much that in talking of paradigms one is talking metaphorically, although obviously one is, but that paradigms are in important senses metaphors. That is what they are all about as they give you a picture, a vision, that goes beyond the purely rational and into the psychological. Paradigms give you a new way of looking at things. So for instance Charles Darwin invites us to see the world as selected. The living world is like a barnyard. As the farmer selects the cows and sheep that he wants, so nature selects the animals and plants that she wants. Darwin (1861) realized this.

> In the literal sense of the word, no doubt, natural selection is a false term; but who ever objected to chemists speaking of the elective affinities of the various elements?—and yet an acid cannot strictly be said to elect the base with which it in preference combines. It has been said that I speak of natural selection as an active power or Deity; but who objects to an author speaking of the attraction of gravity as ruling the movements of the planets? Everyone knows what is meant and is implied by such metaphorical expressions; and they are almost necessary for brevity. (85)[3]

Kuhn grasped what was at play here. Paradigms/metaphors are powerful because they give you new visions—new puzzles to work on. But they do so at least in part by constricting your vision. To use another metaphor, they make you put on blinkers. They direct you to asking new questions, but they do so in part by making other questions not so much wrong or unanswerable in principle but irrelevant and unanswerable within the system. It is as though they say: "Don't waste time on these issues. Get on with the job in hand." So if I say my love is a red, red rose, then I am telling you something about her beauty and her freshness and (perhaps if I am joking) that she is a bit prickly. What I am not telling you is whether she is a Christian or an atheist and whether she is good at mathematics or a dunce. It is not that she is or is not a Christian and it is not that she is a math whiz or not. She may well be an ordained minister or she may well be a distaff Richard Dawkins. She may well be a Field Prize winner or she may well be totally lost with figures. These are perfectly meaningful abilities and attributes and attainments. It is just that the metaphor of her as a flower has nothing to say on the subjects. Things like this are just not part of the present discourse.

Go back now to the metaphor of the world as a machine and it is here that we get to the punch line. The metaphor is going to direct us to ask one set of questions and other sets are going to be ruled out as irrelevant. The mechanical

---

3. Darwin added this to the third edition, published in 1861, two years after the original edition of the work, to answer critics who argued that, in speaking of selection, he was implying a God who did the selecting.

model or metaphor is simply not going to address them. It is not going to address them and say that they lead to falsities. It is just going to be silent. So the issue now is what sorts of questions is the metaphor going to address, or more particularly what sorts of questions is the metaphor not going to address? And at this point, I am probably going to upset the purists, because I don't think that in itself there can be a fixed list, with ever-lasting criteria for inclusion or exclusion. I think any answers are going to be a little bit historical and depend on how we regard the metaphor. I can imagine someone more learned about roses than I might mean something rather different if he spoke of his love as a rose. He might for instance be thinking "infested with parasites" although I do rather hope not! In the machine metaphor I don't see why ends were necessarily excluded although as it happens they were because they didn't lead to interesting questions. (Actually in the case of organisms, we might we speak of a mechanism as having an end. The heart is a pump for circulating blood. It is just that overall in the context of science organisms, including humans, have no ultimate purposes.)

QUESTIONS NOT ASKED

So what questions or areas does the machine metaphor of science ignore or exclude? Let me offer four.[4] First, where did it all come from in the first place? Or if you like: Why is there something rather than nothing? Of course when dealing with machines you can ask about origins. Was the car made in Japan or in Mexico? Did the iron ore come from Canada or Australia? And you can ask about origins when dealing with the world. That is what evolution is all about and the same goes for the Big Bang. But there comes a point with machines when you stop asking questions because it is simply not relevant. Like Hannah Glasse, you first take your hare. At some point, the materials themselves have to be supplied and then you get on with the job of building the machine and getting it to work or function. Second the morality of the machine. Machines are. They are in themselves neither good nor bad. It is how they are used and why that makes them good or bad. This is the simple Humean point: you cannot go from "is" to "ought." I personally cannot think of a good use for an electric chair except perhaps in horror movies and even there you could use a facsimile. But I live in a state (Florida) where most of my fellow citizens would happily pull the switch on many more than they already do. As Dawkins says, under the model or metaphor the world just is. It is neither good nor bad nor is there anything else to it.

Third, and here I recognize I get to contentious ground, I don't think that machines think. Not in the sense of having sentience. They are not conscious. Leibniz (1714) was right on this point.

> One is obliged to admit that *perception* and what depends upon it is *inexplicable on mechanical principles*, that is, by figures and motions. In imagining that there is a machine whose construction would enable it to think, to sense, and to have perception, one could conceive it enlarged while retaining the

---

4. I follow here the basic pattern introduced in Ruse (2010).

same proportions, so that one could enter into it, just like into a windmill. Supposing this, one should, when visiting within it, find only parts pushing one another, and never anything by which to explain a perception. Thus it is in the simple substance, and not in the composite or in the machine, that one must look for perception. (Section 17)

Fourth, as we have seen as the machine metaphor functions in modern science, there is no purpose to it all. The world is just matter in motion. It does not exist for some end. The physicist Steven Weinberg (1977) has said: "The more the universe seems comprehensible, the more it also seems pointless" (1977, 154). Precisely! The metaphor of the machine as it functions in modern science excludes ends or purposes. That is why you are not going to find them.

Now I appreciate that this has all been very quick so let me go over things a little more slowly. With respect to the first question, often known as the "fundamental question," why is there something rather than nothing, a lot of people starting with Wittgenstein (1965) think that it is a bogus question. It is a bit like asking why Tuesday is tired. I cannot see that this is so. Is the Goldbach conjecture (every even number is the sum of two primes) true? I don't know and I don't know that it can be proven one way or the other. But I don't think it meaningless to ask the question. The same is true of the fundamental question. I would agree that if you are going to answer it successfully you are probably going to have to do it in terms of necessary existence (what is known in the trade as "aseity") because otherwise you will be caught in an infinite regress. I am not sure that this makes sense, although as somewhat of a Platonist about mathematics I am not going to rule it out *a priori*. The point that matters here, however, is that a lot of people think that the question is meaningful and that it is important and it is not answered by science because science is not in the business of answering that sort of question. It can ask whether there was something before the Big Bang. It cannot or does not ask about the very existence of stuff itself.

Morality is a bit of a tricky one, especially for someone like myself whose chief claim to immortality seems to be that once (Ruse and Wilson 1985) I said that morality was an illusion put into place by natural selection to make us good cooperators! I still think that, so I am not going to dodge the issue that way. The problem seems to be that if I am right, then matters of fact do explain morality and that is an end to things. You don't need to go beyond the machine metaphor. I agree with that, but notice that what I want to do is explain morality away. I am not doing what Hume thought illicit, namely trying to justify morality by science. (Interestingly, I think my fellow illusionist Wilson thought that he was doing precisely that!) I rush to say that I don't think I am giving you a license to rape and pillage. With Hume, although I am a skeptic about foundations, I think psychology steps in to do the job. Morality is an illusion but it only works because we think that (thanks to natural selection that) morality is objective, something out there and binding upon us. So I am going to be burdened with a conscience like the rest of you and just as tense and miserable when I cheat on my wife or the taxes, and I don't see the point of being tense and miserable just to make a philosophical point. So the point is that I am not denying the existence of an objective, true morality. It is just that I claim that I don't need it and that if others feel that they do need it that science has not ruled this out for them.

If morality is tricky, sentience is a real puzzler. I am what I believe is known as a "new mysterian" (see McGinn 2000), meaning that I don't think the problem of sentience is ever going to be solved. I base this on the belief that, for all the effort expounded, we have not yet started to scratch the problem. Of course we know a lot about the brain and its effect on the mind. Why we should get thought from a chunk of meat is another matter entirely. It is true that there are those who think we are on the way to a solution. There are even those who think we have found a solution.[5] This seems to me a bit like the way that the United States should have ended the Vietnam War. Declare victory and go home. So I remain unconvinced. I will say that if I am wrong, I will not be unduly worried. (Actually I should be delighted.) I have said that my list is not written in stone and it could be that the metaphor of the machine is more powerful than I think and that it could be extended in an acceptable way to solve the problem of sentience. I just don't see it at the moment.[6]

Finally, meaning and ultimate purpose. Again, I don't see this as a phony question. Indeed, given that we are using the machine metaphor I can see how it would fit in. As an automobile is for traveling so the world is for—well, whatever you decided it is for. It is just that, as I have pointed out, the way that the metaphor was developed was one that made such questions improper. I should say that for all that he argues that science gives no ultimate meaning, this seems to be Weinberg's position.[7] He is not against meaning as such. In fact he thinks we can get it in human relationships and so forth. He is just against getting it from science. And in this I concur.

SKEPTICISM

So where does this lead us? I do not think it forces us into religious belief. I think one can be an agnostic or a skeptic. This is my own position. I should say that I start from the fact that we humans are the product of evolution and that I see no guarantee that evolution would produce in us beings who are able to solve the ultimate mysteries of creation. "Modern physics teaches us that there is more to truth than meets the eye; or than meets the all too limited human mind, evolved as it was to cope with medium-sized objects moving at medium speeds through medium distances in Africa."[8] I think the wonder is that we can solve as much as we

---

5. For example, Dennett 1992 and Churchland 1995.

6. I am inclined to think that free will is one of those issues that might be on the list. I personally am happy with a compatibilist position, so I am happy to think of it from the vantage point of the machine metaphor; but I could imagine someone saying that free will just isn't one of those things captured by the machine metaphor.

7. He discusses this on a PBS show, "Faith and Reason," first aired around 2000. <http://www.pbs.org/faithandreason/transcript/wein-frame.html>

8. Dawkins 2003, 19. The reader will have noted that I take a malicious satisfaction at using the ideas of the New Atheists to draw conclusions with which they would not agree. The reader will learn that I am ecumenical in that I am happy to extend this honor to Christians also.

can, not that we cannot solve every problem. So if I say that I just don't know, I don't see this as an impossible or silly position to take. It doesn't mean that I should give up on trying to solve problems, but it does mean that the admission that there are problems not solved is not crushing. The eminent population geneticist J. B. S. Haldane mused about this: "My own suspicion is that the universe is not only queerer than we suppose, but queerer than we *can* suppose" (1929, 286).

Why is there something rather than nothing? I simply don't know. It seems to me mysterious and wonderful. That is at least part of the reason why I am not an outright atheist. But that is all I can or will say. Perhaps there is a reason for existence. Perhaps there is no reason. I just don't know. As you have seen, I am more confident on the morality issue. I don't think you can justify moral claims, but I do think you can explain why we have them and why they are so compelling. Does that mean that there are no objective moral claims? That there are no Platonic Forms or nonnatural properties of the kind supposed by G. E. Moore? I personally don't think there are, for apart from anything else I think they would be redundant. But I cannot deny them absolutely nor do I want to. I am really just a skeptic on the subject. As far as sentience is concerned, let me make it clear that I am not into something that in some sense is nonnatural. Obviously the mind is connected to the brain. But what it is I don't know and I don't think anyone else does either. There are days, frankly, when I am drawn to Cartesian dualism, but that has massive problems of its own. I don't think the mind is spooky. I just don't think we can explain it. And the same goes for purpose. Weinberg is absolutely right. Science gives us no answers. Weinberg is also right about what this entails. We can put in our own answers if we wish. I personally always pull away from humanist-type answers that try to link purpose to human happiness and so forth. On the one hand, it all smacks of a bit of a faux religion to me. On the other hand, I am not sure that it gives an answer of the kind that we are seeking. I see no purpose. Is there one? I don't know. And if I did claim to know, I would be worried. "With me the horrid doubt always arises whether the convictions of man's mind, which have been developed from the mind of the lower animals, are of any value or are at all trustworthy. Would anyone trust in the convictions of a monkey's mind, if there are any convictions in such a mind?"[9]

CHRISTIAN ANSWERS

None of this seems very propitious for religious belief, but if you are a believer I very much doubt that my worries are going to trouble you. Let me plough on to the climax of my argument. Science is metaphor-impregnated. The root metaphor today is that of the machine. This leaves a number of questions unanswered. Why is there something rather than nothing? What is the nature and foundation of morality? What is sentience? What is the ultimate purpose of it all? I am a skeptic on answering these questions. There is an opening here for the religious person to offer his or her own answers. Nothing in science can stop them doing so. You may

---

9. Charles Darwin to William Graham, July 3, 1881. Darwin Correspondence Project, 13230.

want to counter such a person on philosophical or theological grounds. That is another matter. A word of caution, however. Although I think it is open for the religious person to offer answers, what they must not do is offer scientific or science-competing answers. In the case of the body–mind problem, for instance, the religious answer cannot be of the same kind as say the materialist who simply wants to reduce consciousness to molecules in motion. It must be a different kind of answer entirely.

This said, I want to complete the circle by pointing out that religious people do try to offer answers to my four questions. I have not arrived at my destination to find that what I have to say and offer is a matter of indifference or irrelevance to the religious. To the contrary, my questions are matters of very great concern and interest to the religious. I am not pretending that I didn't sense this before I started, but I do think that the link up is significant in that it suggests that I have found a theoretical underpinning to what many (religious) people intuit or assume without much argument. They know what they are about, even if they cannot say why they know what they are about.

Why is there something rather than nothing? The Christian (I will stay with them for brevity) answer is that because a necessary being—a being that needed no further justification for its being—created out of an act of love. "I believe in God the Father Almighty, Maker of heaven and earth."[10] Now, as I have said, you may not like this answer. I am not sure that I do very much. I am uncomfortable with necessary beings and I don't see much love in a universe that contained Adolf Hitler. But I don't want to get into philosophical or theological arguments here. I know and respect the fact that believers think they can answer these objections and others of the same kind. My point simply here is that this is not a scientific answer, it does not pretend to be, and nothing in modern science prevents the believer from offering it as an option. You don't have to accept it. But you cannot reject it on the basis of science.

Morality falls into the same category. At some level, the believer is going to relate morality back to the will or design of God. You should do what God wants. Again, this is not a scientific argument and I don't think that science can stop you from making it. I realize that there are major philosophical objections—theological, too, if you think of some of the imperatives of the Old Testament. The classic problem, raised by Plato in the *Euthyphro*, is whether God wants something because it is good (which means that He is not the ultimate authority) or whether it is good because He wants it (which makes morality a subjective whim of the deity). My own feeling is that the Thomistic natural law position speaks successfully to this problem. God created and now He wants us to follow that creation—to do what is natural. So when God says "Don't kill just for kicks" He is not being arbitrary. He is simply asking us to conform to our nature. We are social beings and killing for kicks is against our nature. Of course there are still lots of arguments about what is "natural"—we don't need reminding of this with today's raging debates about sexual orientation. But that is really not my problem at the moment.

10. This is the opening of the Apostles' Creed, probably written by Saint Ambrose, around 390, given in the Anglican version, from the *Book of Common Prayer*, 1662.

I just want to say that if you feel the need for an objective morality and you want to invoke God to get it, nothing in science can stop you.

The question of sentience explains beautifully the point I am making. I have major differences with the noted Christian (Calvinist) philosopher Alvin Plantinga, but I agree entirely with his comments about naturalistic accounts of the nature of mind: "A theist may be able to learn a good bit from this; but fundamentally he will ask different questions and look for answers in a quite different direction" (1999, 19). The Christian answer to the problem of mind or sentience is that we have them because we are made in the likeness of God. "And God said, Let us make man in our image, after our likeness: ... So God created man in his own image, in the image of God created he him; male and female created he them."[11] Medieval theology separated out "image" and "likeness," with the former having to do with attributes and the latter with morality, but post-Reformation this distinction has been less popular. However you take the exact meaning, the fact is that it is not a scientific answer. And science does not speak to it.

What is the meaning of it all? "I believe in the Holy Ghost; the holy Catholic Church; the communion of saints; the forgiveness of sins; the resurrection of the body; and the life everlasting."[12] Well, that is one answer. God created the world for our dwelling place. He created us out of love that we might in return love and honor Him. And at the end of it all, if we behave ourselves He is going to offer us eternal life in some kind of relationship with Him. It is this, of course, that really gets under the skin of the New Atheists, and basically of most nonbelievers. They see this as a ploy or strategy by one group of people to control another group of people. Do what we say—mess up your sex life, don't try to upset the social order even though you are a have-not, give us your money, offer us major social status—and we promise you pie in the sky after you are dead. As one who went to a Christian high school and who had a headmaster who pushed all of this and a lot more, I have considerable sympathy for this complaint. But my objections—and your objections—do not follow from science. At least they do not in the central sense. To take one of my headmaster's obsessions, science shows that masturbation does not lead to the physical and psychological degeneration that he claimed. But the authority he claimed—God will get you if you don't stop now—is certainly not science-based. So here again I argue that science as such cannot stop the believer having the beliefs that he or she holds.

CONCLUSION

So this in the end is why, although I share the beliefs of the New Atheists, I cannot altogether accept their arguments. You may think I am trying to have my cake and eat it, too. Perhaps so. My defense comes from that very Christian poet T. S. Eliot in *Murder in the Cathedral*: "The last temptation is the greatest treason: To do the right deed for the wrong reason." I would say the same of beliefs. If we are to hold a position of importance, let it be for the right reasons.

11. Genesis 1, 26–27, KJV.
12. This is the conclusion of the Apostles' Creed.

REFERENCES

Black, Max. 1962. *Models and Metaphors*. Ithaca, NY: Cornell University Press.
Boyle, Robert. 1996. *A Free Enquiry into the Vulgarly Received Notion of Nature*, ed. Edward B. Davis and Michael Hunter. Cambridge: Cambridge University Press.
Braithwaite, Richard. 1953. *Scientific Explanation*. Cambridge: Cambridge University Press.
Churchland, Paul M. 1995. *The Engine of Reason, the Seat of the Soul*. Cambridge, MA: MIT Press.
Clark, Andy. 2000. *Mindware: An Introduction to the Philosophy of Cognitive Science*. New York: Oxford University Press.
Darwin, Charles. *On the Origin of Species by Means of Natural Selection, or the Preservation of Favoured Races in the Struggle for Life*. London: John Murray, 1859.
———. 1861. *Origin of Species*, 3rd ed. London: John Murray.
Dawkins, Richard. 1976. *The Selfish Gene*. Oxford: Oxford University Press.
———. 1995. *A River Out of Eden*. New York: Basic Books.
———. 2003. *A Devil's Chaplain: Reflections on Hope, Lies, Science and Love*. Boston, MA: Houghton Mifflin.
Dennett, Daniel C. 1992. *Consciousness Explained*. New York: Pantheon.
Dijksterhuis, Eduard Jan. 1961. *The Mechanization of the World Picture*. Oxford: Oxford University Press.
Haldane, John B. S. 1929. *Possible Worlds and Other Essays*. London: Chatto and Windus.
Hesse, Mary. 1966. *Models and Analogies in Science*. Notre Dame, IN: University of Notre Dame Press.
Kant, Immanuel. 1951. *Critique of Judgement*, trans. James H. Bernard. New York: Hafner.
Kitcher, Philip. 2007. *Living With Darwin: Evolution, Design, and the Future of Faith*. New York: Oxford University Press.
Kuhn, Thomas. 1962. *The Structure of Scientific Revolutions*. Chicago: University of Chicago Press.
———. 1993. "Metaphor in Science." In *Metaphor and Thought*, 2nd ed., ed. Andrew Ortony, 533–42. Cambridge: Cambridge University Press.
Lakoff, George, and Johnson, Mark. 1980. *Metaphors We Live By*. Chicago: University of Chicago Press.
Leibniz, Gottfried Wilhelm von. 1973 [1714]. "Principles of Nature and of Grace Founded Upon Reason." *Leibniz: Philosophical Writings*, ed. George Henry R. Parkinson. London: J. M. Dent.
McGinn, Colin. 2000. *The Mysterious Flame: Conscious Minds in a Material World*. New York: Basic Books.
Pepper, Stephen C. 1942. *World Hypotheses: A Study in Evidence*. Berkeley: University of California Press.
Plantinga, Alvin. 1999. "Augustinian Christian Philosophy." In *The Augustinian Tradition*, ed. Gareth B. Matthews, 1–26. Berkeley: University of California Press.
Ruse, Michael. 2010. *Science and Spirituality: Making Room for Faith in the Age of Science*. Cambridge: Cambridge University Press.
———. 2013. *The Gaia Hypothesis: Science on a Pagan Planet*. Chicago: University of Chicago Press.
———, and Wilson, Edward O. 1985. "The Evolution of Morality." *New Scientist* 1478 (1985): 108–28.
Weinberg, Steven. 1977. *The First Three Minutes: A Modern View of the Origin of the Universe*. New York: Basic Books.
Wittgenstein, Ludwig. 1965. "A Lecture on Ethics." *The Philosophical Review* 74: 3–12.

So What Else Is Neo? Theism and Epistemic Recalcitrance[1]

DAVID SHATZ

Fanaticism, whether secular or religious, is often said to exhibit a feature that I call "come-what-may." This feature is manifest in three ways: First, it is said, fanatics hold on to their beliefs no matter what counterevidence arises; second, they act out the consequences of their beliefs no matter whether their actions conflict with widely accepted moral principles, such as principles forbidding the taking of innocent lives; and third, in many cases, they act out the practical consequences of their beliefs no matter what damage such acts inflict upon their self-interest.[2] Fanatics also display other features—most prominently, thinking in dichotomies (us/them) and intolerance.[3] While I would not venture to advocate a full set of necessary and sufficient conditions for fanaticism, it is plausible to treat at least the conjunction of these characteristics as sufficient conditions for

---

1. In a playful spirit, I thought of the title of this paper well before I had any idea of what its subtitle would be—that is, well before I knew what aspect of neoatheism I would be writing about. As things turned out, it does indeed fit my discussion. To see why, the reader must wait a bit.

2. To explain, it is true that religious suicide bombers often seek rewards that await them in the hereafter, and thus act out of self-interest. But—and this is what I mean by "in many cases"—many suicide bombings have been secular. Further, not *all* suicide bombings by religious people are motivated by prospects for the hereafter. In fact, some analysts think—controversially—that even suicide bombings that are ostensibly motivated by aspirations for the hereafter or religious ideals are in truth secularly motivated. For discussion of this question, see, for example, R. Scott Appleby, "Religious Violence: The Strong, the Weak, and the Pathological," *Practical Matters*, no. 5 (Spring 2012): 1–25, and the responses in that issue.

3. Some would add fervor to this list. But fanatics can be cold and calculating.

© 2013 Wiley Periodicals, Inc.

fanaticism in most people's minds, and to posit at the least a commonly felt association between most or all of the individual items and fanaticism.

Are all religious believers fanatical, using these criteria? Is *religion itself* inherently fanatical?[4] In this paper, I will examine these questions as regards two of the features that neoatheists impute to religionists—epistemic recalcitrance (come-what-may with respect to counterevidence) and moral recalcitrance.[5] These two are connected, for moral recalcitrance is in part a type of epistemic recalcitrance, insofar as a moral claim such as *There is a duty to kill infidels* or *There is a duty to kill abortionists* may be held in a manner that seems impervious to contrary evidence or argumentation. In a nutshell, the atheist's charge is not just that religionists base their beliefs on faith instead of rational grounds; it is that religionists can't be reasoned with, no matter what the state of the evidence or argumentation. Richard Dawkins writes about "fundamentalists"[6] that they "know what they believe and they know that *nothing will change their minds*" (again, my italics). Fundamentalism "debauches the scientific enterprise. It teaches us not to change our minds."[7] The word "delusion" in the very title of Dawkins's book was chosen to imply epistemic recalcitrance.[8] Christopher Hitchens' words are that adherents of religion possess an "*unalterable* system of belief" (my italics).[9] To cast the

---

4. Brian Leiter summarizes what he believes are the defining characteristics of religion as (reversing his order to match mine) "insulation from evidence" and "categoricity of religious commands." His "categoricity" can be subdivided into my second and third features. See Leiter, *Why Tolerate Religion?* (Princeton, NJ: Princeton University Press, 2013), chap. 2. He is defining religion; I am at the moment speaking about fanaticism.

5. On the third type of come-what-may, see Moshe Halbertal, *On Sacrifice* (Princeton, NJ: Princeton University Press, 2012), part 2.

6. Fundamentalism and religious fanaticism might be distinguished, but for present purposes, I'll treat them as equivalent.

7. Dawkins, *The God Delusion* (Boston: Houghton Mifflin, 2006), 19 and 321, respectively. See also pp. 28, 319. Below, I discuss Dawkins's restriction of his claim to fundamentalists. See also Leiter, chap. 2. Leiter is very clear about drawing a distinction between how believers behave and what religion requires (see pp. 34–35), and also clear that the normative claims affect how believers behave. Both of these points, which I developed independently, become important later. Georges Rey states that "[i]t is the maintenance of the claims despite an understanding of the errors that leads me to speculate there must be something else going on, and this has led me to wonder whether they really do believe them." Rey suggests that what may be "going on" is self-deception. See Rey, "Meta-Atheism: Religious Avowal as Self-Deception," in *Philosophers without Gods: Meditations on Atheism and the Secular Life* (New York: Oxford University Press, 2007), 244. See also Jonathan Adler, "Faith and Fanaticism," in the same collection, esp. 278–83. I find it implausible in the extreme that, say, the members of the Society For Christian Philosophers—think of names like Adams, the late William Alston, Plantinga, Stump, and van Inwagen—are all victims of self-deception. Given their stress on evidence, it is striking that neoatheists harbor stereotypes and oversimplifications—religion is theism, religious people won't change their minds, religion is all based on faith, believers are self-deceived.

8. See *The God Delusion*, 28. Other terms for epistemic recalcitrance could be dogmatism, belief perseverance, and closed-mindedness.

9. Hitchens, *God Is Not Great: How Religion Spoils Everything* (New York: Twelve, 2007), 250. In context, Hitchens is not discussing questions of evidence and rationality per se, and the sentence is about totalitarianism, not religion. But the context makes clear that he intends the remark to apply to religion as well.

complaint in the familiar language of contemporary epistemology, theists fail to respond appropriately to undefeated defeaters.[10] And not to be open-minded, Daniel Dennett admonishes, is "immoral."[11]

This is not the first time in the recent history of philosophy that religionists have confronted charges of epistemic recalcitrance—remember logical positivism and the problem of falsifiability? Given this precedent, we might ask about the charge of recalcitrance, "So what else is neo?" However, there is something new. Logical positivists insisted that religionists were saying things that were *cognitively meaningless* because they were empirically unfalsifiable. Far from charging meaninglessness, neoatheists who charge theists with epistemic recalcitrance maintain and *underscore* that at least many religious statements are cognitively meaningful (atheism, after all, is a *denial* of a meaningful claim). Dawkins goes so far as to say that "[t]he most basic claims of religion *are* scientific. Religion is a scientific theory."[12] He does not mean that believers reason scientifically (on the contrary, many believe on faith, religious experience, or intuition), but that theism can be assessed as a scientific theory. Why does Dawkins stress this? Well, it is precisely his willingness to, as it were, "dignify" religion as giving a competing scientific theory (or hypothesis) that enables Dawkins to launch his attack. A scientific claim has to be judged by scientific criteria; theism fails miserably.[13] The strategy here contrasts sharply with the positivists': Religion isn't nonscience; it's bad science.[14] In addition to whatever weaknesses there are in the theistic "theory" and its alleged support (Dawkins takes no prisoners in

---

10. Alvin Plantinga highlights defeaters in his numerous writings on religious epistemology.
11. Daniel Dennett, *Breaking the Spell: Religion as a Natural Phenomenon* (New York: Viking Penguin, 2006), 295.
12. Quoted from a 1992 debate with the archbishop of York in Mark Johnston, *Saving God: Religion after Idolatry* (Princeton, NJ: Princeton University Press, 2009), 46. Jerome Gellman suggests four alternatives to Dawkins's categorization of religious belief as a scientific hypothesis. See Gellman's critical review in *Philo* 11(2) (2008): 193–202.
13. In addition, Dawkins's conception of theism as a scientific theory facilitates his rejection of Stephen Jay Gould's thesis that science and religion are "nonoverlapping magisteria." That view would give credit to religion in its realm (value and meaning), and mute the conflict between religion and science over facts. See *God Delusion*, 78ff.
14. In similar fashion, Larry Laudan finds it pointless to seek a demarcation criterion for science as opposed to pseudo-science. Laudan argues that rather than distinguish science from pseudo-science, we should distinguish good science from bad science. Many of the worst scientific theories in history were open to falsification—which is indeed how they came to be fals*ified*. See Laudan, "The Demise of the Demarcation Problem," in *But Is It Science?* ed. Michael Ruse (Amherst, NY: Prometheus, 1996), 337–50.

There is another difference between neoatheism and positivism, or rather some writings by positivists. After arguing that statements purportedly about God are not subject to verification and falsification, Richard Braithwaite maintained that religious statements express intentions to act in accordance with certain moral commitments, such as a commitment to *agape*. (See Braithwaite, *An Empiricist's View of the Nature of Religious Belief* [Cambridge: Cambridge University Press, 1955]). Neoatheism argues that religion not only makes false metaphysical claims, it makes moral claims that, a far cry from *agape*, are execrable and lead to horrific actions and terrible dangers for the society. This moral critique—indeed, neoatheism itself—was given obvious impetus by 9/11.

that regard), theists fail to meet a prime requirement of *good* scientific theorizing, namely openness to revision.[15]

I've had trouble understanding how positivists could move from the allegation that *believers* are epistemically recalcitrant—that no evidence can dissuade them—to the conclusion that their *utterances* are not falsifiable (and hence not cognitively meaningful). If a *statement* is falsifiable, it seems irrelevant whether *those who make it* would ever say that it is false. Presumably, too, positivists themselves believed that with respect to religious statements, there is a point at which believing the statement would become irrational—an insult that fits best with its having cognitive content. Perhaps the best construal of the positivist critique is that, when challenged, theists defend their claims in such a way as to *render them* meaningless.[16] I'll return to the believer/belief distinction later.

Be all that as it may, I'd like to subject atheistic charges of recalcitrance to scrutiny. I will first suggest that we draw a distinction between empirical and normative versions of the charge of recalcitrance, as well as between two types of recalcitrance. Although readers may already sense in the section on empirical versions that normative versions will be needed to surmount the problems facing empirical ones, I beg their indulgence in that section so that the empirical version(s) and their problems can be formulated with care. I argue that, as commonly formulated, the charges are either false, or do not generate a difference between theists and atheists. The point that atheists can be recalcitrant has often been made, particularly in popular literature, but a close analysis of the matter is called for.

Some notes on terminology: For the most part, I'll be using the terms "atheist" and "neoatheist" interchangeably, but will use only "neoatheist" when I'm talking about the specific individuals (Dawkins–Dennett–Harris–Hitchens) who compose the group known by that name. Importantly, since neoatheism tends to define religions as committed to belief in supernatural beings, I will very inaccurately use "religion" interchangeably with "theism" until it becomes relevant late in the paper to point out that this equation is a mistake.[17] (It is a mistake both because religious practice and feelings exist in many cases without metaphysical beliefs and because metaphysical beliefs in many cases exist without religious practice and feelings.) Finally, the term "counterevidence" or "contrary evidence" will refer not only to what we normally call data, but also to counter*argument* that proceeds without introducing new data, building instead on data already known.

---

15. Some atheists spin matters differently, at least as regards creationism. Thus, on the witness stand in an Arkansas case in 1982 about teaching creationism in schools, Michael Ruse testified that creationism is not a scientific theory because it is unfalsifiable. See Ruse's court testimony in *But Is It Science?* ed. Ruse, 301–06.

16. I thank Alex Sztuden for this suggestion.

17. For nuanced and mostly critical examinations of the notion that metaphysical beliefs play a significant role in religious life, see Howard Wettstein's essays in his *The Significance of Religious Experience* (New York: Oxford University Press, 2012).

EPISTEMIC RECALCITRANCE: EMPIRICAL VERSIONS

Consider the following picture: (1) theists base their beliefs on faith, atheists on reason; (2) atheists are open to refutation 24/7, while religionists are recalcitrant until their dying day. The evidentially grounded but nonetheless tentative and revisable nature of scientific theories stands in stark relief to religion, on both counts, and theists are thus doubly criticized.

Something is wrong with this picture. But first let us distinguish two types of epistemic recalcitrance. In cases of *actual-world* epistemic recalcitrance, a person has already been presented with good evidence against her belief—evidence that makes the belief irrational on the total evidence—but has not changed the belief. To attribute *counterfactual* epistemic recalcitrance is to say not that right now the total evidence goes against the belief, yet the believer, knowing all this evidence, has not changed her mind, but rather that no matter what counterevidence *were* to arise that would make the belief irrational on the total evidence, and no matter how familiar the person were to be with this evidence, the person would not revise the belief. Neoatheists (and predecessors) believe that theists are guilty of both actual-world recalcitrance—that is, there is currently good reason, on the total evidence, not to believe, but it leaves theists unmoved—and counterfactual recalcitrance.[18] For example, theists (so might atheists say) not only do not surrender their beliefs despite the evil that exists in the actual world, but they also would not surrender their belief even were a doomsday scenario to take place in which the world has been nuked to the point of near extinction and the remaining people endure unmitigated agony.

Note that, whereas a charge of actual-world recalcitrance impugns the *truth* of the proposition that is believed, since it references the actual state of the total evidence, a charge of purely counterfactual recalcitrance does not carry an implication of falsehood. The charge relates not to the content of the belief, but to the believer, in particular the *style* with which the believer holds the belief. Even if the belief can be rationally defended, the counterfactually recalcitrant believer seemingly (1) is irrational to *some* degree, (2) lacks a sense of epistemic responsibility, and (3) is deficient in epistemic virtue. Given the lack of entailment between counterfactual recalcitrance and falsehood, one may wonder why it is important for neoatheists to attribute counterfactual recalcitrance as opposed to being content with showing that theism is false. We will return to this question at the end of the paper. Another criticism of epistemic recalcitrance could be that when believers possess counterfactual recalcitrance, their beliefs and doxastic habits have negative utility for the society; the social consequences are pernicious or dangerous.[19] (I will obviously have to omit discussion of the claim that no belief can be refuted by counterevidence because one can always tinker with background assumptions.)

---

18. Obviously, it could happen that S gives up a belief on the basis of evidence E even though no other, counterfactual evidence would sway S.

19. W. K. Clifford, in his 1877 essay, "The Ethics of Belief," used utility arguments to augment his case for the principle that "it is wrong, always, everywhere, and for anyone to hold a belief with insufficient evidence."

Let's return now to the two pieces of the picture we started with, to wit (1) theists base their beliefs on faith, atheists on reason; and (2) atheists are open to refutation 24/7, while religionists are recalcitrant until their dying day. With regard to the first claim—that religion is based on faith, science on reason—certainly one objection is that there are theists at the academic, clerical, and lay levels who hold their theistic beliefs on the basis of evidence, for example, evidence of fine-tuning.[20] Some of these theists would not be committed to religion were it not for this evidence.[21] So claim (1) is not true of all theists. Furthermore, the current debate over whether beliefs can be justified without evidence has to figure into whether (1) generates a good criticism. True, one might distinguish between believing on faith and believing on something like direct perception of truth or on intuition, regarding believing on faith as irrational and believing based on the other sources as rational. But no matter how we slice it, a simple insistence on basing beliefs on evidence will not carry the day absent vigorous argument.[22]

More important for my purposes is the charge of counterfactual recalcitrance (CR). Let's try a first formulation:

(CR1): Religious believers would not revise their beliefs under any circumstances. In psychologists' terms, their thinking shows rigidity and no flexibility.

As a universal generalization, this statement, while oft heard, is false: after all, theists *often* not only revise some of their religious beliefs while staying "within" their religion (such as by interpreting certain biblical narratives figuratively), but also switch religions, or even defect and leave religion altogether. The Pew Survey shows that 28 percent of American adults "have left the faith in which

---

20. Cf. Peter van Inwagen, "Is God an Unnecessary Hypothesis?" in *God and the Ethics of Belief: New Essays in Philosophy of Religion*, ed. Andrew Dole and Andrew Chignell (Cambridge: Cambridge University Press, 2005), 131–49. Van Inwagen denies that *God exists* is a hypothesis at all.

21. Cf. Leiter, *Why Tolerate Religion?* 39–40, where he maintains that intellectualism does not "capture the character of popular religious belief," and that those in the intellectualist tradition would not change their beliefs in the light of new evidence. The first claim (about popular belief), I think, underestimates how much the classic pro-theistic arguments have become woven into theistic belief at the popular level, with all sorts of popular books espousing simplistic versions of, for example, the cosmological and design arguments. The second allegation (of unrevisability) is no doubt true in many cases, but certainly in many other cases the "intellectualist" theists are open to contrary evidence—some or many defect from theism when the counterevidence or counterarguments pile up.

22. The conception of faith in this paragraph—as believing a proposition without having evidence for it—is highly simplistic, both because faith requires more than this (for example, wanting the proposition to be true) and because some philosophers do not think that faith entails lack of evidence or even that it requires belief. Recent examinations of faith that show its complexity include: Lara Buchak, "Can It Be Rational to Have Faith?," in *Probability in the Philosophy of Religion*, ed. Jake Chandler and Victoria S. Harrison (New York: Oxford University Press, 2012), 225–48; Daniel Howard-Snyder, "Propositional Faith: What It Is and Is Not," *American Philosophical Quarterly* 50 (4) (2013): 257–71; and Jonathan L. Kvanvig, "Affective Theism and People of Faith" (in this volume).

they are raised in favor of another religion or no religion at all ... Constant movement characterizes the American religious marketplace."[23] Movements from being a believer to being an atheist are evident in numerous of the essays by the secular philosophers who wrote for the book of autobiographies called *Philosophers Without Gods*, as well as uncountably many other biographies and autobiographies.[24] In fact, even people we characterize as fanatics defect on occasion (which makes me skeptical whether the elements of "come-what-may" that I mentioned at the outset characterize all those whom we call fanatics). A Google search of "former Muslim extremist" yields many articles and books by people who left Islamist extremism for moderate religion, at times because they came to witness up close the consequences of extremist views, for example brutal murders, or because they gained evidence that mitigated their demonization of the West.[25] Interestingly, whereas when they raise charges of recalcitrance scientists and philosophers place much weight on recalcitrant *adherence* to religion, and ignore defection, psychologists and sociologists recognize both phenomena. Is this a case of selective attention? It will be of no use to atheists to change the first words of (CR1) to "*Some* religious believers" because no doubt some *atheists* likewise would never abandon atheism, some scientists and historians would never abandon certain of their theories, and so on. Note that migrations do not have to cross a canyon: Some theists move only from an attitude of subjective certainty to belief tinged with doubts, or to agnosticism, and some continue to believe but start inching away by making moral decisions without consulting their tradition.[26] Admittedly, it seems odd to defend religion against charges of irrationality by pointing out that people defect from it, but such is the dialectical situation with regard to the atheist's claim about belief perseverance among theists.[27]

It might be retorted that theists abandon theism and revise their beliefs only because of life experiences, such as acculturation, loss of interest, exposure to new pursuits, over-involvement with work, a desire to be free of restrictions on sex and free thought (along with attendant guilt feelings for violating those restrictions), resentment of authority, bitterness, aging, depression, diminution of social support, and so on. Some situations of these types, to be sure, foster reasoning, but not necessarily reasoning about evidence; rather, some people living a life with many demands may reason that they cannot make religion very important in their lives,

---

23. <http://religions.pewforum.org/reports>. However, lack of affiliation (the "nones") does not entail lack of belief in God, and most of the "nones" have a religious orientation but free themselves of institutionalized religion. My thanks to Michael Berger and Stephen Tipton for guidance on this issue.

24. *Philosophers without Gods: Meditations on Atheism and the Secular Life*, ed. Louise M. Antony (New York: Oxford University Press, 2007).

25. My thanks to Robert Eisen for mentioning this.

26. Michael Berger raised this point.

27. The notion encouraged by some neoatheists that religious believers are less intelligent than atheists (see Dawkins, 127–29; Dennett calls secularists "brights," but denies he is disparaging them [p. 21]) is absurd on its face, as if those pejoratives could justly be applied to, say, The Society of Christian Philosophers (to mention specifically people who have thought through the arguments for and against theism in a professional capacity). Cf., nonetheless, the studies of scientists cited by Dawkins, ibid.

and some with a family may reason that religion is very important.[28] In sum, when religionists change their beliefs, atheists might claim, it is not because of contrary evidence. This retort forces atheists into a revision of (CR1):

> (CR2): Religious believers would not revise their religious beliefs on the basis of contrary evidence, although they would revise them due to certain causes other than the acquisition of evidence.

The famous psychological research of Leon Festinger et al., although oddly not found in the indexes to the books by Dawkins, Dennett, Harris, and Hitchens,[29] would seem to support (CR2). Festinger et al. identified psychological mechanisms that lead to epistemic recalcitrance. Under certain conditions, encountering contrary evidence can cause increased fervor and even intensified efforts at proselytization.[30] Because religious faith tends to be so deep and impactful on a person's life and to enjoy social support, the likelihood of this result is understandable.

Nonetheless, (CR2) is defective as formulated because there must be constraints on what sorts of contrary reasons are being imagined. If S would give up her belief in God if and only if S were to see an elephant, would that solitary irrational responsiveness to reasons allow S to escape a charge of counterfactual recalcitrance?[31] Such niceties aside, (CR2), like (CR1), is false: It is quite obvious that believers sometimes defect on the basis of contrary evidence, a proposition for which I can supply much anecdotal evidence from my own observations. Also, the cases of extremists mentioned earlier involved belief changes that were due to an appreciation of moral consequences and of misinformation concerning the West. Importantly, if (CR2) were true, *how could neoatheists hope to persuade anyone that theism is false*? The very fact that they write their tracts *with the aim of changing the minds of believers* indicates that they too do not really endorse (CR2).

---

28. My thanks to Shalom Carmy for this last point. Most of the "life experiences" I mention appear on a list of eighteen reasons in Solomon Schimmel, *The Tenacity of Religious Belief: Fundamentalism and the Fear of Truth* (New York: Oxford University Press, 2008), 212–13, citing a variety of works on the psychology of religion.

29. It is drawn upon, however, by Schimmel: see *The Tenacity of Unreasonable Belief*, 212–13.

30. See Festinger, Henry W. Riecken, and Stanley Schacter, *When Prophecy Fails: A Social and Psychological Study of a Modern Group that Predicted the Destruction of the World* (New York: Harper & Row, 1956); also Festinger, *A Theory of Cognitive Dissonance* (Stanford, CA: Stanford University Press, 1957).

31. The problem here parallels a problem in "reasons-responsiveness" approaches to moral responsibility. See John Martin Fischer and Mark Ravizza, *Responsibility and Control: A Theory of Moral Responsibility* (Cambridge: Cambridge University Press, 1998). Another complication: if captured by a cult composed of atheists, and bombarded all day by specious atheist arguments, a religionist might change his or her mind because of those arguments, but only because they were drilled in by brainwashing and not by true appreciation of their force. Atheists would, therefore, need to pack additional conditions into (CR2) to accommodate such cases. Finally, an atheist might defend (CR2) by arguing that, because theistic beliefs aren't based on reasons but instead on faith, they will not be revised on the basis of reasons. This strikes me as patently fallacious, although the fallacy does not affect the truth of (CR2). But all these tweaks are tangential since (CR2) is false anyway, even with refinements.

Dawkins indeed writes, "I believe there are *plenty of* open-minded people out there" (my italics), and his website RichardDawkins.net includes "Converts' Corner," in which erstwhile believers tell their stories.[32] The larger the number of theists whom an atheist thinks he can convince by evidence/argument, or, better, has convinced, the more counterexamples that atheist must admit to (CR2).

But wait, you say: Aren't neo-atheist remarks like Dawkins's about epistemic recalcitrance expressly confined to fundamentalists and fanatics and "dyed in the wool faith-heads"[33]? Isn't imputing to neoatheists the view that *all* religionists are guilty of counterfactual recalcitrance a straw man? Perhaps Dawkins did not entertain the thought of changing *everyone's* minds by his arguments, but only to change the minds of nonfundamentalists. I'll grant that. But we then need to ask: who counts as a fundamentalist? If a fundamentalist is a theist who is both actually and counterfactually recalcitrant, then it is a tautology that all fanatics are recalcitrant. If "fundamentalist" is supposed to be defined by other criteria, for example adherence to biblical literalism or desire to kill infidels, and the claim is that fundamentalists are recalcitrant, then we must again proffer, this time against (C2), the counterexample of defectors from literalism and from a policy of violence against infidels.

Perhaps the pertinent question is how many recalcitrant believers there are relative to the whole religious population,[34] which brings us to a third understanding of recalcitrance:

(CR3): *Most* religious believers would not revise their religious beliefs on the basis of contrary reasons.

Do we know whether (CR3) is true? How are observers supposed to judge what someone else would believe in counterfactual circumstances? How do we collect data? I suggest the following support for (CR3). Festinger's studies suggest that commitments that are held with special depth, foster identity, impact on actions and life, and enjoy social support are commitments likely to remain firm in the face of contrary evidence. Religious commitments are of this kind. Moreover, the Pew Studies suggest that while there is defection from institutionalized religion, defection from a belief in God or in some other spirit or force is uncommon.

But even if (CR3) is true, religious believers might put forth a *tu quoque* that we have already adumbrated. They might charge that notwithstanding their projecting themselves as open-minded, *most* atheists would not revise their atheistic beliefs on the basis of contrary reasons,[35] particularly if they are invested in them

---

32. Dawkins, 28. Dawkins mentions Converts' Corner to refute charges that he cannot achieve more than preach to the choir, but he goes on to explain the benefits of preaching even to a choir (17–18).

33. Dawkins, 28.

34. Atheists very likely feel that the only way to explain why theists so much outnumber them is to attribute counterfactual recalcitrance to most of them.

35. As alleged by critics like Leon Wieseltier, "The God Genome" (a review of Dennett, *Breaking the Spell*), *The New York Times*, February 19, 2006, and David B. Hart, "Daniel Dennett hunts the snarks," *First Things*, no. 169 (January 2007): 31, who writes of the assertion that atheists and philosophers are open to all ideas that it "accords with no sane person's experience . . ."

and have lived a life reflecting that investment. Hitchens wrote somewhere—I don't have his exact words—"If ever I were to convert, it would be so that when I die there'll be one less believer in the world."[36] Of course, he meant this as a clever quip, which it is, but it may be revealing. Hence, a *tu quoque* is in order as regards (CR3). (Obviously, I use the Hitchens case to illustrate, not to prove a generalization.) Atheists, naturally, will claim that if they seem epistemically recalcitrant regarding religion, it is because they have not been presented with any *good* reasons to revise their views. Their actual-world recalcitrance, they'll say, is justified, but they are not guilty of counterfactual recalcitrance, for were *good* reasons for revision to come to their attention, they would revise. But if this is the atheist response, why can't religionists say the same thing to defend their own recalcitrance? The charge of recalcitrance, recall, was a charge about the style with which certain beliefs are held; if one defends oneself against charges of recalcitrance by saying that all proffered contrary reasons have been unconvincing, our discussion becomes one about content, not style.

The mechanisms identified by Festinger don't operate only in the case of religious people, and it is only to be expected that secularists are thought by religionists to be counterfactually recalcitrant. Dawkins admits that not all scientists live up to the ideal of counterfactual openness, even when they pay it lip service.[37] But even scientists who are open to revision about scientific theories, and include such openness in their self-image, may not be open to revision when it comes to their beliefs in the nonscientific domain. Think first about philosophers: Philosophers are supposed to be open-minded and take arguments wherever they lead. Reportedly, two thirds of philosophers reject moral relativism.[38] Yet how many of these philosophers would maintain their anti-relativism no matter what philosophical arguments were brought for relativism? Many, I suspect. How many even now can refute relativism, especially if they do not specialize in ethics?[39] We have no reason to think that scientists who believe in an objective ethics are different from philosophers—an atheist scientist who is an ethical relativist (or absolutist!) may be closed to revision with regard to these beliefs, which lie outside the domain of science and are not controlled by its ethos.[40] Perhaps many such individuals are similarly recalcitrant *vis-à-vis* religion (I am not forgetting Dawkins's characterization of religion as a scientific theory; I still believe that the scientist may be less open to change in the case of religion.) In other words, even if scientists would change their *scientific* views in the face of contrary evidence, their doxastic conduct may be different when it comes to switching to a metaphysical outlook, especially one that entails burdensome practices, can involve a major

---

36. I do not know the source of this remark.
37. *The God Delusion*, 321.
38. A frequent theme in the book *Philosophers without Gods* is that, contrary to stereotype, atheists (or at least atheistic philosophers) believe in an objective ethics.
39. Cf. Dennett, 375–76.
40. See Kwame Anthony Appiah's review of Harris's *The Moral Landscape* in *The New York Times Book Review* (October 1, 2010), available at <http://www.nytimes.com/2010/10/03/books/review/Appiah-t.html?pagewanted=all&_r=0>.

change in identity, destabilizes their social relations, etc. In these circumstances, they may be counterfactually recalcitrant.[41]

We may press further with our consideration of moral beliefs, moving from meta-beliefs about relativism to beliefs about substantive moral principles. The literary critic Terry Eagleton, in a book devoted to refuting the duo he playfully calls "Ditchkins" (Dawkins and Hitchens), quotes Hitchens as saying that humanists' beliefs are open to revision but theists' beliefs are not. He then parries the charge with a *tu quoque*: "One takes it, then, that Hitchens stands ready at any moment to jettison his belief in human liberty, along with his distaste for political tyrants and Islamic suicide bombers."[42] Eagleton continues:

> In fact of course, he [Hitchens] turns out to be a skeptic when it comes to other people's dogmas and a true believer when it comes to his own. There is, by the way, nothing wrong with dogma, which simply means "things taught." The liberal principles of freedom and tolerance are dogmas, and none the worse for that. It is simply a liberal paradox that there must be something closed-minded about open-mindedness and something inflexible about tolerance.[43]

This is not to deny that some humanists and Westerners can be radicalized into rejecting their (prior) values. But it is to assert that there may be many, Hitchens among them, who would not reject those values no matter what the evidence—or at least that such an assertion is not less defensible than(CR3).[44]

In other words, the neoatheist moral critique of religion is *itself* founded on certain principles with respect to which atheists are recalcitrant.[45] How many philosophers would complain about people who would hold on come-what-may to the belief that it is wrong to kill innocent people just for the heck of it? Atheists cannot respond that humanist beliefs, unlike religious beliefs, are universally held because the whole point of the neoatheist moral critique of religion was that humanistic beliefs are *not* universally held—that is, that many adherents of religions don't hold them. To say that humanistic beliefs aren't based on evidence, and therefore are not subject to counterevidence, would make things still worse for

---

41. An intriguing example was proposed by David Berger: What would atheists do if the (in fact extremely implausible) enterprise of "Bible codes"—of "decoding" the text and discovering therein hidden references to much later events in world history—turned out (contrary to fact!) to succeed so dramatically and inexplicably, with minutely detailed and unambiguous descriptions, that atheists had no explanation of the predictions' success? How many of them would be prepared to embrace the Bible's divinity?

42. Terry Eagleton, *Reason, Faith, and Revolution: Reflections on the God Debate* (New Haven, CT: Yale University Press, 2009), 127.

43. Ibid.

44. Dennett (23–24) speaks of values that are for him "sacred" (democracy, justice, life, love, and truth), and between which he must prioritize. The neoatheist stress on scientific method puts them into a difficult position when it comes to explaining the possibility of objective values and especially placing them in a hierarchy.

45. This isn't to say that theists dispute the moral principles, or don't show recalcitrance regarding them—very roughly, moderates don't dispute the principles, extremists do.

atheists, as then they would be admitting that they hold beliefs that are not founded on evidence and not subject to counterevidence.

Let me add something here—that even modulated and qualified moral principles may be adhered to in recalcitrant fashion. Although moral principles may admit exceptions, a qualified version of the principles could nonetheless be held recalcitrantly—as could a qualified version of the already qualified version. Ultimately, even the qualified moral beliefs and qualified principles could be held unconditionally. This strengthens the case for saying that with regard to *some* moral principles, even philosophers are recalcitrant. And what about the commitment to openness itself? Is that revisable? I doubt that many of religion's critics would drop the commitment. Again, they cannot justify their recalcitrance by saying that the commitment to openness is universally endorsed, for it is rejected by extremists.[46]

Tu quoque arguments do not justify a procedure or behavior pattern, but neither do they merely score debater's points. Rather, a *tu quoque* suggests that the people who made the original accusation (in this case atheists) should reflect on how they would defend their own procedures or behavior patterns, and ask themselves whether the same defense could be used by their target. At the risk of sounding unduly cynical, I put forward a suspicion: that one's attitude to recalcitrance depends on whose ox is being gored. Actual-world and counterfactual recalcitrance are *perceived* as faults only when the recalcitrant believers hold a belief that the perceiver deems false. When atheists or marginal believers become radicalized by religious (or for that matter secular) extremists and commit mass murder, the neoatheists would wish that these individuals were not so open-minded and would see no merit in their being so. They won't say, "Well, bravo to them. At least they're openminded." Their reaction to content determines their appraisal of the significance and value of a recalcitrant style; your being open-minded is praised as a virtue only when your mind is open to what the assessor deems the correct view. Or so I suspect. The thinking would go: Because I think my present beliefs are well-founded (be they based on reason or on faith), I believe I have earned the right to be recalcitrant, and to expect it from others.[47] And that way of thinking, a form of conservatism, may be present on both sides of the debate over theism.[48]

Consider another version of CR:

(CR4): The percentage of atheists who will become theists over a given time period because they acquire contrary evidence exceeds the percentage of

---

46. It could be asked as well: What about the commitment to the supreme value of truth as opposed to other goods? Could that be withdrawn in the face of contrary evidence? Yes, if S would accept arguments for pragmatic justifications in certain cases. Neoatheists disparage pragmatic justifications, however. On truth, cf. Dennett, 376.

47. My thanks to Alex Sztuden for this point.

48. There is a glaring connection between this topic and a puzzle put forth by Saul Kripke: If I know that *p*, I know that all contrary evidence is misleading, and therefore I should not revise my belief because of such evidence. The puzzle is why knowledge does not thus entail dogmatism. See Kripke, "On Two Paradoxes of Knowledge," in *Philosophical Troubles*, Vol. 1 (New York: Oxford University Press, 2012). Buchak discusses the rationality of not inquiring into further evidence, but unfortunately her rich paper came to my attention too late to incorporate its insights into my text.

theists who will become atheists during that period because they acquire contrary evidence.

We would need data to establish or refute (CR4). But would it not be embarrassing to atheists if the result of open-minded inquiry by atheists was that many jumped to the other ship? And what would (CR4) show if true? Theists will claim that the reason the percentage of defection among theists is lower than for secularists is that they hold the truth. Atheists will find that claim outrageous. But if they do, then it is not the style of the theists that is at fault, it is the content of their beliefs.

Because of the problems plaguing empirical versions of the atheists' imputation of counterfactual recalcitrance to theists, and because of the difficulties neoatheists will have in distinguishing theists from atheists with regard to recalcitrance, it will serve the atheists' purposes better to attack *norms* of theism that would justify recalcitrance—not only in order to show that religion has objectionable epistemic norms, but also to argue that the presence of those norms makes it more likely that *empirically* a theist will be more counterfactually recalcitrant than a secularist will. Let us turn, therefore, to norm-centered versions.

EPISTEMIC RECALCITRANCE: NORM-CENTERED VERSIONS

Norm-centered versions of the charge of epistemic recalcitrance do not claim that believers *won't* change their minds in the face of contrary evidence, but rather that the logic of theism does not *allow such change*. The critic's claim can be summarized, thus:

> (CR5): Religious believers endorse certain norms that preclude revision of their beliefs. Specifically, the norm of *unconditional commitment* (UC) requires believers to be both actually and counterfactually recalcitrant. Norm UC implies that a believer's disregard of challenges to faith is meritorious. Because such norms are not part of secular belief systems, including secular moral systems, secularist believers are not duty bound to ignore contrary reasons, and indeed are duty bound by the ethics of belief not to ignore them.

The requirement of unconditional commitment amounts to a fanatic's credo. Dawkins admits that not all scientists would follow in practice the scientist's credo—*be always open to revision*—"[b]ut all pay lip service to it as an ideal."[49]

Ostensibly, it indeed is irrational to accept UC. UC can close you off to truth. Notice that the ostensible irrationality of accepting UC does not entail that flesh-and-blood religious believers are irrational, irresponsible, or lacking in epistemic virtue, since many believers violate UC *in practice*, as is manifest when they defect from theism.[50] Observers may suspect, in fact (although admittedly this is the sort of armchair speculation that I critiqued earlier), that not many

---

49. *The God Delusion*, 321.
50. See also Leiter, 35.

believers, whether they defect or not in the actual world, are so strong in their faith that *no* counterevidence *would* move them *were* it to be presented. Put another way—UC is honored in the breach. So if the atheists' aim is to indict believers as opposed to the content of religious belief, (CR5) appears unsuited for the purpose. But we can separate the critique of theism from the critique of theists; whereas empirical versions of the charge of recalcitrance criticized *believers*, normative versions criticize the religion's principles. (Ironically, perhaps atheists should commend theists who do not live according to UC.) And it is not just that UC is irrational; on the heels of that objection, theists who accept UC confront another objection, a charge of inconsistency: If UC is irrational, how could a perfect God dictate it?

Religious believers have several ways to deal with these objections.

A. Post-Kuhn, it is widely held that in the case of large-scale scientific theories, scientists are not irrational if they hold on to their theories despite contrary evidence.[51] Basil Mitchell draws an analogy between the conservatism that Kuhn attributes to scientists who are working within a "paradigm" and the conservatism exemplified by religious believers. Just as scientists embrace large-scale scientific theories, theists embrace large-scale metaphysical systems based on many evidential considerations, and just as in the scientific case conservatism is justified, so too in the religious one. Mitchell, thus, pleads for parity between science and religion, a common pattern of argument in contemporary philosophy of religion, as well as parity with such fields as history and literary interpretation.[52]

Eagleton, too, points to the reasonableness of conservatism:

> It is not usual for a life-long conservative suddenly to become a revolutionary because a thought struck him. This is not to say that faith is closed to evidence, as Dawkins wrongly considers, or to deny that one can come to change one's mind about beliefs.... It is just that more is involved in changing really deep-seated beliefs than just changing your mind. The rationalist tends to dismiss the tenacity of faith (other people's faith, anyway) for irrational stubbornness rather than for the sign of a certain interior depth, one which encompasses reason but also transcends it. Because certain of our commitments are constitutive of who we are, we cannot alter them without what Christianity traditionally calls a conversion.... This is one reason why other people's faith can look like plain irrationalism, which indeed it sometimes is.[53]

---

51. See Thomas Kuhn, *The Structure of Scientific Revolutions* (Chicago: University of Chicago Press, 1961). Mitchell and Eagleton view conservatism as rational. Kuhn often was accused of viewing science as irrational or the product of mob psychology, but this is an image he sought to combat. Any evaluation of conservatism as irrational must confront the cases drawn from science.

52. Basil Mitchell, *The Justification of Religious Belief* (New York: Seabury Press, 1973). Mitchell's work is also drawn on by Douglas Groothuis in his "Obstinacy in Religious Belief," *Sophia* 32(2) (1993): 25–35. I thank Michael Bergmann for this reference.

53. Eagleton, 138–39.

Of course, religious believers generally do not rehearse these arguments, but our interest is in whether UC—the principle itself—can be justified. Mitchell's and Eagleton's defenses go a distance toward vindicating UC, and for that matter toward justifying secularists' resisting conversion to a religious perspective.[54] But in its strongest form, UC would dictate a conservatism that goes far beyond what these advocates of conservatism have in mind. Mitchell and Eagleton concede that at a certain point conservatism is not warranted, whereas UC requires that the theist's belief not be given up at any point. Even so, Mitchell and Eagleton, I believe, reduce the irrationality of UC. (Note, as an aside, that given the psychological realities Eagleton describes, it is not easy to see how advocates of one religion could expect others to convert readily.)

B. Believers might jettison the requirement of unconditional commitment. Robert Merrihew Adams, responding to the supreme value that Kierkegaard assigns to unconditional commitment—Kierkegaard deems an irrational unconditional religious commitment as more religious than rational religion, if the latter is religious at all—submits that "[i]n a tolerable religious ethics some way must be found to conceive of the religious interest as inclusive rather than exclusive of the best of other interests—including, I think, the interest in having well-grounded religious beliefs."[55] Adams, of course, does not deny that faith is a virtue,[56] but he is seeking to modulate its role (without here specifying how). I may be overstating his position, but insofar as UC demands that the believer put reason aside, it is perhaps not "a tolerable religious ethic."[57] As Louis Pojman once noted, Kierkegaard implies that the crazier a belief system is, the more religious it is—so that Charles Manson's cult is more religious than Roman Catholicism, and a religion in which God is a bionic rat surpasses most others in religiosity.[58] Perhaps UC is, therefore, untenable.

---

54. A suggestive fact: People fault politicians for flip-flops, for changing their minds on issues. One would think that if we want open-mindedness, mind changes are entirely expected and indeed praiseworthy. Granted, criticisms of flip-flops are grounded in suspicions of pandering, or political interests of the critic, but I suspect the negativity strangely would exist even without those factors. We do expect firmness and stability of belief. When minds change in politics, we suspect duplicity. Cf. Dawkins, 321.

55. "Kierkegaard's Arguments against Objective Reasoning in Religion," repr. in Adams, *The Virtue of Faith* (New York: Oxford University Press, 1987), 39–40. Adams presents other considerations against UC on pp. 32–33.

56. See the title essay of *The Virtue of Faith*, 9–24.

57. Adams may not himself give up UC. In "The Leap of Faith" (in *The Virtue of Faith*, 47), he says that, although people with faith might seek objective reasons, "the possibility of actually giving up her central convictions is felt by the believer as remote." And, more to the point, he then says that if in the inquiry the believer feels the belief is at risk, then Kierkegaard "is on firmer ground in holding that while the investigation lasts, the investigator cannot have a fully confident religious faith." I'm not sure whether this is adopting UC as a norm, but it could be read as adopting UC as a necessary condition of "confident religious faith," and if "confident religious faith" is required of a believer, as it *prima facie* is, then UC is a norm. Still, regardless of Adams's actual position, his concern with well-grounded beliefs and with the matters he raises on pp. 32–33 undermines a UC requirement. Aaron Segal noted that someone could adopt a policy of not seeking objective reasons for belief while denying UC.

58. See Pojman, "Rationality and Religious Belief," *Religious Studies* 15 (June 1979): 168–69.

C. In lieu of rejecting the unconditional commitment requirement or alternatively embracing it in its usual meaning, a theist may reconstrue it. Mitchell suggests understanding UC as a matter of *trusting* in God no matter what dangers and difficulties one faces, rather than a matter of believing in God no matter what evidence appears. "Although there is a Christian duty to trust in God, this does not imply a duty, let alone an unconditional duty, to go on believing that there is a God.... This is to say that the requirement of unconditional faith is one which has its place within the system of theistic belief and cannot properly be interpreted as an obligation to embrace the system itself."[59] It seems hard to grasp how one could unconditionally trust in someone when one does not unconditionally believe in the existence of the one trusted. But I think Mitchell's suggestion is coherent: the trust is unconditional within a certain context and background (viz., where there is belief in God).

D. Only unconditional commitment enables a person to pursue the consequences of the belief in full devotion and increase the chances for achieving an ideal.[60] Of course, we don't want extremists to pursue *their* ideals unconditionally on this basis, but the need for wholehearted devotion suggests a measure of rationality in adopting UC.

E. Aaron Segal noted (in correspondence) that S could accept UC but be ready to deny UC if presented with good reasons for doing so. If S thus gives up UC at the meta-level, ultimately S is not unconditionally committed.

F. Theists might try to remove the charge that UC is irrational as follows. Suppose that theism is *true*. Would a good God want to let people relinquish the religious truths that they hold in hand? No. On the contrary, He would impose norms that are likely to lead them to persevere in their belief. God's wish to have believers believe the truth about His existence, a belief that not only is true but also can lead to varied sorts of benefits (not only dished-out rewards, but also meaning, security, moral motivation, faith, and spirituality), trumps concerns about the irrationality that UC seems to allow. And so God prescribes UC. It is not entirely clear how this attempt to make *God* reasonable translates into a defense of the rationality of *believers* who submit to UC, but it does suggest that theists need not be troubled by the existence of UC in their system. Only by refuting theism—that is, only by shifting from style to content and showing that God does not exist—can critics of theism prevent this appeal to God's goodness from serving as an underpinning for UC. Thus, UC makes sense within theism. A question that arises is whether an analogous argument can be made in the case of secular belief—heads of state who are certain of a particular political position might, on that grounds,

---

59. Mitchell, *The Justification of Religious Belief*, 140. C. S. Lewis maintains a similar position in "On Obstinacy in Belief," *Sewanee Review* 63(4) (October/December 1955): 25–38. He contends that once a person believes in God, it makes sense to trust Him unconditionally—so UC is rational. The notion that trust in God means believing that all will turn out well is discussed critically in Rabbi Aharon Lichtenstein, "Bittachon: Trust in God," in *By His Light: Character and Values in the Service of God*, adapted by Rabbi Reuven Ziegler (Jersey City, NJ: Ktav and Alon Shevut, Israel: Yeshivat Har Etzion, 2003), 134–61.

60. Jerome Gellman suggested this response, and it appears as well in Adams, "Leap of Faith," 45–46.

demand unconditional commitment to it. But then again, it is one thing for God to be certain of His own existence (!) and another for a leader to be certain of a political position.

It may be countered that it is unreasonable of God to demand unconditional commitment because it is too difficult to attain that level of commitment, or for that matter, some lesser degree of recalcitrance. One counter to this counter is that even though God imposes the norm of UC, He appreciates the difficulty of adhering to it, and will excuse many of those who give up their commitment in circumstances in which it is very hard to sustain such commitment. If He does this, He is not being unreasonable. However, someone who remains committed in the face of circumstances, data, and arguments that challenge his faith may ultimately feel closer to God.

I don't see a clear winner here. Atheists (who, frankly, are probably tearing their hair out in frustration over the theist's posited response; belief in God, they think, is silly enough, but sillier still is to impute to Him all sorts of calculations like wanting us to have truth and being ready to excuse those who do not attain unconditional commitment) could say that, even if God exists, it is worse for Him to influence people to adopt bad habits of belief perseverance than to demand that they never give up the truth. But the theist's contrary weighing is, I think, reasonable *from a theistic perspective*.[61] Alternatively, theists might choose to drop UC or else construe it *à la* Mitchell. Noteworthy is the fact that none of the theistic responses that have been suggested *vis-à-vis* UC are raised in the neoatheist literature, let alone evaluated.

Another challenge to UC (besides its seeming irrationality) is that the presence of UC makes it more likely that believers will be recalcitrant for too long—and longer than secular people would—in both religious and (due to force of habit) nonreligious domains.[62] Even granted that most believers do not have a religious commitment so firm that their commitment satisfies UC, the risk described will affect many believers. This contention moves us away from the norm-centered charge of recalcitrance and back to empirical forms of the charge. Now, it is likely that religious believers hold on longer because of UC, but already we have seen that many believers leave their religion, and the conservatism of those who stay could be justified. Regarding a potential spillover effect to nonreligious domains, could not an analogous spillover argument be made about people who are counterfactually recalcitrant about moral principles (even granted that morality does not expressly dictate having an unconditional commitment)? Moreover, the fact that someone believes in religion based on strong faith does not, in point of fact, lead that person to be irrational in other areas of life. Atheists themselves

61. It is now very common for theists to stress that in meeting challenges like the problem of evil, theists are entitled to use premises that are peculiar to their system. See, for example, Marilyn McCord Adams, *Horrendous Evils and the Goodness of God* (Ithaca, NY: Cornell University Press, 1999), which is built on this point; Peter van Inwagen, *The Problem of Evil* (Oxford: Oxford University Press, 2006), 5–6. My suggestion applies this approach to UC.
62. The claim about spillover to nonreligious domains is similar to one W. K. Clifford puts forth in his "The Ethics of Belief," where he contends that irresponsible belief formation and gullibility in one case can cause irresponsible and gullible belief formation in others.

often—inadvertently—agree to this. After all, atheists sometimes complain that theists use different epistemic standards when they deal with theism than when they function in other areas of life.[63] This implies that there isn't a spillover effect from religion into other areas. Furthermore, scientists don't always carry scientific standards into other parts of their lives.[64] No one thinks that their relative laxness outside of a professional context will create a bad habit within that context. The same, let me add, applies to historians and philosophers; they do not apply professional standards in everyday contexts, but this does not impair their professional work.

Thus far, we have looked at one norm of theism (UC) that condones and encourages counterfactual recalcitrance. There is another:

> (CR6): Theists maintain that if God says something, it is inerrant. Ergo, any rejection of God's word is wrong. The doctrine of inerrancy has the following consequence: one must follow God's commands even when they are by most people's lights immoral. Our ethics would not trump God's commands.[65]

The result of (CR6) is immorality and moral horror perpetrated in the name of religion. (CR6) doesn't claim that theists are *de facto* counterfactually recalcitrant with respect to their moral positions. After all, they might be swayed into not believing in a morally perfect God, in which case they might disobey divine commands (unless fear of punishment prevails). Also, their conscience may, at some point, render them psychologically incapable of carrying out divine commands. But (CR6) reflects a norm—follow whatever God commands—and atheists find that norm objectionable because it condones immoral behavior.

Given, however, that the believer believes in a perfect God and in the Bible's being His word, can the norm really be faulted? How else should a believer proceed in moral decision making? The atheist argument can't be that theists should sometimes disobey God *even though* by their lights God is inerrant—that would be incoherent.[66] So the atheist argument has to be a *reductio*, a *modus tollens*: If the Bible is inerrant, and in the Bible God commands/permits X, Y, Z, then X, Y, Z are obligatory/permitted; but X, Y, Z are morally objectionable; therefore, the Bible is not inerrant. This argument doesn't show that the person shouldn't believe in a deity who created and runs the world, but it does ostensibly show that he or she shouldn't believe in a *morally perfect* and inerrant one.

Notice that this argument is not really about counterfactual recalcitrance; rather, it imputes actual-world recalcitrance—after all, the troublesome commands that lead to denial of a perfect deity are already out there (or "on the books") in the actual world. As for the *modus tollens* itself, theists have a range of responses

---

63. For example, Harris, 19.
64. As pointed out by Lewis, "On Obstinacy in Belief." See also Schimmel, 203–04.
65. See Dawkins, 317–48; see also Eugene Korn, "Tselem Elokim [The Image of God] and the Dialectic of Jewish Morality," *Tradition* 31(2) (1997): 5–30, and Adler, "Faith and Fanaticism," in *Philosophers without Gods*, 266–85.
66. If the argument is that because religious reasons (in the form of citations of the Bible and authorities) depend on the doctrine of inerrancy they shouldn't be allowed in the public square—that's a different topic altogether.

available.[67] Many theists would reply that because God is perfect, God must have good decisive reasons for those commands that humans find morally troubling. Some would actually construct a justification. Some may defend a divine command theory of ethics. Some may argue that the commands don't mean what they appear to mean, or are not meant to be carried out. Looking at the big picture, however, if the charge in (CR6) is that belief in a perfect God is irrational or false because the Bible contains immoral commands, then technically, my work is done. For my question was not whether the belief that a perfect God exists is rational. It was whether the norm described in (CR6), "Do what God commands" is rational; the answer is—yes, unqualified obedience to God's commands makes sense because God is inerrant.[68] The believer's style—that is, the refusal to be swayed into disobedience by the fact that some of God's commands seem immoral—cannot be criticized independently of criticizing the belief that God exists or that God commands X, Y, Z or that XYZ are immoral. (My argument regarding (CR5) was similar.)

But to stop here would obscure some important points. The approach just outlined permits violent extremists to say, "What I'm doing is rational, given my belief system," and many believers, myself included, would not want to be saddled with that consequence. Moreover, there is a theistic response that permits revision of belief when God's commands seem immoral, and that many theists past and present have adopted. The atheist's *modus tollens* assumes that the word of God comes fully interpreted. But God's word will lead to conduct that people regard as immoral only if after *interpreting* God's word and deciding when and how to apply it, it ends up that His word goes contrary to human moral principles. The possibility of interpreting the Bible to harmonize it with morality leads us now into a larger discussion about religious moderation.

RELIGIOUS MODERATES

In response to a charge of epistemic recalcitrance, Robert Merrihew Adams writes:

> The history of religious thought, in all religious traditions that I know about, is centrally a history of revision of more and less fundamental religious beliefs, in view of new experiences, new situations, new cultural developments, new knowledge about the world. Modern evolutionary biology, for example, has been rejected by some conservative Christians; but others, many of them quite conservative in other ways, have embraced it, revising their interpretations of Scripture in a new intellectual situation. Medieval writers spoke of such a process as "twisting the wax nose of authority." Because documents and

---

67. For articulations of both the challenges to biblical morality and possible theistic responses, see Michael Bergmann, Michael J. Murray, and Michael C. Rea, eds., *Divine Evil? The Moral Character of the God of Abraham* (New York: Oxford University Press, 2010); Paul Copan, *Is God a Moral Monster? Making Sense of the Old Testament God* (Grand Rapids, MI: Baker Books, 2011).

68. I am assuming here that the Bible accurately reports God's commands. If it doesn't, the atheist argument against a morally perfect being falls away anyhow.

traditions cannot be appropriated and applied without interpretation, authority cannot fail to have a "wax nose." In such a process, of course, revisions are meant to formulate a core of belief that can be expressed verbally but is more stable than any of its verbal formulations.[69]

Examples of reinterpretation abound: gradual acceptance of evolution and heliocentrism, the denial of anthropomorphism, the limiting of divine intervention (which predates modern times)—with respect to all these subjects, theists interpret the Bible in the light of scientific and philosophical principles. Adams goes on to analogize between the process of revising in religion and the process of revision in science. An atomist physical theory is treated as a revision rather than a rejection of belief in "solid bodies." Galileo says the Bible doesn't err, only its interpreters do, and advocates having science guide interpretation.[70] Perhaps we can apply the same approach to morally problematic commands.

Let us employ the term "religious moderates" to denote those theists who, on principle, refuse to interpret biblical texts literally when the literal reading conflicts with reason or moral principle, and who therefore do not hold extremist beliefs. The process of reinterpretation is shaped by the interpreter's background beliefs, and changing interpretations reflect either changes in background beliefs or discoveries of how long-standing background beliefs bear on the text being interpreted. For example, as we learn more about the Hebrew language, interpreters revise prior interpretations of biblical verses in the Hebrew Bible; as modern literary scholarship sensitizes us to literary techniques in the narratives—for example, the use of the same keywords in two distinct narratives suggests they must be construed as parallel or intertwined—our interpretations of biblical narratives become more robust and cogent.[71] So, too, moderate theists argue, beliefs are revised in the face of new scientific discoveries, including not only evolution, which necessitates a nonliteral reading of Genesis 1, but also, say, psychological theories about family dynamics, which create new interpretive options *vis-à-vis* certain narratives. Reinterpretation can likewise affect how immoral-sounding texts are understood.

One would think that neoatheists would embrace religious moderates with open arms. Far from it. Sam Harris criticizes the moderates in a striking way. He thinks (in my words, not his) that *real* theistic religion is extremist cognitively and morally, so that moderate religion is (my word) ersatz.[72]

---

69. Adams, review of Brian Leiter, *Why Tolerate Religion?*, *Notre Dame Philosophical Reviews*, January 10, 2013, available at <http://ndpr.nd.edu/news/36599-why-tolerate-religion>.

70. See his letters to Castelli and the Grand Duchess Christina in *The Galileo Affair*, ed. Maurice A. Finocchiaro (Berkeley: University of California Press, 1989), 49–54 and 87–118, respectively.

71. Robert Alter pioneered this approach to reading the Bible, and it has become standard. See Alter, *The Art of Biblical Narrative* (New York: Basic Books, 1981).

72. See Harris, 15–23. He defines moderates as people who tolerate extremists, but his discussion makes clear that they also engage in reinterpretation of texts of the sort we are considering. Dawkins writes that "even mild and moderate religion helps to provide the climate of faith in which fanaticism flourishes" (342). Dennett is critical of moderates (297–300) but does not wish them out of existence.

Religious moderation is the product of *secular* knowledge and scriptural ignorance—*and it has no bona fides, in religious terms, to put it on a par with fundamentalism* [my italics]. . . . By their light [the light of the texts] religious moderation appears to be nothing more than an unwillingness to fully submit to God's laws. By failing to live by the letter of the texts, while tolerating the irrationality of those who do, religious moderates betray faith and reason equally.[73]

In the same vein, Harris states that "[m]oderation has nothing underwriting it other than the unacknowledged neglect of the letter of the divine law."[74] So, religious moderates are unfaithful to their own professed commitments to their religions, because if they truly adhered to their tradition they *would be* extremists. Dawkins registers the same argument when (in Michael Ruse's paraphrase) he views Pope John Paul II as a hypocrite for endorsing Darwinism.[75] Apart from accusing moderates of infidelity to their own traditions, Harris maintains that their pluralist, tolerant attitude—an attitude that, for him, is the defining characteristic of moderates—leaves extremists to do as they please. Criticism of moderates by neoatheists is so widespread that even the atheist Ruse complains (to Dawkins's irritation) that "[a]theists spend more time running down sympathetic Christians than they do countering creationists."[76]

Are neoatheists right that a religious moderate view is inauthentic?[77] Traditions are built through interpretation, yet Harris opposes the very idea of a religious tradition that is dynamic and adaptive, and believes—in effect—that religions must remain in a state that Jerome Gellman calls arrested development.[78] As Lord Jonathan Sacks, former Chief Rabbi of the United Kingdom, writes in his critique of religious extremists:

Interpretation is as fundamental to any text-based religion as is the original act of revelation itself. No word, especially the word of God, is self-explanatory. Exegetes and commentators are to religion what judges are to law. . . . Living traditions constantly interpret their canonical texts. That is what makes fundamentalism—text *without* interpretation—an act of violence against tradition. In fact, fundamentalists and today's atheists share the same approach to texts. They read them directly and literally, ignoring the

---

73. *The End of Faith*, 20–21.
74. Ibid., 18.
75. See Dawkins, *The God Delusion*, 92. Dennett, *Breaking the Spell*, 297–301, bids moderates to work "from within" to curb extremism, as opposed to wanting them out of the picture.
76. Ibid., quoting an article by Ruse in (of all places) *Playboy*.
77. A minor irony is that if only biblical-texts-read-literally define Christianity and Judaism, then since the Bible speaks of God anthropomorphically, *genuine* theistic religions should be absolved of believing in immaterial beings, whereas neoatheists assumed religion involves belief in supernatural beings. I don't think this point harms the neoatheist's case.
78. See Gellman's review of Wettstein, *The Significance of Religious Experience*, at <http://ndpr.nd.edu/news/38428-the-significance-of-religious-experience>.

single most important fact about a sacred text. Namely that its meaning is not self-evident.[79]

This theme, that religious texts require interpretation, did not begin with modernity; it is prominent in ancient religious sources. There is something unfair about neoatheists excoriating believers for reading the Bible literally, and then not allowing them to develop a more rational and moral form of their religion by reading it nonliterally, especially when so many precedents are available within traditions to legitimate such interpretations.[80] If the Bible is divine, and God does not want us to neglect reason, harmonizing the two seems requisite; if one accepts the Bible as true but allows for other sources of knowledge and trusts in human reason, one will seek harmonization through interpretation. The neoatheist critique of moderates would maintain that Judaism began and ended in the Ancient Near East, where the only true form of their religions existed. But no religion has to call a halt to its growth. Should we brand Augustine, Averroes, Maimonides, and Aquinas—exemplars of the process of which Adams and Sacks spoke—as insufficiently faithful adherents of the religions with which they are associated? We discern a straw man when atheists claim that religions are immune to counterevidence—because, according to moderates, religions are set up as interpretive communities precisely to incorporate change, flexibility, innovation, and so forth.[81] Thinkers who believe this do not use it as a mantra; they develop the approach with rigor. Speaking only of the religion I know best—Judaism—a gigantic literature exists in both English and Hebrew that explicates the notions of interpretive tradition, canon, authority, interpretive autonomy, interpretive charity, justification in law, parallels between interpretation in religious law and interpretation in secular law, change, development, the history of biblical interpretation, and more. Obviously I can't rehearse this literature here, but no indictment on a charge of inauthenticity can be lodged until the large and enormously complex discussions in the literature are engaged.

To be sure, Sacks fails to note that fundamentalists, too, have a tradition of interpretation—to wit, a literalism that promotes extremism. Literalism may be attractive, in fact, as a way to prevent the "anything goes" problem that arises if one allows reinterpretation; seemingly, literalism allows for the comfort of certainty.[82] But aside from the fact that even the literal meaning is often ambiguous, both literal *and* nonliteral traditions are traditions. Neoatheists might characterize statements like Sacks's as mere apologetics, but even if we accept this cynicism, it is hard to see how that leads to the conclusion that the world is better off without moderates.

For consider: Surely neoatheists are not naïve about what their books can accomplish. Surely, they recognized when they wrote them, and still recognize, that their writings will not rid the earth of literalists, fundamentalists, extreme religion-

---

79. Sacks, *The Great Partnership: Science, Religion, and the Search for Meaning* (New York: Schocken Books, 2011), 252, 254.
80. Daniel Rynhold suggested this formulation in correspondence.
81. I thank Alex Sztuden for this formulation.
82. I thank Michael Berger for pointing this out. Subsequently he and Brooks Holifield provided extremely generous and valuable correspondence about literalism and inerrancy.

ists, or call them what you will. Religions are here to stay. (Not to mention the unimaginable dislocation and massive traumas to society if religion leaves the world.) Given that, what is the logic in dissuading people from being moderates? Neoatheists need all the friends they can get in their assault on extremism. Reducing the ranks of moderates, therefore, seems self-defeating. Religious moderates, contrary to the neoatheist critique, can have some success trying "from within" to dissuade extremists or prevent people from embracing extremism. The basis for Harris's skepticism may lie in his *definition* of moderates—they are those who tolerate extremists. If we define moderates as I did (in terms of openness to reinterpretation), then moderates don't, by definition, leave extremists to do as they please—they may well not tolerate extremism. They would then be doing something that is useful and good even by neoatheist lights, and it can be argued that secularists would have less likelihood of achieving. Note also that it may be psychologically easier for extremists who want to leave extremism to do so when a moderate form of their religion is available than when secularism is the only option. (I noted earlier that some extremists do become moderates.) For neoatheists to crave an earth without moderates is a paradigm of throwing out the baby with the bathwater. Questioning moderates' fidelity to their own religion or even their motives is consistent with wanting them to remain in existence.

Admittedly, there is something manipulative about not protesting against those you think are inauthentic (which is how Harris views moderates) merely because they are providing you with some gains in the form of some converts from extremism. But Harris himself takes a utilitarian stance about right and wrong,[83] and in those terms his desire to quash moderates is self-defeating. Further, what of the dangers that polarization breeds, when all we have is extremist religion and a highly combative secularism?[84] A true belief can have dangerous social consequences, a false one can have good social consequences; neoatheists could place moderate religion in the latter category. Add to this the moral good that moderates do, and the case for keeping moderates grows stronger. It has been suggested that the neoatheists' real discontent with religious moderates is that they threaten to give religion a good name.[85] Dennett offers precisely this fear of giving religion a good name as the reason why "brights" do not channel their good deeds through religious groups.[86]

It is even more difficult to see what objections neoatheist critics of moderates can register against religious approaches that regard the Bible as humanly authored (although divinely inspired), and therefore occasionally errant; or against nonrealist forms of religion—the "religion without metaphysics" approaches that mark Continental philosophy and have champions in analytic philosophy as well; or approaches that utilize religious texts to provide images, symbols, and metaphors that lead to certain feelings and a particular way of life, without metaphysical commitments. If there is no personal being named God, as in some of these forms,

---

83. See especially *The End of Faith*, chap. 6, and *The Moral Landscape* (New York: Simon and Schuster, 2010).
84. See also Sacks, 264–65.
85. Sacks, *The Great Partnership*, 264.
86. Dennett, 300–01.

then the notion of an inerrant text, so alarming to atheists, falls away. Furthermore, no one can coerce anyone into believing in God if the coercer doesn't believe in God either. There can be coercion to conform to religious practices, but we don't see this in practice among religious nonrealists. In these theologies, the Bible is not literal truth. I do not advocate the views just mentioned, but what, for the neoatheists, would be wrong in a world in which those groups remained? What could justify their scorched earth approach? Has their equating religion with supernaturalism hidden nonsupernatural forms of religion from the neoatheists' view?[87]

In addition, it is not clear to me what justification there is for saying that moderates tolerate extremism, unless one *defines* moderate as espousing tolerance for extremists. Moderates polemicize against extremists and seek to persuade them; what more should they do? Mobilize an army? Or, as Dennett demands, "name names"?[88] Do neoatheists do these things in *their* confrontation with religious extremism? And are all or even most moderates pluralists who let extremists do as they please? Yes, there are religious pluralists among the moderates, but also plenty of anti-pluralists who (despite being exclusivist with regard to truth claims) are not extremists.[89]

The foregoing discussion suggests a new normative formulation of epistemic recalcitrance, one that captures what moderates are up to:

(CR7): Religionists *should* revise their beliefs in the face of counterevidence. Any revision of religious belief must take place through reinterpretation of authoritative texts by an interpretive community and its authorities. The core statements in those texts should never be given up (abandoned), only reinterpreted.

There is much unclarity about what counts as a community and who counts as an authority; those questions are explored and debated in the literature on these topics that I referred to earlier. Neoatheists may object to the idea that texts are never abandoned, only reinterpreted. It suggests to us that not everything is up for grabs; neoatheists may want nothing to be sacrosanct. I won't undertake a response to that here, but I think there are certain parallels that a theist may suggest to the case of moral commitments.[90] My point is only that (CR7) is an accurate rendition

---

87. Cf. Simon Blackburn, "Religion and Respect," in *Philosophers without Gods*, 179–93. Blackburn sees destructive potential in nonrealist religion too. By that point in the discussion, he ought to be comparing nonrealist religion's potential to the actual behavior of secular ideologues.

88. Dennett, *Breaking the Spell*, 299. Dennett's excoriation of moderates for not doing enough is more extensive than Harris's (see 297–301).

89. In the Modern Orthodox Jewish community, condemnations of extremism are routine and numerous, and likewise for Conservative and Reform.

90. A paper by Alasdair MacIntye in a recent Festschriftt for Rabbi Sacks is of relevance. See "Torah and Moral Philosophy," in *Radical Responsibility: Celebrating the Thought of Chief Rabbi Lord Jonathan Sacks*, ed. Michael J, Harris, Daniel Rynhold, and Tamra Wright (London: London School of Jewish Studies, The Michael Scharf Publication Trust/YU Press and Maggid Books, 2012), 3–16.

of the principles adopted by moderate theists—and it allows for changes in interpretation based on revision of belief, a far cry from the stereotype of rigidity and recalcitrance.

FINAL THOUGHTS

It may seem that the atheistic claim about counterfactual epistemic recalcitrance on the part of theists is but a small and dispensable cog in a large atheist machine. The really big issues raised by neoatheists, it will be said, are the weak state of evidence for theism, contrary evidence based on scientific findings (or absence of findings), the problem of evil, the unfathomable killings perpetrated by organized religions through the centuries, the weighty, perhaps disproportionate, influence that religion carries in the society, and the society's provision of special legal protections for religions. Hence, even if theists successfully parry the charge of counterfactual recalcitrance (in both empirical and norm-centered versions) in the ways I suggested, atheists might simply end their own erstwhile recalcitrance on the subject and drop the charge. They may add, "No big deal; we haven't given up anything important. The imputation of counterfactual recalcitrance isn't central to our case the way it was for positivists."

But denigrating the significance of the charge within atheistic argumentation is, I think, glib. The charge of counterfactual epistemic recalcitrance is not trivial, and surrendering it *is* surrendering something of importance in the atheists' case. First of all, by positing counterfactual epistemic recalcitrance, atheists magnify the extent of theists' (and theism's) irrationality and epistemic vice, and place theists outside the frame of rational debate. In addition, imputing counterfactual epistemic recalcitrance plants suspicions about the plausibility of theists' *actual-world* recalcitrance. For atheists may discredit theistic replies to actual-world objections by insinuating that theists will have an answer for everything—this, not because the theists are defending the truth (which is after all one possible explanation for having an answer for everything), but merely because they approach issues of truth with a certain style, a style that doesn't really value truth but instead closes off serious attempts to think and participate in rational discourse. The charge of counterfactual epistemic recalcitrance cuts to the heart of neoatheists' understanding of what theistic religion is all about: mindless, intransigent faith. To surrender the charge and/or to recognize that it applies to both sides *is* to surrender something of importance. This, even though attacks on believers' counterfactual recalcitrance are attacks on believers (*ad hominem*) and not on belief. The focus on discrediting believers is reminiscent of positivism, for I mentioned earlier that positivist claims about unfalsifiability seem to be leveled at believers rather than their utterances.

In its present state, the debate over theism in analytic philosophy shows vitality on both sides. Both sides land punches. But atheism is very far from the dominating position it was 50 or 60 years ago. In the debate over evidentialism, for example, the notion that nonevidentially based religious belief is *ipso facto* irrational has taken a hard hit. Mark Johnston avers (speaking in general terms and not referencing evidentialism or recalcitrance) that "one can readily understand why

Dawkins and Hitchens would feel that if only the old arguments were repeated *over and over again*, the halcyon days might return."[91] Granted, the neoatheists' uses of biology and neuroscience (the notion of the God gene, for example) are new, as is the prominence they give to moral critique. So, not all the neoatheist charges are old hat. But surely counterfactual epistemic recalcitrance ranks among the old complaints.

I don't know whether the label "neoatheism" was coined to disparage the Dawkins–Dennett–Harris–Hitchens axis by pejoratively implying "here we go again," or to distinguish these authors by their aggressiveness,[92] or to praise them as providing new arguments. Despite the neoatheists' implicit repudiation of positivism, my reaction to the charge of counterfactual recalcitrance is "So what else is neo?" I hope I have removed this persistent charge from the table, or at the very least clarified both it and the challenges to its cogency.[93]

---

91. Johnston, *Saving God*, 38.

92. Bergmann, Murray, and Rea, in their introduction to *Divine Evil?* (3), speak of neoatheism's "evangelical fervor" as the "new" element.

93. I thank Shalom Carmy, Daniel Rynhold, and Alex Sztuden for their comments on an earlier version of this paper, and Michael Berger for extensive discussion of several issues. My thanks as well to David Berger, Michael Bergmann, Yitzchak Blau, Robert Eisen, Brooks Holifield, Michael Murray, Aaron Segal, and Stephen Tipton for valuable correspondence.

Religious Agnosticism

GARY GUTTING

My approach in this paper differs in two ways from standard philosophy of religion. First, I begin not with "Is religious belief rationally justified?" but with "Is atheism rationally justified?" This makes sense since today most people claiming that they have a strongly rational basis for their view on religion are atheists (e.g., Richard Dawkins and his followers). Also, although these claims don't stand up to philosophical scrutiny, we will see that answering them sets important limits to what believers can claim on behalf of religion.

Second, turning to the case for religious belief, I ignore traditional master-arguments designed to convince any rational being and instead look at the reasons informed, intelligent, and reflective people (in particular, philosophers) actually have for believing. This leads, among other things, to a conception of religious belief that is unusual in analytic philosophy of religion but that I think accords with the implicit attitude of many believers: religious agnosticism.

THE FAILURE AND CHALLENGE OF ATHEISM

I was surprised to learn from the PhilPapers survey that over 60 percent of philosophers responding are atheists (with another 11 percent "inclined" to the view). Agnosticism (the position of about only 5 percent) strikes me as a far more plausible way of not believing. At least, I do not find any compelling case for atheism in the philosophical literature, so I'm not sure if philosophical atheists generally have reasons for their position that would pass professional scrutiny. The personal essays in *Philosophers Without Gods* suggest that they do not.[1] Similarly, as we shall see, philosophical believers do not generally believe primarily because of the results of their professional work.

I will, therefore, begin with the case for atheism that seems convincing to a good number of increasingly vocal non-believers, the case made by "new atheists," centered around Richard Dawkins. (At least one prominent philosopher, Daniel Dennett, has endorsed this case.) I will argue that the case has little going for it as a support for atheism, but it does push more naïve forms of belief in the direction of agnosticism.

The No-Arguments Argument for Atheism

Contemporary atheists, including Dawkins, often assert that there is no need for them to provide arguments showing that God does not exist. Rather, the very lack of good arguments for God's existence provides a solid basis for denying his existence. The case against God is, they say, the same as the case against Santa Claus, the Easter Bunny, or the Tooth Fairy: there are no good reasons for believing in any of them.

At least at first blush, it seems very odd to compare the argumentative case for God with that of cases for Santa Claus et al. There are, after all, well-known arguments formulated by respected philosophers that at least some competent judges have found convincing. No one much over the age of 6 thinks there is a remotely plausible argument for the existence of Santa Claus.

Dawkins himself thinks that the traditional arguments for God's existence are readily refuted and confidently undertakes, in a few embarrassing pages,[2] to carry out the task. He is no more successful than, say, I would be in an effort to refute the theory of evolution. We hardly need Dawkins to show us that there are no compelling arguments for God's existence. The fact is apparent from centuries of serious philosophical discussions of the issue. But the no-arguments argument for atheism requires the sort of facile demolition of theistic thinking that Dawkins purports to provide. Only then does it seem at all plausible to put the existence of God on a par with the existence of Santa Claus et al.

What the history of natural theology in fact shows is that we can formulate various versions of causal and ontological arguments as logically valid deductions, with one or two premises that are disputable but not obviously or demonstrably false. The premises, indeed, often have a certain intuitive appeal. Some people may even, on reflection, see them as obviously correct and would be rational to accept them. But there is no general agreement on the premises' truth, and it can be equally rational to deny them.

Given all this, it follows that philosophical arguments for God's existence fail in the sense that they do not make an intellectually compelling case for God's

---

1. Louise M. Antony, ed., *Philosophers Without Gods: Meditations on Atheism and the Secular Life* (Oxford: Oxford University Press, 2007).
2. Richard Dawkins, *The God Delusion* (Boston: Houghton Mifflin, 2008), Chapter 3. (This book will subsequently be referred to as GD.)

existence: they do not show that any rational person must accept the existence of God. In this sense, their failure supports agnosticism. But why think it supports atheism?

The situation is very like that of a mathematical conjecture for which there is no proof but that does follow given a controversial premise that some find plausible and others do not. In such a case, there is no basis for denying the conjecture on the grounds that it has no proof. Similarly, the status of arguments for God's existence is like that of numerous disputes about scientific theories, political policies, and ethical decisions, where both sides have arguments that they find plausible but the other side rejects. The existence of creditable but not conclusive arguments for God's existence undermines the no-arguments argument for atheism. To the extent that arguments are required for rational belief in God, the failure of the standard theistic arguments supports agnosticism but not atheism.

The Complexity Argument for Atheism

Dawkins does, however, offer one important challenge to theism in what he calls his "Boeing 747 argument" (GD, Chapter 4). The challenge begins as a critique of the standard argument for God as the designer of the universe, but segues into the claim that a divine designer is highly improbable. A Boeing 747 airplane is a premier example of something that could not be produced by chance but requires intelligent design. No one would believe that such a machine could result, say, from winds blowing about in a junkyard. What brings us to the design argument is the thought—classically elaborated by William Paley and by Hume's Cleanthes—that there is no difference in principle between a Boeing 747 and the universe.

Dawkins agrees: we need to explain "how the complex, improbable appearance of design in the universe arises" (GD, 188). But, Dawkins claims, design arguments presuppose that the only possible explanations for complexity are chance (which explains nothing that is highly improbable) and design by an intelligence. He says, however, that there is a third possibility: the gradual development of the complex from the simple, with Darwin's idea of evolution by natural selection as the prime example.

Dawkins uses the Darwinian possibility in a familiar way to squelch the argument from design. Given sufficient time, evolution, particularly by natural selection, explains how complex animals have developed from the simplest living things. Biologists have successfully explained the origins of many particular species, and this success makes it highly probable that all biological complexity can be explained in the same way. Creationists and other critics point to unexplained examples of biological complexity, but they merely highlight future stages of a highly promising research program.

Of course, we need more than biology to explain the universe. We need chemistry to explain how elementary life forms arose from complex inorganic molecules, physics to explain the complex forms of inorganic matter needed for the emergence of life, and cosmology (or perhaps even metaphysics) to explain the origin of matter itself. Dawkins has to admit that the chemical and physical processes that would parallel natural selection are still promissory notes.

Here Dawkins's argument seems to have stalled, but he switches gears and moves it forward, claiming that anything capable of designing and maintaining something as complex as the universe would itself have to be highly complex and so itself require an explanation. Here Dawkins echoes Hume in the *Dialogues*: "a mental world or universe of ideas requires a cause as much as does a material world or universe of objects; and, if similar in its arrangement, must require a similar cause."[3] But Dawkins makes more of the point than Hume does and concludes that the hypothesis of a designing God is a nonstarter. There is, he maintains, no plausible alternative to explaining complexity through its natural development from simple elements.[4] In short, any designer would have to be an instance of the complexity the designer is posited to explain.

Why didn't Hume use his point about a designer's complexity to make a case for atheism? Perhaps because he knew natural theologians understood God as both simple and necessary. The first attribute allows them to deny that God is complex and the second to deny that God requires a causal explanation even if he is complex. So it might seem we can dismiss Dawkins's argument as based on his disdainful ignorance of what natural theologians are about.

The idea that God, unlike other beings, is simple and necessary has been developed with immense detail and subtlety in the grand tradition of metaphysics. The project is perennial, beginning with Plato and Aristotle, continuing through the philosophical theologians of the Middle Ages (Augustine, Anselm, Aquinas, Scotus) to the early modern rationalists (Descartes, Spinoza, Leibniz) and the German idealists (Fichte, Schelling, Hegel), and flourishing today in the work of contemporary analytic metaphysicians such as Richard Swinburne and Alvin Plantinga.

But even believers find it difficult to understand a divine nature that is radically simple (lacking all internal differentiations) and necessarily existent. Simplicity is a particularly difficult hurdle, with even traditional theists balking at the thought. Plantinga, for example,[5] argues that if God lacks all complexity, we cannot distinguish any of his properties from one another, so he has only one property. Moreover, we cannot distinguish this property from his divine nature, so God himself is simply a property. But, Plantinga notes, no property is a person or is capable of actions, so a simple God would be entirely different from the God of Christianity and most other world-religions. Others have noted that simplicity entails unchangeability and have wondered how an unchangeable God could love

---

3. David Hume, *Dialogues Concerning Natural Religion*, 2nd ed. (Indianapolis, IN: Hackett, 1988), 30.

4. Some critics (e.g., Alvin Plantinga) think this aspect of Dawkins's argument makes the mistake of assuming that an explanation that itself requires an explanation is not an explanation. This would be on a par with saying that we can't postulate intelligent early humans to explain the existence of ancient abandoned cities, since the existence of such humans itself requires explanation. But to this Dawkins can rightly reply that the God of religion is understood as an ultimate being, not dependent on anything else for his existence, so that a designer that is itself designed could not be God in, say, the Christian sense.

5. Alvin Plantinga, *Does God Have a Nature?* (Milwaukee, WI: Marquette University Press, 1980).

us, since he would be indifferent to (i.e., unchanging in the face of) anything that happens to us. It is also hard to grasp how an unchangeable God could cause effects in a temporal world.

Necessary existence gains some traction because there's at least some tendency (called "Platonism") to think that abstract entities such as numbers have to exist. But the gap between abstract entities and persons is profound, and we are hard pressed to explain necessary existence in a way that bridges this gap.

Dawkins's complexity argument, then, does not establish atheism, but it does force reflective believers toward a sophisticated metaphysical conception of God. This conception skirts the edge of logical incoherence and is hard to reconcile with the God of scripture and of personal experience. Atheists like Dawkins would like to push the point even further. They think that metaphysical discussions of God's nature are pointless because they are not supported by empirical evidence.

Theism and Empiricism

There is some reason to think that an argument for *God's existence* will require empirical evidence (derived from sense experience). Except for the ontological argument, all standard theistic arguments are based on facts, as Aquinas put it, "evident to the senses," such as the existence of motion, of causes and effects, or of contingent things. But why should a discussion of *what kind of a being God would be* have to be based on empirical evidence?

This would make sense if we already knew that God exists as, say, the creator of the world and were trying to infer his nature from the nature of the world. But the natural theologian's question is whether God could be a being radically different from the ones we know from sense experience. How could such a discussion be decided by sense experience? From sense experience alone we could only draw conclusions about the kinds of beings that can be known by sense experience, whereas our question is whether there are other kinds of beings.

Some atheists would short-circuit such metaphysical discussions by maintaining that there can be no beings other than the ones knowable by sense experience (that, in other words, everything is empirical). But, as before, how could this claim itself be known from sense experience, which can tell us only about what is knowable by sense experience? For anything not knowable by the senses, sense experience has nothing to say—not even that it does not exist or is not possible. In the same way, our sense of sight alone cannot tell us whether there are or could be things that are invisible.

Dawkins can, however, retreat for one last stand. Make God as ontologically different as you like. Still, if he has causal effects on the material world, his existence must be detectable by empirical methods. As Dawkins puts it, "a universe with a supernaturally intelligent creator is a very different kind of universe from one without." From this he concludes, "the presence or absence of a super-intelligence is unequivocally a scientific question" (GD, 82). Therefore, if science does not find any evidence of God's existence, he does not, in all probability, exist.

Here we need to distinguish the case of a deistic God who creates the world and never miraculously intervenes from the case of a creator who also from time to time performs miracles. Dawkins claims that even the existence of a nonintervening creator is a "scientific hypothesis": "a universe in which we are alone except for other slowly evolved intelligences is a very different universe from one with an original guiding agent whose intelligent design is responsible for its very existence" (GD, 85). Two such universes are, as he says, "irreconcilably different," since one is created by an intelligence and the other isn't.

But Dawkins offers no features *detectable by science* that must distinguish the one universe from the other. Supposing, for example, that the Big Bang is a radically spontaneous eruption of a material universe into existence, with no creative agent, there is no reason that such a universe could not be identical to such a universe created by an immaterial God. It is by no means clear that the mere claim that God has created the universe is subject to disconfirmation by scientific results.

In the case of miracles Dawkins is on stronger ground. Science does have something to say about whether, for example, someone has miraculously recovered from an illness. One of the strongest points against accepting most allegedly miraculous cures is that they involve the healing of conditions that are not fully understood by science, such as cancer and paralysis. For such cases, we are not certain whether an apparent cure is due to some as yet unknown natural factor. By contrast, there are conditions, such as an amputated limb or a person born without eyes, that we are confident could not be cured by unknown natural processes. Why, nonbelievers rightly ask, are there hardly ever reports of miraculous recoveries from such conditions?

It may well be, as Dawkins says, that most believers think God does miraculously intervene in the universe, at least by answering prayers. If so and if such believers base their belief that God exists on the occurrence of miracles, then their belief is open to refutation by scientific debunking of the alleged miracles. In many cases, however, people who claim that miracles occur do not base their belief in God on that claim. They identify certain events as, for example, God's answering prayers because they *independently* believe that there is a God who cares about us and so expect that at least some prayers will be answered. In such a case, God does make a difference in the universe, but there is no strong evidence for this unless one already believes in God. Only if a belief in God logically depends on the occurrence of miracles does it need to answer to scientific evidence.

Dawkins's failure to refute atheism does not mean that his argument has no effect on theistic belief. The argument makes a good case that God cannot be just an extrapolation, a "superized" version of the kind of intelligent beings we are familiar with. Such a being could not be the ultimate (unexplained by anything else) explanation of the world's design. Nor is there any strong evidence for thinking that such a being exists. The case is on a par with that of superior space aliens. Theists cannot plausibly think of God as a superized human but must try to understand him as a radically different sort of being: immaterial, necessarily existing, and, perhaps, entirely simple. But, as we have seen, this radical view faces its own set of problems, arising both from logic and from religious life itself.

Atheism and Evil

The oldest and most affecting of all arguments for atheism, the argument from evil, makes these problems much more intense. In any effective form, the argument depends on thinking of God as far more good and powerful than humans, but only in ways that do not seriously alter our expectations about how he will act. God is like, for example, a medical researcher who knows a simple cure for any malignant brain tumor. If such a researcher were in the room with a child dying from such a tumor and were not a moral monster, we would of course expect that he would bring about the cure. Accordingly, if someone maintains that there is a good-intentioned doctor in the child's room who knows how to cure her cancer, we would rightly demand strong evidence for such a claim, since we already have strong evidence that the claim is false from the very fact that the child has not been cured.

Atheists are entirely correct that there is no evidence at all for the existence of a God conceived along these lines. For a theistic religion to have even minimal plausibility, it must admit that our expectations of what good human beings would do if they could are not a helpful guide to what God will do. Its God cannot be a "superman," linearly extending current human projects to alleviate ravages of diseases, natural disasters, and large-scale human atrocities. Just as there is no evidence that someone like the comic-book Superman exists, there is no evidence for a superhuman God who picks up in the struggle against evil where our powers fail.

There is also no point to the theist's responding that we cannot be judged by human standards of morality. If God is good in some sense quite distinct from what we mean by "good," then there is no reason to praise, rely on, or be consoled by his goodness. The divine "goodness" no longer responds to the questions and longing that lead us to religion. Our God must agree with our judgment that human suffering is a great evil, one to be eliminated to the maximal extent possible.

The problem, however, is that we do not know the extent to which God is able to eliminate human suffering (and other evils). The decision to eliminate any particular evil depends not only on the judgment that the evil in itself deserves elimination but also on whether eliminating it would produce greater evils or eliminate goods that outweigh the evil. It might be said that this consideration applies only to finite agents, who cannot do everything and must choose between, say, putting out a fire or blocking a flood, not to God, who has no limits to his power. But even God cannot produce logical contradictions (e.g., make something simultaneously both exist and not exist), and there may be evils that are logically necessary for certain goods that outweigh these evils. (For example, bearing pain magnificently requires the evil of pain; genuine human freedom may require allowing the evil of a wrong choice.) Given this, God may not eliminate evils that we would, not because he does not see them as evil but because he, unlike us, knows that they are necessary for greater goods. The difference may not be that God is not good in our sense but that he knows a lot more than we do about the goods that exist in the universe and the evils that are logically necessary to have them.

Given the hypothesis of evils necessary for offsetting goods, the fact of evil does not make it unlikely that God exists. Further, since our knowledge is extremely limited, we have no firm idea of how likely or unlikely this hypothesis itself is. It follows that evil makes God's existence unlikely only if some evils are not necessary and we are totally uncertain whether this is so. The logical conclusion is that the existence of evil gives us no good reason to think that God does not exist.

This philosophical escape from the problem of evil is, however, a two-edged sword. The appeal to our ignorance of God's knowledge avoids the apparent contradiction of a world created by an all-good God that contains evils. But it also restricts much of what many theists would like to say about God. Here I have specifically in mind frequent religious appeals to what "God would want." To take a random example, Una Kroll, writing in the *Guardian* (July 11, 2010) in defense of a proposal to ordain women bishops in the Anglican Church, argues that the proposal would be an "example of how it is possible to live in a community that is based on mutual love and respect despite profound differences." She then clinches the point by saying: "that, I believe, is what God wants us to learn to do."

Now it may well seem to us that God would want us to learn to live in communities based on love and respect among people who have deep differences. But no more than it would seem that God would want to save innocent children dying from cancer. Once the appeal is made to the gap between God's knowledge and ours, we cannot move from what we *think* God would want to what he *does* want.

It is not, as I have emphasized, that God is beyond the basic principles of morality. Rather, the application of such principles will typically depend on specific facts about the situation in which are acting. "Thou shalt not kill" does not typically forbid my shooting at a target for practice, but it does if I know there is someone in the near vicinity of the target. Precisely because God knows so much more than we do, we can have no idea how his superior knowledge will affect his actions, even if he acts according to the same moral principles as we do.

However, God's omniscience does allow for the possibility that his knowledge of moral principles is far superior to ours and may even contradict what we think we know about morality. Of course, we remain obliged to act on what we honestly see as the correct moral principles. But there is no way to know that these principles reflect God's perfect knowledge of morality. Here it's natural to maintain that God would never let us be deceived about essential moral principles. But such a response itself ignores our lesson about the gap between God's knowledge and ours.

Although the problem of evil does not make an effective case for atheism, it does require theists to reject conceptions of God that put him on a moral plane with humans. Just as refuting Dawkins's Boeing 747 argument requires thinking of God as radically different from humans on the metaphysical level, so disarming the problem of evil requires thinking of God as radically different from humans on the ethical level.

Coming to terms with the problem of evil requires one more turn of the screw for the theist. The great theistic religions respond to deep human hopes, most importantly our hope to be ultimately safe (saved) in a world of peril. This is not to say there's nothing to religion beyond this hope, just that a worldview that does not provide it will not be religiously fulfilling. Our salvation may depend on our free choice (e.g., to accept divine grace), but given the right choices, salvation is assured.

God, of course, must be the sure source of that salvation. He must be good in the sense of fully committed to working for our salvation (given any free cooperation needed from us) and powerful to the extent of assuring that no external circumstances (factors outside his and our wills) will interfere with our salvation. These are what we might call the *conditions of religious adequacy* on a concept of God.

It's natural to think that a God defined by the properties of traditional natural theology (omnipotence, omniscience, and omni-benevolence) meets these conditions. But this is not so. First of all, the omni-properties are not necessary to guarantee our salvation. God could be totally committed to saving us, even if he, say, lacked appropriate moral attitudes to other beings. Similarly, he might lack power over forces that are irrelevant to human salvation.

More importantly, the omni-properties of natural theology are not sufficient to guarantee our salvation. Omnipotence assures the divine power to do whatever is needed to save us. But omni-benevolence could prove an obstacle to our salvation.

Here is where the unavoidable response to the problem of evil comes in. The only viable answer to the question "How could an all-good and all-powerful God allow the evils of our world?" is that such a God may have knowledge beyond our understanding. As Hume suggested, the problem of evil is solved only by an appeal to our ignorance.

To come to terms with evil, theists must admit that an all-benevolent being, even with maximal power, may have to allow considerable local evils for the sake of the overall good of the universe. But—and this is the crucial point—we have no way of knowing whether we humans might ourselves be the victims of this necessity. We do not, for example, know whether there is or will be some other, far more advanced, species for whose sake God will allow us to be annihilated or suffer endlessly.

It's true that an all-good God would, of course, do everything possible to minimize the evil done to us, but we have no way of knowing how great that minimum might be. Some have suggested that when God allows suffering it must ultimately be for the benefit of the sufferer. But what basis do we have for thinking that this is the way God, in his omniscience, sees it? The free-will defense, for example, emphasizes that the freedom of moral agents may be an immense good, worth God's tolerating horrendous wrongdoing. We have no way of knowing whether destroying our happiness might turn out to be an unavoidable step in the soul-making of a super-race whose eventual achievements make our ultimate loss of salvation acceptable to God.

My conclusion is that, given standard ways of responding to the problem of evil, even knowing that there is an all-good and all-powerful God does not guarantee our hope that (assuming we live a good life) we will be saved.

PHILOSOPHERS WHO BELIEVE

Atheists fit right into the standard approach to philosophy of religion because the traditional arguments matter to them. They are typically convinced (rightly) that the theistic proofs don't establish God's existence and (again rightly) that the problem of evil is a serious challenge to theism. They are wrong in concluding that no sort of divine being exists, and should be content with the skeptical stance of agnosticism. But this is only because there may be a divine being so different from the beings we are familiar with that there is no reason to expect that we could find strong evidence for it in our experience of the world. Anthropomorphic atheism (the denial of a superized human that designs and controls the universe) stands on solid ground.

Correspondingly, religious belief, if at all tenable, will have to acknowledge —as it typically does—the mysterious otherness of God and will have to base itself on something (call it "faith") with far less evidential or argumentative force than, say, a compelling scientific case. This, in fact, is what we find in the lives of even philosophers who believe. Does this mean that religious belief is not an option for intellectually serious people? Should they retreat to an agnostic position? My paradoxical answers are: no and yes.

The Reasons of Philosophers Who Believe

I base my discussion on some remarkable essays published about twenty years ago in which philosophers who are religious believers tried to explain how and why they believe.[6] Although every story is different, there are some widely shared features that give a good sense of how it is that people with a strong commitment to rational reflection become or remain religious believers.

An Attractive Way of Life

First of all, believers are attracted to religion as a way of life. Sometimes this is just a matter of having been born into a certain religious community and always finding it comfortable and rewarding. David Shatz, for example, was raised as an orthodox Jew and has remained content with that way of life. "My commitment is not rooted in the (naïve) notion that reason vindicates my beliefs. It is rooted rather in what Judaism provides me with: intellectual excitement, feeling, caring for others, inspiration, and a total perspective that is evocative and affecting" (GP, 184).

In other cases, nonbelievers gradually move into a religious community. The move often begins with knowing believers whom they respect and admire. Basil Mitchell, for example, notes that when he began teaching at Oxford, "I met for the first time Christian thinkers who were imaginative and articulate and also philosophically sophisticated" (PWB, 36). Here, "in the company of committed

---

6. Kelly James Clark, ed., *Philosophers Who Believe* (Downers Grove, IL: InterVarsity Press, 1993) (this book is subsequently referred to as PWB); Thomas V. Morris, ed., *God and the Philosophers* (Oxford: Oxford University Press, 1994) (this book is subsequently referred to as GP).

Anglicans, I felt entirely and immediately at home" (PWB, 38). There is also almost always a sense of satisfaction with participation in a religious community (liturgy, fellowship). An important step for Peter van Inwagen, for example, was simply learning that "I like going to church and that an unconscious fear of churchgoing was no longer a barrier between me and the church" (GP, 37).

William Alston offers a fuller account. In his mid-50s, after fifteen years of "secular life," while visiting at Oxford he began going to church and found wonderful music very important for "communication with the divine" (GP, 23). Back at Princeton, he kept up church going but didn't "make an intellectual assent to Christian doctrines." But his new openness to religion was having an effect, especially in his relation to people: "I began, for the first time in my life, to get a glimmer of what love means." He went to a new parish and found a new pastor who was "a living example of what spirituality can be" in our time. He next joined a "low-key" Episcopal charismatic group and came to see that "these people were really in touch with God as a more or less continual presence in their lives." So he now had "a whole bevy of role models for the Christian life." He joined a "hard-core" charismatic group: received the "gift of tongues" and came to "a new and more vivid sense of the presence of the Spirit," which never entirely deserted him. He drifted away from the charismatic movement (due to what he calls a "cultural gap"). But at this point, he was fully and permanently a member of the Christian church (GP, 25).

Alston, in fact, says that what brought him to faith was a call to enter a Christian community, where he found an "experience of the love of God and the presence of the Spirit" (GP, 28). "It was like having one's eyes opened to an aspect of the environment to which one had previously been blind." Life within this community involves growing in understanding by studying and thinking about Scripture and theological tradition, prayer and contemplation, reception of sacraments, Christian fellowship, living a life of love.

Religious Experiences

Also important for many believers are what we might call "experiences of transcendence." These are hardly ever visions or visitations. They vary in specificity, intensity, and frequency, but always amount to at least a strong sense that there is "more" to the universe than a materialist account allows. Alvin Plantinga, for example, recalls an event, while he was a freshman at Harvard, and dealing with "doubts and ambivalences" about his religious faith:

> Suddenly it was as if the heavens opened; I heard, so it seemed, music of overwhelming power and grandeur and sweetness; there was light of unimaginable splendor and beauty; it seemed I could see into heaven itself; and I suddenly saw or perhaps felt with great clarity and persuasion and conviction that the Lord was really there and was all I had thought. The effect of this experience lingered for a long time; I was still caught up in arguments about the existence of God, but they often seemed to me merely academic, of "little existential concern," as if one were to argue about whether there has really been a past . . . or whether there really were other people. (PWB, 51–52)

Plantinga reports many similar, though usually not as intense, experiences of what he calls "the presence of God": "in the mountains, at prayer, in church, when reading the Bible, listening to music, seeing the beauty of the sunshine on the leaves of a tree or on a blade of grass, being in the woods on a snowy night" (PWB, 52).

Metaphysical and Historical Arguments

Philosophical believers also often, though by no means always, rely on what they see as the plausibility of theistic metaphysics. William Wainwright admits to a "skeptical temperament" that has led him to question all metaphysical positions. But, he says, his considered view is that "classical theistic metaphysics survives criticism at least as well as, and probably better than, its competitors" (GP, 78). He does not say that classical theism (the theism of Christianity) is more likely to be true than not; it may not, as far as he can see, be more probable than the disjunction of naturalism, Buddhism, and other metaphysical views. But it is more probable than any of these taken individually and so the most probable explanation. Further, he thinks that "when plausible explanations are available . . . it is reasonable to adopt *some* explanation rather than none" (GP, 80). Nonetheless, he retains a "sense of the wretched insufficiency of our reasoning about anything except the most mundane matters" and particularly about "the ground of all being," about which—especially given Marxist, Freudian, and even Christian bases for distrusting our reasoning about fundamentals—it is hard to avoid suspecting that "even our best formulations are only 'straw' " (GP, 78).

But here Wainwright's skepticism also works in the opposite direction: he is inclined to question the demands of what we might call a "narrow rationality" that ignores the prompting of faith and feeling. "My congenital skepticism couldn't help but make me suspect that I might be duped if I *didn't* trust what James called my *believing tendencies*. In other words, I have never been able to repress the suspicion that (as he says) the 'heart' may be 'our deepest organ of communication' with reality" (GP, 79).

Richard Swinburne has, in his philosophical work, gone the furthest of anyone down the path of traditional apologetics, from proofs of God's existence through historical arguments for the truth of Christian revelation. But he makes it clear that he was a believer before he had serious arguments: "My intellectual development has been largely a matter of systematizing and justifying what I believed in a very vague way forty years ago. Although my views on lesser matters have changed, my worldview has not" (PWB, 199). Nor does he seem to think that prior rigorous proofs are needed for responsible belief: "The practice of religion . . . does indeed involve giving your life generously for supremely worthy purpose. But it needs to be shown that the purpose is indeed worthy . . . ; and that involves showing that the Christian theological system . . . has some reasonable chance of being true" (PWB, 181). Correspondingly, he does not claim that his apologetic efforts provide a decisive proof of his religious belief: "I am less than absolutely confident that [the central claims of Christian faith] are true . . . But I judge that there is a significant balance of evidence in favor" (PWB, 199–200).

Failures of Nonbelief

Most philosophers do insist on plausible defeaters for important objections to their beliefs. It's not surprising, then, that philosophical believers have devoted much of their professional activity to discussing the problem of evil and other objections to theism. The idea, however, is not necessarily that every difficulty must be removed. As Terence Penelhum put it, "a philosophical believer does not have to have answers to all objections to his faith: he does not have to suppose that all the difficulties . . . are resolved; only that some of them can be and have been, and that the rest are not altogether intractable" (PWB, 236).

Philosophical believers also typically emphasize the questionable materialist or naturalist commitments of most forms of atheism, which they see as simply assuming that such views can make sense of realities such as consciousness and objective moral values. They are also often pushed toward religion by what they see as the arrogance and complacency of academic nonbelievers. Van Inwagen is particularly disdainful: "I know I was becoming more and more repelled by the 'great secular consensus'. . . . What made it so repulsive to me can be summed up in the schoolyard *cri de coeur*: 'They think they're so smart!' I was simply revolted by the malevolent, self-satisfied stupidity of the attacks on Christianity that proceeded from that consensus" (GP, 36).

What Sort of Case Is There for Belief?

The intellectual capstone of a philosopher's faith is often an appeal to the ability of religious belief to make coherent sense of our world as a whole. Belief, in other words, provides an understanding that is not matched by either agnosticism or atheism. This understanding is the intellectual complement of what we have already seen as the moral attraction of a religious way of life. Indeed, helping us understand the goodness and power of this life is not the least merit of this understanding.

In fact, as I see it, the philosophers generally make a case for belief (beyond the ethical project of living a religious life) based on the understanding belief brings, not on reasons for thinking that the account this understanding provides is literally true. It is, we might say, a matter of *understanding* rather than *knowledge*, where "knowledge" implies a historical/metaphysical account of supernatural realities that solidly justifies claims about the existence and operation of a divine power in the universe. "Understanding," by contrast, means a fruitful way of thinking about things, without implying that there are no alternative ways of thinking (both theistic and nontheistic) that would be equally fruitful.

The only elements in the testimonials we have been looking at that might support what I'm calling knowledge-claims are experiences of the divine and traditional metaphysical and historical arguments for God's existence and action in the world. The experiences are common among believers, but not sufficiently wide and deep to provide anything near the certainty of, say, sensory perceptions and nowhere near specific enough to support traditional claims about the nature of God or his plans for us. The metaphysical and historical arguments play a role only for a few believers—most notably Swinburne—but even then they are seen as at best making a plausible but not decisive case. At a minimum, they do not decisively support the full-blooded belief expressed, for example, in Christian creeds.

Belief without Evidence?

Most philosophical believers realize this and defend their full-blooded beliefs by claiming that they have a right to hold them without evidence, just as we hold many other beliefs. Alvin Plantinga, of course, has been the primary proponent of this sort of case for the rationality of religious belief. This is not the place for a full-scale discussion of this position, but let me try to formulate briefly one reason why I think it is not successful.[7]

The claim that we hold many beliefs without evidence is supported by appealing to various beliefs that play a special basic role in our noetic structure: belief in what we perceive by the senses, in the existence of other minds, in the reliability of inductive inferences (to stick to examples involving existence claims). But all of these examples should in fact be thought of as supported by evidence, although not quite in the way of other beliefs, which are derived from the basic beliefs. Basic beliefs arise, as Plantinga often points out, from experiences that lead to their formation. He also rightly points out that this formation is not a matter of logically inferring these beliefs from (propositional expressions of) the experiences.

But there is more to say about the process of formation. In every case, the formative experiences exist as a cohesive and mutually supporting whole. Once a basic belief is formed, it is typically confirmed by other basic beliefs, which are themselves confirmed by the initial belief. So, for example, I hear a roar outside my window and form a basic belief that someone is running a lawnmower; getting up to see who it is, I form a basic belief that my neighbor is mowing his lawn. I mention this to my wife, who tells me that he's been mowing his lawn every Saturday, which leads me to remember that he mowed it last Saturday. Here we have various basic beliefs—auditory, visual, testamentary, and recollected—working together to support one another.

Sometimes, of course, a given basic belief fails to be confirmed by further experiences; then there is need for noetic revision by dropping and/or adding various beliefs. Beliefs that continue to be supported by this process become more deeply embedded in our noetic structure. Notice also that this system of mutual support connects all our various sorts of basic beliefs with one another. To sum up: basicality is a function of connectivity.

The problem with claiming that religious beliefs are properly basic is that they do not exhibit connectivity to anything like the extent of unproblematic basic beliefs. (1) An individual's religious experiences are typically highly intermittent, occurring at disparate times and often not repeated in essentially similar circumstances; (2) religious experiences are seldom shared by two or more individuals,

---

7. For further discussion of this, see my *What Philosophers Know* (New York: Cambridge University Press, 2009), Chapter 5.

even when they are in the same situation; (3) there are many occasions when religious experiences are expected but don't occur; (4) many people, even among believers, seldom or never have such experiences; (5) none of our other systems of basic beliefs (even ones not directed to the material world) connect up with religious experiences. For all these reasons, it seems wrong to claim that religious beliefs are properly basic in the sense that paradigm examples of such beliefs are.

Belief without Knowledge

At this point, let me try to sum up my assessment of the religious faith of philosophical believers. Their testimonies suggest that religious belief might have three distinct aspects. There is a religion of love, a religion of understanding, and a religion of knowledge. Religious love offers a moral orientation within a community that many believers see as transforming their lives for the better. Religious understanding offers a way of making sense of the world as a whole and our lives in particular. Religious knowledge offers an historical/metaphysical account of supernatural realities that, if true, shows the operation of a benevolent power in the universe.

Many believers are entirely justified in accepting a religion of love; that is, in believing that their life in a specific religious community—or in accord with a specific religious tradition—is of great moral value. They are, however, not justified in an exclusivist reading of this belief, implying that the form of life they live is the only one that might have been morally fulfilling for them or that it is the only or best life of moral fulfillment for everyone.

Many believers are also justified in holding that their religious viewpoint provides a viable understanding of the main features (cognitive, moral, aesthetic) of our lives, that it offers a coherent and fruitful way of thinking about everything that needs thinking about. Once again, however, there is no justification for a claim of exclusivity.

Finally, the claim to religious knowledge is not, as the new atheists maintain, risible, on a par with the claim that the tooth fairy and Santa Claus exist. But the sort of "evidence" for it—metaphysical arguments from disputable premises, intermittent and fairly vague experiences, historical arguments from very limited data—does not meet ordinary (common-sense or scientific) standards for postulating an explanatory cause. It seems to me that agnosticism—even if sympathetic and open to something more positive—is the best judgment about claims of religious knowledge.

AN AGNOSTIC'S RELIGION

Nonbelievers—and many believers themselves—assume that, without a grounding in religious knowledge, there is no foothold for fruitful religious understanding. But is this really so? Is it perhaps possible to have understanding without knowledge? Here some reflections on the limits of science, our paradigm of knowledge, will be helpful.

It may well be that physical science will ultimately give us a complete account of reality. It may, that is, give us causal laws that allow us to predict (up to the limits of any quantum or similar uncertainty) everything that happens in the universe. This would allow us to entirely explain the universe as a causal system. But there are aspects of our experience (consciousness, personality, moral obligation, beauty) that may not be merely parts of the causal system. They may, for example, have meanings that are not reducible to causal interactions.

This is obvious for moral and aesthetic meanings: even a complete account of the causal production of an action will not tell us that it is good or beautiful. The same is true of semantic meaning. We might be able to predict the exact physical configuration of the writing in a text that will be composed a million years from now in a language entirely unknown to us. Looking at this configuration, we would still not be able to understand the text.

Similarly, although we do not presently have anything like a complete causal account of consciousness, we have a fairly good idea of what such an account would look like from a third-person objective perspective, looking at the brain as just another physical system. But we have almost no idea of how to incorporate into such an account the first-person subjective perspective of our concrete experiences: what it is like (from the inside) to see a color, hear a symphony, love a friend, or hate an enemy.

At a minimum, we at present do not have anything like an adequate causal account of such experiences. Nor can we know that such an account is forthcoming. Atheists who ground their position in materialism may believe that such an account will someday be given, but that belief is no more knowledge than the religious claim that God exists as the ultimate causal power of the universe.

It doesn't, however, follow that we have no ways of understanding our first-person experiences. Not only our everyday life but also our art, literature, history, and philosophy contribute to such understanding. To say that, apart from the best current results of, say, neuroscience, we have no understanding of these experiences is simply absurd.

Every mode of understanding has its own ontology, a world of entities in terms of which it expresses its understanding. We can understand sexuality through Don Giovanni, Emma Bovary, and Molly Bloom; the horror of war through the images of "Guernica"; our neurotic behavior through Freudian drives and complexes; or self-deception through Sartre's being-for-itself, even if we are convinced that none of these entities will find a place in science's final causal account of reality. Similarly, it is possible to understand our experiences of evil in the language of the Book of Job, of love in the language of the Gospel of John, and of sin and redemption in the language of Paul's epistles.

The fault of many who reject religious ontologies out of hand is to think that they have no value if they don't express knowledge of the world's causal mechanisms. The fault of many believers is to think that the understanding these ontologies bring must be due to the fact that they express such knowledge.

As in the case of morality, there is no exclusive or infallible mode of understanding, religious or otherwise. Religions should, and increasingly do, accept other modes of understanding and try to integrate them with their own. Expressions of religion in art and poetry (Fra Angelico, John Donne) have always implicitly done just this.

I suggest that "non-believers" who express serious interest in and appreciation of religions, are thinking of them as modes of living and of understanding. Both they, and the believers who welcome their attention, should keep in mind that this says nothing at all about claims to religious knowledge.

Knowledge, if it exists, adds a major dimension to religious commitment. But love and understanding, even without knowledge, are tremendous gifts; and religious knowledge claims are hard to support. We should, then, make room for those who embrace a religion as a source of love and understanding but remain agnostic about the religion's knowledge claims. We should, for example, countenance those who are Christians while doubting the literal truth of, say, the Trinity and the Resurrection. I wager, in fact, that many professed Christians are not at all sure about the truth of these doctrines—and other believers have similar doubts. They are, quite properly, religious agnostics.

How to Vanquish the Lingering Shadow of the Long-Dead God[1]

KENNETH A. TAYLOR

> After Budda was dead, his shadow was still shown for centuries, in a cave—a tremendous gruesome shadow. God is dead; but given the way of men, there may still be caves for thousands of years in which his shadow will be shown—And we—we still have to vanquish his shadow.
>
> —Nietzsche, *The Gay Science* 108

Though Nietzsche happily declares the death of God, in *The Gay Science*, he also laments that we still live in "his tremendous, gruesome shadow." Finally and decisively vanquishing that shadow, he seems to believe, is key to the cultural transformation of the Europe of his time. Now it is worth being clear about just what sort of event Nietzsche intends to be announcing when he announces the death of God, and also worth puzzling over just what he is referring to when he refers to the "shadow" of the dead God. Presumably, as an avowed atheist, Nietzsche believes that there never was a living God in the first place. So he cannot really be intending to declare the actual historical demise of some once living transcendent being. But I think even the most diehard atheist will have to acknowledge that at least the concept of God once played, and for many continues to play, a vital role in undergirding certain cultural practices and formations, including

---

1. Earlier versions of this paper were presented at the Baylor Conference on the Philosophy of Religion, at the University of Nevada Las Vegas, and at Pacific University. I am grateful to the members of those audiences for many comments and suggestions.

© 2013 Wiley Periodicals, Inc.

practices and formations which are not directly or explicitly religious in nature.² I take Nietzsche's claim about "the death of God" to be a claim about the diminishing role of the concept of God in supposedly undergirding certain cultural formations. What Nietzsche proclaims is what might be called a cultural death, not so much of a once living being, but of a once thriving concept. Nietzsche is claiming, that is, that the concept of God has lost its cultural relevance for enlightened Europeans of the nineteenth century.

As a historical claim about the role of the concept of God in undergirding nineteenth century European culture, Nietzsche's claim strikes me as plausibly correct. But even if that is a mistake, it will be of little consequence for the current essay. For even if you think that Nietzsche's declaration of the cultural death of the concept of God is premature, then you can take the reflections contained in the essay to have a hypothetical character. Now suppose, at least hypothetically, that Nietzsche is correct. Suppose, in particular, not only that there is not now and never was a living transcendent God, but also that the very concept of a living God has largely lost, for good or for ill, its cultural currency in our time. What exactly could it then mean to suggest that nonetheless we still live in the shadow of God? Why might God's shadow prove so difficult to vanquish? Would finally vanquishing the shadow of God be, on balance, a good thing or a bad thing for our lives? These are the sorts of questions I shall address in this essay.

I should make it clear from the outset that, although I shall be framing my discussion in a way that is deeply inspired by my reading of various passages in Nietzsche's *The Gay Science*, it is not my aim to give a scholarly exegesis and interpretation of that text. Nor do I claim to systematically explicate and defend Nietzsche's own understanding of the claim that we moderns lamentably still live in the lingering shadow of a long-dead God. Mainly, I take Nietzsche as a jumping-off point for a set of extended reflections on the nature of what I call the human normative predicament in the face of the presumed absence of God and the presumed cultural irrelevance of the very concept of God. Nietzsche's wide-ranging ruminations about the human normative predicament in light of both the cultural death of God and our inability to fully vanquish God's shadow run

---

2. For example, though we tend these days to think of religion and science as opposing tendencies, there is a strong case to be made that the rise of Christianity played a decisive role in the eventual rise of science. Nietzsche himself gives great credence to such views. See, for example, *Gay Science* 300. And also this at *Gay Science* 344:

> But you will have gathered what I am driving at, namely, that it is still a *metaphysical faith* upon which our faith in science rests—that even we seekers after knowledge today, we godless anti-metaphysicians still take our fire, too, from the flame lit by a faith that is thousands of years old, that Christian faith which was also the faith of Plato, that God is the truth, that truth is divine—But what if this should become more and more incredible, if nothing prove to be divine anymore unless it were error, blindness, the lie—if God himself should prove to be our most enduring lie.

I will not stop to interpret Nietzsche's various claims about science. But it seems clear that despite his admiration for science and its achievements, he believes that even science—with its commitment to objective truth—has not fully escaped the "shadow of God." I shall not attempt to say to what extent Nietzsche is either right or wrong about science.

very deep in my estimation. Those ruminations may help us to look right into the teeth of our normative predicament.

I start with another passage from *The Gay Science* in which Nietzsche announces what he calls the "problem" of morality:

> It is evident that up to now morality was no problem at all but, on the contrary, precisely that on which, after all mistrust, discord, and contradiction, one could agree—the hallowed place of peace where our thinkers took a rest even from themselves, took a deep breath, and felt revived. (*Gay Science* 345)

To take morality as a "hallowed place of peace," lying beyond all mistrust, discord, and contradiction is, I think, to construe morality as a realm of objective truths and one that is discernible by all sufficiently unclouded, reflective, right-thinking, or right-feeling minds. Nietzsche clearly thinks that such a view of morality is deeply mistaken on at least two different fronts. First, he clearly thinks that morality never was, in fact, a hallowed place of peace to begin with. Our collective failure to "problematize" morality, by as he puts it, "examin[ing] the *value* of that most famous of all medicine ... morality ... and ... for once to *question* it" (*Gay Science*, 345) has, he thinks, all along blinded us to the true nature and function of morality. But he seems to believe that we compound the error when we continue to endorse morality as a hallowed place of peace once the concept of God has been vanquished from its foundational role in our culture. After God has been exiled from the foundations of culture, continued belief in the very possibility of such a hallowed place of peace amounts not just to ordinary error, confusion, or a failure to raise questions that ought to have been asked all along, but to a kind of false consciousness and bad faith.

Now Nietzsche's claim that continuing belief in morality as a hallowed place of peace in the face of the cultural death of God can only be a matter of false consciousness is not entirely unproblematic. The view that morality is precisely such a place of peace has a very deep hold on the human mind—deeper even than Nietzsche himself may have appreciated. It has roots not just in the pronouncements of revealed religion, and speculative philosophy, but also in the plain deliverances of common sense and common decency. Its hold on us is both deep and nonaccidental. Only the depth of that hold would seem to explain why certain moral judgments come so easily and without hesitation to so many. Who can doubt, for example, that it is morally wrong—really and truly wrong—to kill the innocent for mere personal gain? We would shun anyone who would engage in such killing as unfit for human society. We would condemn any religion that sanctified such killing as archaic and benighted. And we would dismiss any philosophy that pretended to justify such killing as extravagant and perverse.

Still, we should not, I think, take either the depth or the apparent inevitability of the hold of the very idea of morality as a place of peace on the human mind to show that therefore that idea must be apt or true. The human mind is, unfortunately, subject to many perhaps inevitable, all but inescapable, and thoroughly gripping illusions. So it may well be that the widely shared invincible conviction that there are objective moral truths is itself the result of nothing but such an illusion. So we should be wary of taking the deliverances of common sense at face value and of accepting them on their own terms. I have, in fact, argued at length for such a view elsewhere and will return to this theme briefly below. For the nonce, let me try to soften, just a bit, our perception of the aptness of the belief that morality is a hallowed place of peace open to any sufficiently unclouded, right reasoning, or right feeling mind.

I begin by recalling that there have always been, and no doubt will always be, many who stand outside and apart from our shared moral consensus. Think of religious traditions that promise rewards in the great hereafter for the commission of unspeakable horrors. Think of history's great pantheon of murdering and marauding tyrants or of revolutions from below that culminate in the slaughter of millions in the name of some ever-receding ideal of liberation and empowerment. Think of the agents and enablers of the gulag, the concentration camp, ethnic cleansing, and slavery. Now suppose that even in the face of such pervasive and enduring darkness, we, nonetheless, continue to believe, that morality is not, as Nietzsche puts it, a problem, that it really does subsist as a hallowed place of peace, a realm of objective moral truths, beyond dispute and division. On what positive evidence, considerations, or arguments might we base such a belief?

It is no doubt tempting to sidestep the question, to appeal, instead, to what I earlier called an invincible conviction. We may confidently insist that moral truths are somehow manifest and discernible by all sufficiently unclouded and/or reflective minds. After all, we confidently grasp them. Do we not? And it need be neither a matter of stubbornness nor mere browbeating of those who disagree, we tell ourselves, to insist that anyone who stands outside and apart from the moral consensus must lack either the capacity or the will to acknowledge the plain moral facts—however exactly those facts are ultimately discerned by us. Perhaps they see with eyes beclouded by ignorance, prejudice, passion or ideology. Perhaps they listen with ears deafened to the imploring voices of reason, fellow feeling, or divine command.

My point here is that the very idea that morality is a hallowed place of peace, where disputation will inevitably come to an end, would seem to presuppose that we have a capacity for reliably and systematically discerning moral truth. But it is certainly fair to wonder what such a capacity might consist in. I do not deny that many different answers have been offered to that question—right reasoning through the spontaneity of the intellect; right feeling and the receptivity of the heart; or a faith that hears the whispering God amidst the blaring cacophony of our mere humanity. That some such capacity could somehow, at least in the limit, enable us to reliably and systematically track the moral truth and thereby enables us, at least in the limit, to bring resolution to all moral disputes is part and parcel of the very idea of morality as a hallowed place of peace.[3]

---

3. I do not mean to suggest that the bare fact of moral disagreement decisively shows that there can be no objective moral truth. That would certainly be a hasty and fallacious inference. Even if we could not in principle hope to convince the rational other of the objective moral truth, that need not mean that, therefore, there is no objective moral truth. See Boghossian (2006) for an anti-relativist tract that makes many correct points against more or less standard forms of

My aim here is not to decisively refute all such views. But it does not require an extravagant degree of moral skepticism to doubt that any such capacity is actually resident in humans. So let us ask, with utter seriousness, what if there is no hallowed place of moral peace, either in heaven or on earth? What if there is no merely human capacity by which we might reliably discern such a place even if there was one? What if there is no transcendent God whose whispered commands reliably direct us toward that which is unquestionably good? What if the finite, merely material universe is all there is and that it contains nothing that might stand in for the whispered divine command? What if, to put it differently, the nonexistent God casts no shadow whatsoever so that, after all, the finite merely material universe contains nothing of intrinsic moral worth or objective value? What if this merely material universe is governed by nothing but the blind mechanical laws of morally indifferent nature? What if the voice of human reason and/or human sentiment and fellow-feeling sing not the sweet harmony of an all-embracing brotherhood, but a cacophony of competing and irreconcilable ends? What then?

These questions are intended to give us a sense of the human normative predicament, as Nietzsche seems to understand it. It is these questions which we must answer, I think, if we are to embrace the human predicament and finally extinguish even the shadow of God.

I hasten to add that although my understanding of the human normative predicament is deeply influenced by Nietzsche, I admit to finding no satisfying formula for dealing with that predicament in Nietzsche's own prescriptions. For my own taste, Nietzsche pays too little heed to what I call the problem of common life. That is, he gives too little thought to fact that the human normative predicament is faced not just by each of us taken one by one, but by humanity as some sort of collectivity or other, if only a collectivity struggling to constitute itself. We must determine, from within our normative predicament, not just how our own individual lives are to go, but how we are to go on together. Nietzsche's own solution to the problem of common life, such as it is, would seem to call for the domination by those with what he believes are higher natures over those with what he believes are lower natures. He apparently believes that if the human spirit is to flourish, some must become tools and instruments of others. I find that I cannot endorse that solution.

So how, then, *are* we to live and thrive within the human normative predicament? Some may doubt that there is any way forward at all, if the human normative predicament is as I take it to be. The prospect that our predicament might be as Nietzsche takes it to be may fill some with a certain horror and dread, a horror and dread from which they naturally recoil toward what they take to be embracing arms of a loving God—or if not of God himself, then at least of his shadow. But I hold that both the comfort of the divine and the comforts of the various immanent stand-ins for the divine are one and all false comforts. We should not recoil from the human predicament. We should learn, rather, to embrace it, to live and thrive within it.

---

relativism. I claim, however, that there is a form of relativism—what I call intolerant relativism—which withstands all such criticism. I elaborate on the distinction between tolerant and intolerant relativism in my *A Natural History of Normativity* (Taylor, in progress).

MORE ON THE HUMAN NORMATIVE PREDICAMENT

Let us say more about the nature of the human normative predicament. Begin with what I call the Dostoyevskyan conditional. If God is dead, Doystoyevsky has Ivan Karamozov say, then everything is permitted. But if everything is permitted, then there really is no distinction at all between what is permitted and what is forbidden, no distinction between right and wrong. In the absence of God, the thought seems to be, we are faced with the bleak conclusion that we live in a universe utterly devoid of meaning, purpose, and value.

The Dostoyevskyan conditional is most often on display in theistic reasoning about God and morality.[4] One can easily imagine a theist arguing from the truth of that conditional and what she takes to be the evident fact that the bleak conclusion is false, that there really are objective moral truths that, therefore, God must, after all, really exist. For once we both acknowledge the conditional and grant that there really and truly are moral absolutes and objective value in the universe, it follows immediately, the theist will say, that we must also acknowledge the God who is the sole possible source and author of an objective moral order. According to this reasoning, we simply cannot have it both ways. Either we view our lives and the universe as governed by moral absolutes and suffused with objective value—and thereby acknowledge the God who is the sole possible author of all value and all morality—or we deny the existence of God, and resign ourselves to the bleak conclusion and lives utterly devoid of meaning and value, in a universe governed by no moral law.[5]

Of course, there are also plenty of atheists who deny the existence of God, while rejecting the bleak conclusion and accepting the reality of absolute morality and objective value. Such sunny atheists, as I will call them, thus reject the Dostoyevskyan conditional. And if one rejects the conditional, one can consistently deny God, while rejecting the bleak conclusion of the Dostoyevskyan conditional. Now sunny atheists are no doubt right to point out that there are many potential grounds for rejecting the Dostoyevskyan conditional. Chief among them is the much-discussed Euthyphro dilemma. Suppose we assert that the objective moral order exists because God freely wills that order into being. And suppose we think that this order is an objectively good thing. We may now intelligibly wonder whether the moral order is good merely because God wills it or whether God wills the moral order because it is independently good. If the latter, then the goodness of the moral order would seem to be independent of God's will. And the independent goodness of that order would seem to explain rather than to be explained by God's willing of it. But in that case we need to be told some independent story about what makes the moral order good. On the other hand, if the moral order is

---

4. Though see Anderson (2007) for a deft attempt to turn the conditional against the theist.

5. Theological voluntarism—which encompasses divine command theories of morality—comes in many different flavors, which differ in important ways from one another. For a guide to the complexity of the dialectical landscape occupied by the various versions of theological voluntarism, see Murphy (2012). For a nuanced and sophisticated defense of one version of theological voluntarism, see Quinn (1978). For a theistic approach that rejects theological voluntarism (and also natural law theory), see Murphy (2011).

good solely because God wills it, we may now intelligibly wonder why the mere fact that God chose to usher this moral order rather than some other into being should suffice for its goodness. To be sure, God, if he exists at all, may have the biggest stick—since he may condemn to hell all who will not cleave to the divine program— and the juiciest carrots—since he puts on offer everlasting bliss in union with the divine for all those who will do so. But neither the size of one's stick nor the sweetness of one's carrot *ipso facto* suffices to endow one's will with trumping normative authority.

I do not mean to argue either for or against the divine command theory here. But I do maintain, contrary to much received philosophical wisdom, that the divine command theorist may be no worse off—but also no better off—than the sunny atheist who believes in moral truth and objective values and seeks to ground them in something immanent rather than transcendent.[6] On my view, neither the theistic believer in objective value nor the sunny atheistic believer in such values has an easy way to locate the source of such values in the total order of things. If appeals to divine nature, divine wisdom, divine love, or divine command are found wanting as the ultimate sources of meaning, value and normativity, it is not obvious how anything in brute configurations of immanent nature could more adequately suffice. The sunny atheist could, of course, take objective truths about moral facts to be brute and irreducible constituents of the immanent order of things. But the advantage of that fantasy over approaches which attempt to ground morality and value in transcendent facts about the divine seems to me to have all the advantages of theft over honest toil. Moreover, I would argue—though I lack the space to do so here—that approaches that see the facts about objective value as nonbrute and so attempt to ground such facts in something less mysterious and magical— including such potential grounders as human reason, human sentiment, or human agreement—simply fail to deliver what they promise to deliver. It is not, however, that I think that all such attempts to ground value deliver nothing. Indeed, I argue elsewhere that such potential grounders deliver all the normativity it is worth our while to care about.[7] It is just that such normativity as they do ground falls very far short of constituting a realm of absolute moral truths and objective values.

I do not expect these passing remarks to be persuasive as they stand. But it can hardly be denied that saying how absolute morality and objective value manage to subsist in a merely material universe, devoid of either an intrinsically authoritative divine will or a metaphysically primitive, but still immanent stand in for such a will, is a daunting task. I say this while openly acknowledging that over many centuries now, since the question "why be moral?" was first ushered onto the philosophical stage by Plato, philosophers of a sunny but still atheistic

---

6. At least one sort of atheist claims, in fact, that the divine command theory is *better* off than any naturalistic alternative with respect to grounding objective morality and value. See, for example, Mackie (1977) and Mavrodes (1986). Atheists of this sort see the divine as something that could possibly, if it were to exist, ground objective morality. It is just that they think that there is no such thing as the divine. On the other hand, they think nothing in merely material nature could possibly serve as a ground of objective morality. Nietzsche himself might be read as holding a view of this sort.

7. I argue for this claim at length in Taylor (in progress).

disposition have devoted considerable energy and great ingenuity to just that daunting task.[8] Though I suspect that all those prodigious philosophical efforts ultimately come to naught, I will not try to establish that point in detail here.[9] For the space of the current argument, we can afford to proceed in a more hypothetical vein. We can suppose that all efforts to ground absolute morality and objective values in something immanent rather than transcendent are bound to come to naught, and then investigate what exactly follows from that supposition.

Since we are hypothetically assuming that both attempts to ground objective value in something transcendent and attempts to ground value in something immanent come to naught, we are, in a way, faced with the worst of both worlds—the combined weight of both the Dostoyevskean Conditional and the Euthyphro Dilemma. That combined weight may seem to force on us the bleak conclusion that both the theist and the sunny atheist sought to avoid. It would be one thing to deny the dilemma—for example, if we were willing to allow ourselves to be thrown back toward the divine as the only possible source of the objective value. But we are, in effect, rejecting the divine, while also denying the dilemma. That is, we may seem to want to have it both ways. But if we hold that there is neither a transcendent nor an immanent ground for objective value and moral absolute, how are we to forestall the bleak conclusion that everything is, after all, permitted and nothing is, after all, forbidden and the correlatively tempting conclusion that human life must be entirely without ultimate meaning, purpose, or value? Can we possibly resist this bleak conclusion, without appealing to either an immanent or transcendent ground for objective values? I submit that we can. And I submit that seeing how we can amounts to seeing just what we must do to fully and finally vanquish the still lingering shadow of the long-dead God.

Let us begin by granting, if only for the space of the current argument, that we live in a finite, merely material universe, containing at its core nothing of intrinsic or objective value. Let us grant that the universe is governed by no purpose, that it neither contains nor rests upon anything sufficient to ground universal or absolute moral law. Still, whatever else the universe does or does not contain, *we* exist in it and through it. And we are what I shall call value and norm-mongering creatures. We are creatures who pervasively and persistently value things. This propensity to value things, to take things as mattering, is, I think, built into our evolved biological and psychological natures. Find a creature that values nothing at all and that creature will, I submit, be hardly recognizable as a human being. To be sure, we do not, on the picture I am painting, find or *discover*

---

8. The force of the question "why be moral?" is in part due to the worry that morality might have its ultimate source in something merely external to the self and thus have no particular claim to command the self. Nietzsche clearly evinces this worry in dismissing morality on the grounds that to hew to morality is to make oneself an instrument of the herd. Similarly, Plato's famous ring of Gyges is grounded in the worry that the benefits of morality are primarily external—being moral will give you a good reputation and the company of others. But these goods leave open the question of whether morality has any intrinsic value for those who are subject to it. Partly as a consequence of the potential externality of the demands of morality, Nietzsche and Plato both worry that taking morality as a guide to life can lead to a kind of self-alienation.

9. I give an elaborate argument to this effect in Taylor (in progress).

value in the universe, as if value were antecedently present there, independently of anything that we do or are. Value and meaning are not hidden in some deep reaches of the order of things, waiting merely to be uncovered by the inquiring human mind. Rather, we *create* the values that we monger. And we create them more or less *ex nihilo*. We do so simply by engaging in the merely human and entirely natural activity of *taking* things to matter *to us*. By *taking* things to matter we thereby *make* them matter. We make them really and truly matter, at least to ourselves.

Now many philosophers, as well as many theologians, have thought that at least some of our valuings stand in need of external "vindication" as "worthy" of having. But I insist, to the contrary, that the values that we constitute through our human, all-too-human value mongering remain always and only values of our own. There is not and need not be anything either within or without the merely material universe to externally "vindicate" our merely human valuings—not God, not a transcendental realm of objective goodness, not a realm of natural rights, not a system of categorically binding commandments of cold, impersonal reason. We may cry out with longing and despair to the cold uncaring universe to embrace our value, to vindicate our *right* to value what we value. But we will hear only silence in return. The universe is mute. It is devoid of all power to either affirm or deny the worth we place on either ourselves or on others. To quote Nietzsche once again:

> But how could we reproach or praise the universe? Let us beware of attributing to it heartlessness and unreason or their opposites: it is neither perfect nor beautiful, nor noble, nor does it wish to become any of these things; it does not by any means strive to imitate man. None of our aesthetic and moral judgments apply to it. Nor does it have any instinct for self-preservation or any other instinct; and it does not observe any laws either. Let us beware of saying that there are laws in nature. There are only necessities: there is nobody who commands, nobody who obeys, and nobody who trespasses ... (*Gay Science*, 109)

If Nietzsche is right—and I strongly suspect that he is—then the universe is not the kind of thing that contains values of its own. And, more to the point, it does not contain anything else sufficient to vindicate our valuings. Indeed, Nietzsche seems often to suggest that it was all along a mistake to think that our merely human valuings need go on parade in search of vindication from elsewhere. With Nietzsche, then, let us say. "So be it." We do not and could not matter *to* the morally mute universe. And just because the universe is morally mute, it is not fit to sit in implicit judgment on the probity of our merely human valuings. Nonetheless, the brute facticity of our nature as value-mongering creatures remains. It remains as a fact that is definitive of our very being in the universe. Things matter to us. We often matter to ourselves. And we sometimes matter to other value-mongering creatures, who sometimes matter to us in return. And that, I submit, is all the mattering, all the value and valuing, that it is worth our while to concern ourselves about.

Now I grant that it is important to distinguish between, on the one hand, that which, by its very nature, goes on parade, seeking external vindication and that which stands in no need of such vindication. At least to the extent that they purport to represent and be answerable to how things stand by a mind-independent world, our beliefs are, by their very nature, on parade in search of validation by the very world they purport to represent. The belief that snow is white, for example, does not stand in splendid indifference to whether snow is, in fact, white. Indeed, the probity of our beliefs is, in a sense, directly hostage to how things are by a world largely independent of mind.[10] If snow is not, in fact, white, then the probity of believing that snow is white is directly undermined—at least to the extent that the facts of the matter shape our evidence. And I cannot, by merely taking snow to be white, restore or rescue the probity of that belief. Now if our valuings were like our believings in purporting to be answerable to how things are, in the way of value, by a mind-independent world, then it would be part of their very nature, too, to parade in search of external validations. Our valuings would then be hostage, for their probity, on whether what we valued was in itself valuable. In that case, thoroughgoing failure to find anything in the nature of things which "answered" to our valuings would thoroughly undermine the probity of those valuings. Our valuings would then be shown up as mere illusions.

But it is, I think, a deep and consequential mistake, one deeply rooted in much common sense and much philosophical elucidation of common sense, to suppose that our valuings must, by their very nature, go on parade in search of external validation or to think that the very probity of our valuings depends on there being "objective" values resident in the nature of things which somehow demand respect by commanding our valuings. Once again, Nietzsche sees the mistake clearly and captures its essence powerfully:

> Life *shall* be loved, because—! Man *shall* advance himself and his neighbor, *because*—! What names these Shalls and Becauses receive and may yet receive in the future! In order that what happens necessarily and always, spontaneously without any purpose, may henceforth appear to be done for some purpose and strike man as rational and an ultimate commandment, the ethical teacher comes on stage, as the teacher of the purpose of existence; and to this end he invents a second, different existence and unhinges by means of his new mechanics the old ordinary existence. (*Gay Science* 1)

Nietzsche, of course, thinks this presumed "second existence" is a mere invention and, as such, that it is entirely illusory. With that judgment, I fully concur. We should reject the very idea there is or must be an ultimate normative ground to human existence, an ultimate ground lying outside our merely human valuings, but

---

10. As Boghossian puts it, "we have no choice but to think that the world out there is what it is largely independently of us and our beliefs about it." Now many hold that the same is true of values. I reject the claim that values are answerable to a mind-independent world in any way like the way that beliefs are. On the other hand, there are also those who claim that beliefs are no more answerable to a mind-independent world than our values are. Rorty (1978) holds such a view. On the score of belief, and their answerability to the world, I side with Boghossian rather than Rorty. Explaining just why beliefs and valuings differ in regard to their "answerability," or lack thereof, to the world is a task I take up in great detail in Taylor (in progress).

endowed, nonetheless, with the power to command, approve, or disapprove those valuings. Our valuings remain always and only valuings of our own constituting. They rest on no normative authority save our own.

The thought that there is no external normative authority that vindicates our merely human valuings may seem dizzying and discomforting. But it need not be. If our valuings need not go parading in search of external validation in the first place, then the "failure" to find anything objective in the order of things that answers to and grounds them would do nothing to "undermine" them. What need have we for the mandate of heaven or of history and tradition or of timeless and impersonal reason, when we have our own inner mandate already ready to hand?

To be sure, down that path I am suggesting for living with and within the human normative predicament, there may appear to lurk the danger of a thoroughgoing relativism. What matters to one may fail to matter to others. If, as I insist, there is no external authority to which we may appeal to decide what is really and truly worthy of valuing, then it would seem to follow that each person becomes the creator and arbiter of her own values and that, consequently, no person has any authority whatsoever to command, criticize, or sanction another. Such relativism, it is often thought, would be the end to all mattering and all morality, rather than a vindication of them. For I may value and esteem my own dear self in ways and degrees that others do not. I may feel entitled; nonetheless, to have others respect the value I place upon myself. I may take this entitlement as more than a mere hope or wish, but as my inalienable right as a human being. And if others disagree, what am I to say to them? How am I to make my right good, if each is really an authority unto herself?

Not entirely without reason, relativism is widely regarded as a bogie from which we must flee. But the threat of relativism arises because of certain intrinsic and inescapable facts about the human normative predicament, facts that give the lie to the most cherished dreams of both theist and sunny-minded atheists alike. But we must not recoil in horror from the facts of our predicament, but rather face them with clear eyes. As a final prelude to offering my view about how we might live with and within the human predicament, let me characterize, as fully as I can, the nature of that predicament. Our predicament arises from the fact that we are value-mongering, norm-mongering creatures. Moreover, we are beset by the urge to parade the values and norms that we monger in search of external validation. Finding none, we are brought short and are presented with certain stark options. We may either surrender our valuings as illusory, sinking into a kind of nihilism of value. Or, recoiling from such nihilism, we may retreat into relativism. But in acknowledging the self-validating nature of our valuings, relativism threatens to make each of us a normative authority unto ourselves, thereby stripping us of the power to command, criticize, or sanction other value-mongering creatures when they disagree. Neither nihilism nor relativism is an entirely attractive option. And for that reason we tend to project onto the morally mute universe that which satisfies our longing that there be a decisive normative authority. And just as Nietzsche says, the names for this projected authority have been many—God, Reason, Tradition, Fellow Feeling, the Good, and so on. But all such names are, I submit with Nietzsche, empty names, with no reference to any real existent. Precisely that is our normative predicament.

MY AUTHORITY, YOUR AUTHORITY, AND OUR AUTHORITY

I do not deny that there is a sense in which each person is indeed the ultimate creator and arbiter of her own values. But the key to understanding how we can live with and within the human normative predicament, without retreating into either a paralyzing nihilism or an intractable relativism, is to recognize that one's own values and normative lights need not be remain always and only values and normative lights merely of one's own endorsing, as if each of us were always destined to be and remain a moral community of one. Human beings collectively have the capacity to constitute moral communities, communities held together by systems of reciprocal obligations and commitments. In fact, there has never been a time when human beings did not find themselves distributed in moral communities of varying scope and complexity. Our ancient progenitors formed themselves into normative communities encompassing only small circles, drawn around kin, clan, or tribe. The rough general trend of human history has been haltingly toward normative communities of ever-increasing scope, so much so that we are now able to conceive of something barely dreamt of in many ages of the past—the real possibility of a global moral community.[11]

But one should let neither the rough general trend of history nor our current capacity to imagine alternative realities tempt one to the conclusion that an all-encompassing moral community is there for either rationally mandatory or historically inevitable.[12] When we survey the long sweep of human history, we find that one, then another moral community has taken its stand, flourished for a while, and then run aground. It is worth granting, of course, that although moral communities are one and all equally creations of human beings, they are not, from our current point of view, all created equal. Some moral communities have been instrumental to what we, here and now, by our own lights, take to be progress. Some have not been. Moral communities are often contested and always contestable. What one moral community regards as moral progress, another may regard as moral decline. But it is part of our predicament that there is no privileged stance, fixed

---

11. For a fascinating account of what he sees as moral progress, see Kitcher (2011). See also Taylor (in progress) for an account similar in spirit to Kitcher's that does, however, claim that moral change is "objectively" progressive.

12. I argue in Taylor (in progress) that we cannot determine *a priori* from first principles alone whether the dialectic of ratification and resistance through which normative change is largely driven has what I call a Hegelian dynamic or an anti-Hegelian dynamic. By a Hegelian dynamic, I mean a dynamic in which rational creatures converge, as a consequence of reason reconfiguring itself over historical time, on something like an all-encompassing normative community. If the dynamic of reason is Hegelian, then we can see normative change as, in some sense, progressive, as a matter of reason throwing off one, then another "irrational" or at least incompletely rational local configuration. The dynamic of reason is anti-Hegelian if there is nothing in the mere work of reason as such that guarantees such convergence. If the dynamic of reason is anti-Hegelian, then reason may ultimately settle into a fragmented landscape consisting of multiple local configurations.

once and for all, outside of history and culture, from which we may determine by which normative lights the "truth" is to be measured in such disputes. This is not to deny that we typically do measure the sweep of history by our own current lights. We may even take ourselves to be justified in so doing. But as dear and as precious as our own normative lights may be, they enjoy no antecedent privilege except that of being our own. There may come a time when our own lights are entirely extinguished and when we are viewed by those who follow as having undertaken merely one more failed experiment in collective existence. With what right shall we then protest the verdict of history?

If each person is really an ultimate arbiter of values and a moral authority entirely unto herself, how have we escaped the bleak conclusion that everything is permitted and nothing forbidden? The answer is already ready to hand. Though there is no external normative authority, either in heaven or on earth, that outweighs our own, that may reliably direct us to that longed-for place of peace, there is, nonetheless, genuine normative authority in the world. There is a normative authority lying within each of us. Each fully mature, intact, and reflective human being has the power to bind himself or herself to a norm and thereby to commit himself or herself to living up to those norms in ways that may even entitle others to hold him or her to the relevant norm. Once one has committed oneself, it is no longer the case that everything is permitted and nothing forbidden. Some things are forbidden to one simply because one forbids them to oneself.

Elsewhere, I spell out in fulsome detail an intricate story about the normative authority that lies within each one of us. That story explains the source and nature of our normative powers, articulates the factors that constrain and govern the exercise of that authority, and outlines the consequences for individual and social life that flow from the exercise of that capacity over both evolutionary and historical time. I lack the space to tell that story in any real detail here. But I need to introduce a small part of my theory of normativity, if I am to be able say how we can avoid the collapse into either a paralyzing nihilism or an intractable relativism.

I begin by saying a bit more about what it takes for a person to be really and truly bound by a norm. The key lies with our powers of reflective endorsement. An agent is bound by a norm N, I claim, if she would endorse N upon culminated competent reflection. To a rough first approximation, one may think of culminated competent reflection is a kind of "ideal" reflection. But talk of "ideal" is prone to carry certain unwarranted connotations. For example, some may be tempted to think of "ideal" reflection as reflection that tracks the "objectively good" whatever exactly that is. Others may be tempted to hold that under "ideal" reflection, agents are guaranteed to converge on endorsements of the same standards or norms. My own talk of "ideal" reflection is intended to carry no such connotations. On my view, there is nothing in the universe that merits the title objective goodness. And I deny that moral convergence is guaranteed to us. Even at some imagined ideal limit of moral inquiry, even assuming the full reflective rationality of all, the norms that one endorses, and by which one's life is thereby governed, may not be endorsed by any other. This is to say that there is the real possibility that the human adventure will culminate in thoroughgoing moral fragmentation and enmity.

Though I reject certain unwarranted connotations that often go with talk of ideal reflection, I concede that not just any form of reflection can bind an agent to a norm. Excessive emotion, illicit substances, mental dysfunction, and immaturity may all disrupt or distort reflection. Under such circumstances, reflective endorsement of a norm would constitute no rational commitment to that norm. Reflection is "competent" only if no such disruptions or distortions obtain. Competent reflection is thus the kind of reflection, whatever it is, that is more or less characteristic of mature, intact, well-functioning human minds. Only competent reflection about the course of our lives could suffice to bind us to norms. To be sure, standards of competence are, as I argue elsewhere, subject to certain variability. What counts as "competent" reflection in a prescientific, preliterate, prephilosophical age may differ radically from what counts as competent reflection in a scientific, literate, and philosophical age. But we need not explore such complications in depth here.

The reflection that binds us to norms must not only be competent, it must also "culminate." Intuitively, the culmination of reflection is a matter of reflection coming to a stopping point, at least temporarily. We may reflect and reflect, but until reflection culminates, we have not bound ourselves to any determinate norm. Very roughly, reflection culminates when it produces an endorsement that is "stable" in light of all currently relevant inputs. Reflection culminates when further reflection would yield the same endorsement at least given the same input. But the stability in which reflection culminates is typically merely a local and temporary stability. The inputs to reflection change in a myriad of ways and for a plethora of reasons. They change in response to social and personal upheaval, in response to new voices, demanding recognition and respect, in response to new discoveries about either our individual lives or about our collective places in the order of things. Reflection is practically inexhaustible. We are subject to constant moral testing, to constant opportunities for discovery, for growth, for failure, for success. What stability and fixity reflection achieves, in light of the constant churning of the moral whirlwind, is likely to be but the fixity and stability of the dialectical moment. Still, in the fixity and stability of the dialectical moment, we have *decisively* committed to a certain norm. For this dialectical moment, we have given that norm our full rational backing. Giving a norm one's full rational backing amounts to decisively undertaking to govern one's life by the relevant norm. It is, I suggest, through such decisive rational commitments that one escapes the Dostoyevskian predicament. In the moment of decisive rational commitment, one has really and truly bound oneself to a norm.

Now I alone have the power to decisively commit myself to live in accordance with a norm. Others may attempt to coerce me into living in accordance with some norm. Such coercion may even play a role in causing me to "obey" the relevant norm. That does not, however, make the norm binding on me. I am bound—really and truly bound—only to norms of my own culminated competent reflective endorsement. But despite the fact that another cannot bind me to a norm, she may nonetheless be *entitled* to *hold* me to certain norms, even to norms by which I am not bound. We must distinguish, that is, between one's being bound by a norm and another's being entitled to hold one to a norm. Moreover, entitlements themselves originate in two different ways. They can be *self-generated* or *granted from the subject.* When *x* entitles herself to hold *y* to *N*, *x*'s entitlement with respect to *y* is self-generated. When *y* entitles *x* to hold *y* to *N*, *x*'s entitlement with respect to *y* is granted from *y*. Many self-generated entitlements with respect to others arise because we sometimes endorse a norm not merely as norm for ourselves but as a norm for others as well, perhaps even as a norm for the entire rational order. These are what I have elsewhere called traveling norms. When one reflectively endorses a norm as a traveling norm—that is, as a norm for the entire rational order—one, in effect, entitles oneself to hold the entire rational order to that norm, whether or not the entire rational order has collectively bound itself to that norm. In such self-generated entitlements, one takes one's own normative authority as a normative authority for all. One takes oneself to be legislating, as it were, for the entire rational order.[13]

Now the urge to take what is merely one's own normative authority as an authority for the entire rational order is both a blessing and a curse. When we give in to this urge, we are often led into moral conflict. But moral conflict may sometimes be a mere way station toward more encompassing moral community. Moral conflict arises when I entitle myself, through purely self-generated entitlements, to hold you to norms by which you are not bound. When I do so, you may entitle yourself to resist my attempts to do so. I may endorse a norm that entails the abolition of slavery everywhere, while you endorse a norm that permits slavery. I may thereby entitle myself to hold you, by whatever means necessary, to my abolitionist norm. You may entitle yourself to resist my so holding you. When that happens we have a deep moral conflict.

I do not mean to say that agents are never mutually and reciprocally bound by a system of norms. When we entitle ourselves to hold the entire rational order to a norm, we, in effect, offer that norm up to others as candidates for their endorsement as well. When agents each accept what is on offer from one another, they achieve *mutual ratification* of a system of norms. Through mutual ratification of a system of norms they thereby make the system of norms mutually and reciprocally binding. Now they do not merely self-generate entitlements. Rather, they grant one another *mutual and reciprocal entitlements* to hold one another to the norms by which they are now mutually and reciprocally bound. When agents achieve mutual ratification of shared norms, they have, in effect, acknowledged each other as equal partners in a normative community. To acknowledge another in this way is for each to say to the other that the normative authority of one is also a normative authority for the other.

---

13. My talk of travelling norms has a quasi-Kantian feel. But my differences with Kant are deep and important. For Kant, to adopt what we might call the ethical stance is, in effect, to regard oneself as legislating for a kingdom of ends. And he seems to believe that when one legislates from the ethical stance, one's legislation will have a certain intrinsic normative authority. For when we adopt the pose of being one legislator among others in a kingdom of ends, all mere particularity somehow drops out. And the reason in me comes, as it were, to speak with the authority of reason itself. I intend to be endorsing no such view here. Still, I do not mean to deny that something like a Kantian community of ends may be one possible configuration in the total space of possible configurations of reason.

None of this is automatic. The initial tension generated by agents competing attempts to hold one another to norms to which they have not yet bound themselves initiates what I call the dialectic of ratification and resistance. The dialectic of ratification and resistance rests first and foremost on self-recognition and self-valuing. Each fully reflective intact rational being recognizes herself to be an original, nonderivative source of reasons for herself. But we are also capable of recognizing, and sometimes do in fact recognize, that other reflective rational agents value themselves in similar ways. To recognize another as a fellow reflective rational being is to recognize that other as an original and nonderivative source of reasons for herself. In this mere recognition of another as a fellow rational being, we have already elevated her above the whole of nonrational nature. Nonrational beings, who lack the power of reflection, are nothing at all either to themselves or for themselves. They are at best derivative source of reasons for any rational being. Nonrational beings can indeed be sources of reasons for us, but only in virtue of the rationally optional interests that we happen to take in them. We may esteem nonrational beings as instruments, as objects of wonder and awe, even as objects of a peculiar kind of sympathy or love. But they are not the kinds of beings for which even the possibility of normative community arises.

The mere recognition of another as a fellow rational being, a being capable of the deepest sort self-valuing, is not yet the achievement of normative community and not yet a stable solution to the mutual ratification problem. In the bare recognition of another as a fellow rational being, one has not thereby reflectively owned the other as a nonderivative rational source for oneself. Recognition does, however, set the question, "What, if anything, shall we do, be or believe together as fellow rational beings?" This happens when we confront each other with concrete demands for respect and recognition of the normative authority that lies within. I claim here and now a right to what I take to be mine. I demand recognition and respect of my claim from you. Correlatively, you claim rights to what you take to be yours. Our claims may conflict and so we are confronted with a question. How, if at all, shall we be reconciled? How, if at all, shall we live together? The struggle to arrive at mutually acceptable answers to such questions, a struggle in which we sometimes succeed and sometimes fail, is what I mean by the dialectic of ratification.

Through a dialectic of ratification and resistance, I try to get you to ratify me and my norms. I try thereby to make it the case that me and my norms govern your life. Simultaneously, you try to get me to ratify you and your norms. You try thereby to make it the case that you and your norms govern my life. When we are each governed by the other, we constitute a normative community. We have made ourselves into original normative authorities and nonderivative sources of reasons for each other.

Normative communities are among humanity's highest achievements. Through the constitution of normative communities, we extend the reach of our own rational powers. For mutually ratified norms are the rails along which reasons may be transmitted from cognizing agent to cognizing agent. Within a normative community, the rational powers of one become rational resources for all. Normative community thus makes possible the emergence of complex cooperative rational activity, including shared forms of inquiry, deliberation, and argument. But contrary to the dreams of, say, Kant, an all-encompassing community of reasons is not an *a priori*, rationally mandatory imperative categorically binding on all rational beings as such. Indeed, there are myriad ways in which we might fail. The norms by which I would see the world governed, that I most urgently offer up for mutual acceptance to the entire rational order, may simply be rejected. That would make them an insufficient basis for normative community. But it would not make them any less deeply held by me. Not out of mere hubris or self-love, but out of deep concern for the entire rational order, we may entitle ourselves to make an unyielding world as we would have it be. We may prefer the force of argument if argument will suffice. But must we simply abandon our deepest convictions about the governance of the world, if argument should fail? Yet, if we succeed merely through coercion in imposing norms upon a reluctant world, we have not achieved true normative community. We have achieved the mere domination of one over another. With fellow rational beings who succeed through coercion in holding me to norms of their own endorsing, despite my abhorrence of those norms, there can only be rational enmity and a discord of reasons. Even if I appear to endorse their domination over me through incompetent or nonculminating reflection, that amounts to a mere semblance of normative community, not its reality.

I do not mean to say that discord and domination are inevitable. I mean to insist that the building of normative community is always an achievement—a local, rationally optional, historically contingent, and politically precarious achievement.

CONCLUSION: VANQUISHING THE SHADOW OF GOD

With this understanding of the sources of normative community in hand, it is time to consider how we might use the only tools at our disposal—our finite and fallible reason, history, and tradition, the warm glue of human sentiment, and even the force of arms—to live with and within the human normative predicament. The story we have so far told will no doubt seem like cold comfort for many of our most cherished ambitions. We reject not only divine command and divine providence, but also the moral fantasies of the sunny-minded atheist. We must begin anew in our search for normative community by acknowledging forthrightly and without hesitation that we possess no simplemindedly uplifting alternative narrative of human history. We recognize that the voice of human reason may speak in a cacophony of competing ends that may never be reconciled. We recognize that it is a real possibility that the human adventure may end in discord and thoroughgoing enmity or in the domination of some over others. Vanquishing the shadow of God requires that we take this real possibility not as a counsel of despair but as an urgent call to arms. The normative order, such as it is, is an order entirely of our own human, all-too-human constituting. If we would build anything like a Kantian kingdom of ends, in which all stand equal before all, in which all are equally valued, then it falls entirely on our shoulders, and on the shoulders of no one else, to constitute that world. The work of building from the bottom up an all-encompassing moral order is heroic work, invigorating work, work that calls upon the best of ourselves, but it is also work fraught with peril, that holds out both the possibility of great joy as a consequence of success and great sadness as a consequence of failure.

There are, to be sure, many with whom we would achieve normative community who will reject from the depths of own rational self-valuing the defining dreams of a secular modernity. And unlike the sunny-minded atheist, we acknowledge that that the fact of resistance from the rational other gives rise to a deep dilemma—a dilemma intrinsic to our normative predicament. If all-encompassing normative community is neither historically inevitable nor rationally mandatory, with what right do we seek to impose that vision on a reluctant world? It is clear that down the path of forceful imposition lies much that we will reject, including Stalin's gulag, Mao's cultural revolution, George Bush's misbegotten invasion of Iraq, and the dark dreams of Al Qaeda. On the other hand, if we merely abandon the dream of an all-encompassing moral community in the face of resistance from the other, do we not open the door to unending discord and division? We might seek a simulacrum of moral peace in a middle ground of a tolerant relativism. Tolerant relativism acknowledges that each person lives by her own normative lights, while recognizing that normative lights may vary from person to person or culture to culture, but it refuses the very idea of holding others to norms which they do not themselves endorse. Such tolerant relativism is, however, no option in our times, not because it is incoherent, as many have alleged, but because the contingencies of history have guaranteed that there are no peoples of the world with whom we can escape asking the question what, if anything, should we do or think, or be together as fellow rational beings. Thanks to the contingencies of history, we have come to be enmeshed with all rational beings in the struggle to constitute ourselves as beings in the world. We are brought into fraught contact through the relentless globalizing of commerce, through the worldwide degradation of the environment caused by our thirst for ever-greater consumption, through the imperial hubris of the world's leading military powers, through the power of the media to bring the suffering and poverty of the world's teeming masses to the attention of distant and indifferent elites, and the corresponding power to make that indifference manifest to all.

So what is the answer? How shall we orient ourselves in a world where nothing is guaranteed to us, where the pursuit of even our deepest most life-affirming aspirations, may lead us into moral darkness? How shall we live in the face of utter moral contingency? I answer that we have no choice but to embrace this thoroughgoing contingency as the stuff out of which our very being in the world is to be made and remade. What could be more exhilarating than to know that it falls entirely in our hands to make the world as we would have it be? If Nazism or Stalinism or Islamic fundamentalism or American imperialism is to be beaten back, only we all too fallible humans can beat them back. If there is to be progress and moral harmony, only we humans, divided and at odds as find ourselves, can bring them about. Is humanity really capable of building an all-encompassing moral order, in which all are valued and respected? Surely if we could, the rewards would be great. Nietzsche once again speaks powerfully to the exhilaration that we may experience when we have refashioned and renarrated the world:

> Anyone who manages to experience the history of humanity as a whole as *his own history* will feel in an enormously generalized way all the grief of an invalid who thinks of health, of an old man who thinks of the dreams of his youth, of a lover deprived of his beloved, of the martyr whose ideal is perishing, of the hero on the evening after a battle that has decided nothing but brought him the loss of his friends. But if one endured, if one *could* endure this immense sum of grief of all kinds, while yet being the hero who, as the second day of battle breaks, welcomes the dawn and his fortune, being a person whose horizon encompasses thousands of years past and future.... [I]f one could burden one's soul with all this, the oldest, the newest, losses, hopes, conquests and the victories of humanity—this would surely result in a happiness that humanity has not known so far; the happiness of a god full of love and power, full of tears and laughter, a happiness that like the sun in the evening continually bestows its inexhaustible riches, pouring them into the sea, feeling richest, as the sun does, only when even the poorest fisherman is still rowing with golden oars. This godlike feeling would then be called—humaneness. (*The Gay Science*, 337)

Can we remake the world? Can we redeem humanity and its centuries of suffering and darkness? There are no guarantees. There is no hallowed place of peace already waiting for us that we are guaranteed to reach merely by reasoning rightly, feeling humanely, or listening closely enough for the whispered command. We are thrown back on nothing but our all too fallible selves. Nonetheless, let us not be paralyzed in despair and doubt. Let us rather try it and see where the trying may lead us.

REFERENCES

Anderson, Elizabeth. 2007. "If God Is Dead, Is Everything Permitted?" In *Philosophers without Gods: Meditations on Atheism and the Secular Life*, ed. Louise M. Anthony, 215–30. Oxford: Oxford University Press.
Boghossian, Paul. 2006. *Fear of Knowledge: Against Relativism and Constructivism*. Oxford: Oxford University Press.
Kitcher, Philip. 2011. *The Ethical Project*. Cambridge, MA: Harvard University Press.
Mackie, John L. 1977. *Ethics: Inventing Right and Wrong*. New York: Penguin.
Mavrodes, George. 1986. "Religion and the Queerness of Morality." In *Rationality, Religious Belief, and Moral Commitment*, ed. Robert Audi and William Wainwright, 213–26. Ithaca, NY: Cornell University Press.
Murphy, Mark. 2011. *God and Moral Law: On the Theistic Explanation of Morality*. Oxford: Oxford University Press.
———. 2012. "Theological Voluntarism." In *The Stanford Encyclopedia of Philosophy*, ed. Edward N. Zalta, <http://plato.stanford.edu/archives/fall2012/entries/voluntarism-theological/>.
Nietzsche, Friedrich. 1974. *The Gay Science*, trans. Walter Kaufmann. New York: Random House.
Quinn, Philip. 1978. *Divine Commands and Moral Requirements*. Oxford: Oxford University Press.
Rorty, Richard. 1978. *Philosophy and the Mirror of Nature*. Princeton, NJ: Princeton University Press.
Taylor, Kenneth. In progress. *A Natural History of Normativity*.

Limited Belief

ANDREW WINER

His first visit to her cell came only a few days after her imprisonment. She had been moved in secrecy during the previous night, out of the women's block, where she'd originally been incarcerated, to a remote part of Clanton-Wade Correctional that hadn't been renovated when the regime converted the old airfield to its prison for political offenders. Both the clandestine nature of her sudden relocation, which had involved traversing a broad cratered tarmac in total darkness, and the distance her jailers seemed intent on putting between her and the main population, had caused her to worry. When she was led into a derelict terminal building, she had feared she was going to be executed. Then, in a hot corridor where doves were sheltering on dead overhead flat screens, she was shuffled past wall maps vaunting flights to long-forbidden destinations, and made to wait while a guard unlocked some kind of equipment room hastily cleared of its truck.

"Your stay will be short," he said.

"On earth?" she replied, staring down into the dishevelment of cords and computers that lay in heaps outside the door.

Once locked in, she discovered a roll-away bed in the corner, opened and covered with a sheet, and a shallow plastic bucket on the floor.

She was meant to rest, and to relieve herself. To continue to live.

God's last act before vanishing on her: condemning her to these days, her very first, without belief.

It was President Eront who woke her the following morning. He threw open the door to her cell, forcing her to sit up and scramble to cover her breasts with the sheet when she couldn't find her prison garb, discarded in her sleep because of the heat. From the moment he'd first learned that the country's last significant religious holdout had finally been captured—that Sybil Miller, his most outspoken critic had actually *turned herself over*—the great atheist must have known he would pay her a visit. In some deep part of her she had known this too. Had expected it as she might a death sentence.

"I think it's the perfect room," she declared, unable to resist the proliferation of meanings.

"You say that as if taking credit for it."

She was a little amazed to hear his voice, so reserved for the masses, filling a tiny room of only two souls. It sounded crushed. Was the *man*? Not physically. Having only ever seen him on screens, she was transfixed for a second by the imposing density of his actual presence, against which she felt herself already building some sort of defense. That he remained standing in the doorway with an alert, self-conscious apartness only seemed to increase the effect. He was appreciably taller than she'd imagined. Her eyes were drawn to his sunburned face, which shone of sweat and exertion, and was grinning at her with significance.

"Aren't you going to invite me in?" he said.

She smiled, as one smiles at a very stupid joke.

He took one step in and looked around theatrically at the room. "You're right—it's perfect."

"And I do take credit for it," she said coldly. Referring not to the room but to what had landed her in it: their public battle, her ten years of resistance and hiding, even her capitulation.

"It's a terrible room," he said. "Cover yourself."

She looked down: the sheet had fallen a little, perhaps even by her own volition, so that her left nipple was partially revealed. When she looked up, she caught his eyes gathering darkness and mass as they alit on her breasts.

"I like it here," she said. "It disallows the possibility of hiding me from *me*."

She was too startled by what was coming out of her mouth to bother about her breasts.

He looked away and wiped something from his cheek with the back of his hand. He said, "I'm sorry about the heat."

"The better to cook the religion out of us."

This upset the great atheist much more than it should have. The door behind him was still ajar, and he seemed to become temporarily conscious of the hallway outside where guards could be heard lingering. Reaching back, he quietly closed the door, sealing the two of them in with an overly determined motion, as if what he really had wanted to do was slam the door shut. He remained facing away from her.

"There are two ways we can do this," he said finally, and turned to measure the effect of these words on her.

The effect was she pulled the sheet up over her breasts.

And said: "I'd have thought the leader of the country would be more imaginative than that."

"I'm not speaking about sexual positions."

"Neither am I."

That was his first visit. What she had been speaking about was how, exactly, and when he was going to kill her. To judge by his next astonishing words to her, he had been speaking about the only way he wouldn't.

"I need you to give me faith in God," he told her intently the following day, again planting his feet just inside her door, his questioning eyes on hers.

She had risen from her bed, and now had to stand there a moment taking this in, the great irony of it. And then she had to sit down. The revealed purpose of her relocation to this windowless hole fell so heavily on her that she couldn't fight an urgent desire to close her eyes for a moment. The great atheist needed God, and he was going to get it here. The Religion Room. No one was to see.

"Will you help me?" came his voice, and she checked the expression on his face. There was no explicit threat in it. If anything, she saw only relief. The full bottom lip was relaxed, turned up slightly at the ends, and there was less depth to the crease of his brow. The look of a man who had just shifted a great, secret burden onto someone else. But behind the relief, she knew there lay need. Now there would be two threats to her: his secret and his need.

"What you need is a minister," she said severely, desperate to impress it upon him. "You have only to go to the men's block." Where they are all locked up, she could have added—the ones that haven't been executed.

He looked at her flatly. "I've tried them."

Of course, she thought. Perhaps in this very room. What had he done with them *afterward*, she wondered, and took a fresh glance around looking for terrible evidence. Except for her bed and bucket, there were only a fallen ceiling panel, two curls of ancient Ethernet cable, and here and there on the drywall, ubiquitous scuff marks. Innocent scraps of modern grimness.

"And?" she said, trying to control her voice. "What happened?"

"They were of no use."

Never had she read so much into the worn phrase.

"They didn't hate me enough," he went on, with a tone of fatalism.

She felt the rise of her heart rate, of her anger, and of an impulse to snicker, which she had to swallow hard. "*That* I don't believe," she let out with a lot of breath, and immediately regretted it.

"It's true. It had been trained out of them—their ability to hate. And I wasn't seeking their *understanding*." The word sounded toxic on his tongue.

Her thoughts returned to her own fate. "Then what exactly did you *want* from them?"

"God."

"Right."

He looked at her. "But it turned out I didn't want *their* God."

"As if there are more than one." She'd almost said, As if there *is* one.

He was still following his train of thought and looked visibly annoyed by it. "The God they spoke of was too small. There was no room for a person like me in Him."

It irritated her that, with this last statement, he was actually starting to make sense. So was his recruitment of her, disturbingly. She said, "You're not giving them enough credit."

His gaze sharpened on her. "I gave them their lives."

Involuntarily, she exhaled. She could feel herself flushing with relief. As if he had just given her *her* life. "No. Someone else gave them that," she said, thinking of parents, or congregants.

"Who?"

"Their 'small God'," she shot back, aware how active with spite her words were.

For a brief second, he faltered. He was still standing by the door, taking her in with amazement, bitterly smiling, his narrowed eyes shining hard at her. She inclined her head, composing herself. Adjusting still, as he surely was, to the shock of proximity. Having exchanged injurious public indictments for years, neither had expected to actually *speak* to the other.

"You have real reason to hate me," he said in a voice she hadn't heard.

"Yes."

That night, the intermittent sound of laughter floated through one of the walls, laughter so extreme it would sometimes explode into coughing that kept wedging itself somewhere between Sybil and sleep. In the darkness, she stood and pressed an ear to the wall. Wailing, not laughter. It sputtered into a wet gasping for air—what she'd taken for coughing—and she pushed herself away. Refinding her mattress in the dark, she tried planting each ear into it. To no effect: the wailing continued. Again like distant laughter. She fell into a passing sleep. Half-dreaming that someone in the next room was telling jokes.

A guard entered in the morning with food and a clean bucket.

"I'm done with your buckets," she said.

He was a large man, impassive and puffy about the eyes. Pausing halfway to her bed, he flung his gaze at the full bucket near her feet. "Where will you—?"

"You'll take me to where *you* go," she said, gestured toward the hallway with her chin. "When you hear me knock from inside."

"I'll have to ask."

"Or I can go on the floor," she retorted hastily.

He made eye contact with her. "I will share it with the President."

"Yes," she replied. "Tell him I said, 'There are two ways we can do this.' "

Save for a brief widening of his pupils, the large man was unresponsive to her provocations, and it made her stare at him all the more rabidly when he went ahead with his task, approaching the bed in order to replace her bucket. He kneeled down gravely.

"There were noises last night," she said.

His eyes rose level with the edge of the mattress—he seemed to know something—but, aware that he was being appraised by her, he shrugged in half-apology.

She pointed to the wall. "Cries."

He didn't hesitate. "I won't talk about that."

This quickened her pulse. Her interest was aroused. She glared at the top of his head, where damp strands of red hair had been combed back from the high forehead. "Because—you aren't allowed to?"

"Because I won't."

More than a week went by and Eront failed to return. So did the sounds from next door. So did her belief. The President *had* granted permission for her to use the old women's room in the hall while the guards stood by just outside, no doubt listening to her relieve herself and clean up as best she could in the sink. But these short trips to the characterless bathroom were all she knew any more of the outside world, and they seemed to conspire with the general indifference of the guards, until the combined oppressiveness of both instilled in her an irrational desire to deal head-on with the President's dissolution—to have him walk into her room with his piercing stares and shocking religious need. She would actually be glad of his human greeting; at least she could try to be useful to someone. If she failed, there would be the intimacy of watching a man coming undone, the satisfaction that it was *this* man.

But the Eront who walked in one very humid morning while she was working on a piece of dry toast was anything but a man coming undone. His khaki shirt was unbuttoned at the neck, his wrinkled trousers appeared to have been slept in, but he was saddled with calm. Too tired to be anything else.

"They've made an attempt on my life," he said, running a hand through his dark hair.

"What?" Setting down her toast, she registered the damp clothy smell emanating from him; all at once, the room's close air was deepened by traces of skin and sleep and strain, was activated with maleness. Something so familiar and certain about it.

"Seems my own offices are no longer safe."

"So it wasn't—"

"Your people?" he asked, finally meeting her eyes. "No. One of my own. We know that now."

She stared down into the floor, as if the larger implications of this fact might be sought in the oxidizing swirls of cement laid down cheaply on some long ago day.

"I used to think I could eradicate evil," he said.

She looked up. He had crossed his arms, and the fingers of his large right hand were tapping the smooth skin where his left triceps pushed out of the shirt sleeve.

"An easy mistake," he continued, "when you control everything from a distance." He was transfixed by some invisible image hovering in the air before him. "But it's something else when evil finds you alone. Inexplicable. Alters you." He slid his eyes to hers. "I feel different."

"What do you feel?"

She was still stranded at the idea of him, of all people, eradicating evil.

"That I was arrogant."

"You mean because in fact you perpetuated ev—?"

"Because I tried to get *rid* of it."

"Ah."

"Or pretended it didn't exist."

Yes, she thought: atheists were more talented at forgetting about evil. Or ignoring it when it disturbed the natural order of things. There had been times when she'd envied them this gift. Even now that she'd lost her belief, she couldn't forget about evil, its fearful otherness. It was why she couldn't really call herself an atheist.

"There's no eradicating it," he added, lifting both heels off the floor and replanting them.

"No," she agreed, watching him tense his right thigh and then his left. "No."

"The look in the man who tried to kill me last night."

"Terrifying?"

"Indifferent."

"Did you know him?"

He shook his head. "There was nothing *personal* about it. But he was very much trying to kill me. Do you understand? He could have been anybody—he *was* anybody, hired by someone in my circle, but *anybody*—and yet he was intent on ending one very particular life. There's no way to explain it."

"You're doing very well."

"No. Because it was completely inexplicable. We're too limited. I was trying to say this when you advised me to see a minister last time. Those ministers—their God believes He can put evil in a neat box."

"Or *they* do." As *you* did, she thought.

"Yes. They go around judging and judging—"

"As they must," she insisted with astringence, staring hard at him. "It *must* be judged, evil."

He blinked at her. "Even if it can never be made to go away? Who does that benefit? Really—*who*?"

Between his logic and his guilt, he wouldn't go *easily* to God. Or *would* he?

She was stern in her response: "It benefits the one who suffers from evil. And the one who perpetrates it."

At this, he turned pale and tremulous. His hands suddenly hung vulnerably at his sides. He said, "The one who perpetuates it suffers from it too."

And he uncrossed his arms and faced her openly as if to let her see what such suffering looked like in a perpetrator.

All her religious learning had taught her that the inflictor of suffering and the sufferer were one—that wickedness could be found no less in the sufferer's nature than in the nature of the person who inflicted it. And for ten years, she'd privately hoped this had applied to the President; she'd wanted to believe Eront was suffering by his atrocious acts. But now that she was confronted by the actual living confirmation of it, she couldn't believe he was *worthy* of suffering.

"Did you catch the man?" she asked.

Watchful of her reaction, he pressed his lips together and nodded in the affirmative.

"What will happen to him?"

All at once, he looked small standing there, as though her question had draped an absurdly heavy blanket of guilt over him.

"It already happened," she said.

He just stared at her imploringly, and she couldn't look at him anymore.

How drained she suddenly felt. Her shoulders and back would no longer hold their tension, and she sank a little into the bed.

"I need you," he said quietly.

She replied in a cold voice. "No you don't."

"There will be more."

"More what. Killings?"

"Attempts on my life."

She couldn't muster a response to this. No feeling came to her.

"Come here," he said, and she looked up. He had taken a step toward her, and all of a sudden the atmosphere in the room had altered. Whatever had prevented him from penetrating more than a few feet into it before was now gone without warning; she felt he might approach her bed. He said it again, "Come here," and by repeating the command he seemed to charge the space between them with emotion and threat. It gave her a dangerous degree of power over him, a power he might abruptly reverse, through a physical act.

"It's *God* I need," he said.

He had read her fears.

And then he reached a hand out toward her and said, "Come," as if she could carry God across to him.

It challenged her—challenged everything she thought she'd understood about the workings of faith in the world—to think that, by virtue of seeking her help, this man (of all people) was forcing God back into her life just when she'd been freed of Him. That it might be some sort of dark grace haunted her, even though experience had deprived her of the belief in a deity who helped the undeserving. It was true she didn't *deserve* the grace of a God she no longer believed in, which was precisely what made her a candidate for it. Or perhaps she was merely meant to assist, for if there had ever been an undeserving human to test the limits of grace, it was Nathaniel Eront. He was exactly the kind that the ministers refused to concern themselves with—which was, she had to admit, an argument for the *necessity* of God and his grace. Otherwise who would help the damned? Had that task fallen to her, now that she no longer believed? Did one have to be damned to help the damned? Was it he or she who needed help?

"Whether you believe or not is beside the point," she told Eront during his fourth visit. "God will still be God."

All through the halting conversation they were having about belief, he had been pacing her room moodily, expressing his doubts, shaking his head, radiating skepticism during the long silences. And now her provocative statement had caught him at the far corner of the room, facing away from her.

"But—if I *don't* believe in Him ... ," he said weakly into the corner. He placed his two large hands on either wall and leaned in a little with his upper body, as though bracing himself. "What then?"

From the bed, she straightened her posture and stared at the back of his head, which looked vulnerable to her suddenly. She took a breath. With a sense of personal threat, she was realizing that a certain kind of reasoning—the kind she was currently engaged in—was doomed. "Well. If there is no God—"

He swiveled around, riveted, concerned, pink with emotion. "If there is no God?" he echoed incredulously. Intently, he searched her face, seeming to suffer at finding no reassurance in it.

If there is no God. She was grappling with having actually *voiced* this possibility. A first for her. And *them*. It put before her with terrific starkness the life she had built up until recently on the opposite possibility. To see if the effect held, she voiced it again: "If there is no God"—starkness, terrific starkness—"then, then your lack of belief won't change anything."

Pressing back into the corner, Eront slid down into the sitting position on the floor, knees jammed against his chest. With his right hand, he took up a nearby stray curl of Ethernet cable, which he held at arm's length and squeezed in his fist with severe concentration. A man trying to transfer his shock to a thing.

"But if there *is* a God?" he asked.

"If there is," she said, controlling her voice because something was actually coming to her, "then you're still okay."

He let the piece of cable fall from his hand and raised his eyebrows doubtfully. "Even if I don't believe?"

"All the better."

"Better how?"

She was still catching up to her own words.

"Better to love Him as an atheist," she said crazily. "Then—you won't *know* you love him," she clarified. Crazily!

Eront stared across at her, helpless, awaiting more.

And then, as if it were so obvious—it was to her, now—she said, "That's the purest love: when the lover isn't *aware* of how he serves the Beloved."

She had intended to console the desperate atheist, but had ended up, she saw, explaining herself to herself. Looking for a way—mad as it sounded—to love the One she no longer believed in.

Eront considered her warily. "But how can I serve Him if I'm not *aware* of it?"

"Don't you see"—as she suddenly did—"that even by *not believing in Him* you serve him?"

Again, he raised his eyebrows. "Because—?"

"Because you no longer constrain Him by your belief. No longer violate His unlimitedness with your notions of Him."

He was visibly at a loss. "But what about my *hope* in Him. My *desire* for Him."

His searing expression of heartbreak.

"They'll finally have an object equal in scope to them," she said. "Finally, there might be *something*—call it God if you want—as unlimited as your hope and your desire."

Eront had risen to his feet and was gazing at the piece of cable on the floor with a look of incomprehension. In turn, he did the same with the bed and the bucket she no longer used, as if he no longer recognized what these simple things were. He seemed to have forgotten she was in the room, and she found herself taking in the length of him until becoming self-conscious, and doing it again.

"Do you—" he started. Then he looked up at her searchingly. "Do you believe in that way?"

His blazing stare seemed to encompass her, and she hesitated. She felt she could no longer fend off his entirely understandable questions, which had buffeted her like a series of invisible blows, leaving her to contend dizzily with the throbbing pulse of blood washing through her face and throat.

She said, "I believe, if there is a God, *He* believes that way."

His foot caught on the cement floor, causing him to falter for a moment, and she realized he was turning to leave without looking at her. She wanted to call out to him. But he was suddenly no longer there, leaving a vacuum in the corner where there had been a dense restless seething.

Only after he was gone did she realize that she hadn't *only* been explaining herself to herself, she had also been trying to get out of giving him what he really wanted from her. That would be God. And not the strange God she'd offered up to him, but *God* God—the One any normal person wanted. She had been called into the Religion Room as a witness, as an advisor in the most important affair in human life. What was Eront doing if not laying bare his soul, trying to find a new home in the unknown? She had always lived there; the varying layers of God's mystery had been her native element, and loving God had alone provided her with the impression of moving through life. But she had felt impossible on earth. Now, she had fallen down to it, and was proving to be useless to a guilty, God-hungry man. One thing was for certain. No one's real needs were clear. And the plain truth was that she felt bad. For him.

But when he didn't return for more than a week, she became frightened that, beyond her unhelpfulness, Eront held her accountable for filling his head with dangerous and confusing theories, and would again view her as his old foe, not his new savior. Perhaps he would resort to his longtime habit of disappearing enemies of the regime, and the Religion Room would become her death chamber after all.

He was extremely quiet when he walked in almost two weeks later and closed the door behind him. Out of fear, she stood up immediately from the bed as he turned his slightly reddened gaze on her with speculation. She couldn't read his expression.

"What you've shared with me," he said, speaking as if he was still trying to figure it out—"you've left me with less than I had when I was simply an atheist. At least *then* I had an idea of God."

"That was your problem."

"Because it was the wrong idea?"

"Because it was any idea."

She permitted herself to breathe. He was thoughtful with weakness, not rage. And he wore a startled expression, like that of an animal chased into a corner.

"Doubt was so much easier," he said.

She looked at him with surprise. "Doubt? I thought you were certain in your disbelief."

"Certain in my doubt."

She lowered her eyes. "Doubt can be as much of a delusion as certainty."

"Don't you have doubt?"

Her eyes suddenly started to well up, but she refused to let him see. "I don't have anything."

What was happening to her? She kept approaching the perilous truth, kept almost unburdening herself to him.

"I'll get them to move you back," he said in response.

She looked up to see his eyes making a quick tour of her paltry cell. He'd taken her for another meaning. "To the women's block," he clarified, smiling when their eyes met. "But you'll still come back here to talk with me, right?"

The sight of him standing there clutching his own arms. She nodded, aware that he was seeing the moisture in her eyes.

"Is it true?" he asked her then.

She was shaking.

He took a step toward her. He said, "You have *nothing*?"

She couldn't speak. She had *thought* she had nothing. The world had been emptied of God and she'd been seeking refuge in it, catching her breath. But she felt herself being pulled back into the thickets and thorns. Paying attention to man this time. To one man.

His eyes were large with understanding, with softness, and he came nearer.

"It's hard," he said, and she nodded, uncertain what she was admitting to.

He was in front of her now, darkening her with his tallness. Without thinking, she reached for his left hand with her right. He stared at it in her grasp.

"I wish the world were a place where no one was guilty," he whispered.

She sniffled in agreement, and had the staggering realization that her belief might return if the world were a place in which this man was not guilty.

It opened something in her.

She took up his other hand.

They were both looking down at their hands.

"Thank you," he said.

"For what?"

She could feel him thinking hard about it.

"For God," he said at last.

Her mouth let out a little wet blast of air. "As though I've created Him."

"Maybe you have."

She put her cheek against his shoulder. "Would you hate me?"

"I already do hate you."

His lips were buried in her hair, and she tilted her head to let him find her neck.

"I hate you," he said again.

Articulation falling away with everything else, they were left with base repetition.

"You hate yourself in me," she corrected him, pulling in closer.

"Yes."

"But you're not in me."

No answer.

"You're not in me," she repeated.

He didn't move.

"Put yourself in me."

Epistemic Toleration and the New Atheism[1]

RICHARD FUMERTON

INTRODUCTION: WHAT'S NEW ABOUT THE NEW ATHEISM?

We hear a great deal these days about the new atheism.[2] Before evaluating it, we should probably try to figure out what it is and how it differs from the atheism that various intellectuals have been defending for thousands of years.

As best I can tell, and painting with a very broad stroke, the new atheists are characterized by taking two aggressive stances. First, they make a very strong and public claim about the epistemic irrationality of religious belief. Second, they warn that irrational religious beliefs have been, are, and will probably continue to be a morally destructive force. Let's look more carefully at both of these claims.

EPISTEMIC RATIONALITY—CAN'T WE ALL JUST GET ALONG?

At first blush one might be taken aback by the suggestion that there is something interestingly new about atheists concluding that their religious opponents have irrational beliefs. In popular culture one sometimes finds people willing simply to segregate science and religion with the understanding that each has its own domain in which it can legitimately reach conclusions (more on this later).[3] But

---

1. I would like to thank my colleagues, Evan Fales and Diane Jeske, for their helpful comments on an earlier draft of this paper.
2. Associated most commonly with the so-called "four horsemen"—Daniel Dennett, Richard Dawkins, Sam Harris, and Christopher Hitchens.
3. See Ruse (2000, 2010) for an attempt to find room for both scientific and religious views.

© 2013 Wiley Periodicals, Inc.

philosophers aren't typically into this sort of compromise, and, on the face of it, for good reason. One might suppose that it is just part of one's reaching the conclusion that rationality supports atheism that one also be prepared to conclude that theists (and, for that matter, agnostics) with whom one disagrees have epistemically irrational beliefs.[4] Atheists have presumably reached the conclusion that the evidence at their disposal makes it rational to believe that there is no God. *If* they are right, and *if* theists have available to them roughly the same evidence, then it is surely equally rational for the theist to believe that there is no God. And if it is rational to believe that there is no God then it certainly isn't rational to simultaneously believe that there is one. Even agnostics should reason the same way. The agnostic thinks that it is epistemically rational to withhold belief on the question of whether or not there is a God. And *if* the agnostic is right, and *if* the theist has roughly the same relevant evidence as does the agnostic, then presumably it would again follow that the theist has an epistemically irrational belief in the existence of God (and the atheist has an epistemically irrational belief that there is no God). For all that, it strikes some that there is an air of epistemological imperialism about these stark charges of irrationality. One might wonder if there might not be good reasons to soften the position.

The crucial claims above are conditional. And a potentially problematic antecedent in one of the conditionals is the supposition that theists, agnostics, and atheists all have access to roughly the same (relevant) evidence. But it is far from obvious that those trying to reach conclusions about the existence of God *do* share all of the same relevant evidence. The question is critical, for it is surely a truism that you can have an epistemically rational belief that P while I have an epistemically rational belief that not-P, where our epistemic difference is explained by the fact that one of us has evidence to which the other is not privy. What is more, it is virtually certain that no two people share *all* of the same evidence. And if that is so, one might wonder whether we can't undercut the presuppositions which might lead atheists, agnostics, and theists to charge one another with epistemic irrationality.

This debate about evidence could easily involve larger, more theoretical debates in metaepistemology. So, for example, if some version of a coherence theory of justification were plausible, it wouldn't be that hard, *in principle*, to imagine that a theist's position is perfectly rational relative to her belief system, while an atheist's position is perfectly rational relative to her belief system. All this talk of rationality, after all, gets translated by the coherentist into claims about how a given belief coheres with the rest of what one believes. It should go without saying that the truth of a coherence theory of justification won't *automatically* save one from having irrational beliefs. I'm pointing out here only that once two people have different beliefs (as the theists and the atheists do), it is trivially true according to the coherentist that they are not in precisely the same epistemic positions vis-à-vis what is relevant to the rationality of their respective beliefs.

4. Whether one should *charge* them with irrationality is another matter. There is surely an etiquette concerning such matters that depends very much on the context in which one is discussing an issue. The new atheists are very public in their epistemic criticisms of both theists and agnostics.

And the coherence theory isn't alone among metaepistemological theories that might seem to increase the chances that perfectly rational people might end up disagreeing on even large, much debated, issues that are of critical concern to anyone who is curious about the world in which we live. Huemer's (2001) "seeming evidentialism" holds that what one is *prima facie* epistemically justified in believing is a function of what *seems* to one to be the case. The seemings he is talking about are supposed to be something different from beliefs, dispositions to belief, or inclinations to believe. We are supposed to understand the relevant concept of seeming by reflecting on the fact that even after we no longer believe that the lines in the Muller-Lyer illusion are of unequal length, there is surely some sense in which they still *seem* to be of unequal length. I'm not sure we need to move beyond inclination to believe in order to accommodate the phenomenological data, but that's not important here. If anything like seeming evidentialism were correct, it wouldn't be hard to imagine a world in which the atheists have perfectly rational beliefs that are a function of how various things seem to them, while the theists have perfectly rational beliefs based on how things seem to them.[5]

Some externalists (process reliabilists, for example) make the justification of one's belief a function of the reliability of the processes that yielded those beliefs. When a process takes as input beliefs, most often the pedigrees of the input beliefs are also relevant to the epistemic status of the output beliefs.[6] Again, there is nothing intrinsically absurd about the suggestion that people are different with respect to both their cognitive "software," and even hardware. Perhaps theists are capable of reliably processing certain input so as to get reliably produced religious beliefs as output, whereas atheists lack that capacity. The process reliabilist can hardly deny the *intelligibility* of such a hypothesis.[7] Indeed, process reliabilists are probably committed to the view that there *could* be a God who, for whatever reason, has revealed himself to some and not to others (through some sort of processing ability with which he has imbued some, but not all).[8] And if that's the way it is, the "chosen" ones will presumably have a source of epistemic justification for their beliefs that the rest of us lack.

---

5. But again, I'm not suggesting for a moment that embracing seeming evidentialism paves the way for the conclusion that all of your beliefs are epistemically unproblematic. Seemings can notoriously turn on themselves. Remember Russell's famous warning that commonsense leads to science and science leads to the rejection of commonsense.

6. An obvious exception is the "process" we might call introspection of our beliefs. On one way thinking about it, when one introspects a belief, the belief is the input and the output is the metabelief that one has the belief. The rationality of the input belief is clearly irrelevant to whether the output belief is justified.

7. I haven't talked about one obvious difference in processing ability that might affect the rationality of outcome beliefs. Some people are obviously less intelligent than others—they can't see connections that others can. Ironically, perhaps, being less intelligent than another can rescue the rationality of some of my beliefs. Given the evidence I am able to process, my belief that P might be perfectly rational even though if I were much brighter I'd be able to take account of evidence that is currently unavailable to me. My thanks to Evan Fales for reminding me of this.

8. The critical modal operator can be interpreted in a number of different ways. It seems to be that the statement is true if the "could" is interpreted as referencing conceptual, deep metaphysical, or epistemic possibility. Causal possibility blows with the empirical winds.

In the above I emphasized the possibility of differing *processing* abilities. But, notoriously in the context of religious epistemology, there is also much discussion about possible differences among people with respect to the kinds of experiences they have, experiences that might be *input* to processes which are, perhaps, just waiting to receive the input that would allow them to "do their work." These experiences might range from a certain sense of wonder at the intricacy and beauty of the world, the strangeness of a consciousness that so obviously resists a successful reduction to the physical, or more controversial mystical experiences that are said by some who claim to have had the experiences to be quite ineffable. I think I do know what the first two sorts of experiences are, and even if I don't know what the last is, I would feel no confidence in denying that there are people who have those experiences. Perhaps those with the experience are like the lone sighted person in the world of the blind. That person has visual experience but is left in the (probably frustrating) position of being unable to explain the character of the experience to anyone who hasn't had it.

So there are all sorts of views that deserve to be taken seriously, any one of which might mitigate against atheists taking too confident a position regarding the epistemic irrationality of theists (and agnostics). Unfortunately, while I think none of these views are frivolous, I also don't happen to think that any of them are true. The coherence theory of justification comes in either an internalist or externalist version. The internalist version leads to regress for one needs access to one's beliefs of a sort one will never get. One will be led to higher and higher levels of meta-beliefs in an endless search for one's lower-level beliefs. And the externalist version of the view is vulnerable to devastating counterexamples. Huemer's seeming evidentialism (and its even more "liberal" close cousin, epistemic conservatism[9]) seems to me to make it far too easy to gain *prima facie* justification. Process reliabilism is the most attractive of the externalist epistemologies but I still think that the new evil demon problem is insoluble.[10]

Obviously, none of the above cryptic comments are intended to be fully developed reasons for rejecting the relevant views that might allow more epistemic "humility" in the evaluation of opposing views in natural theology. But I'm stuck with a version of the kind of internalist evidentialism that Conee and Feldman (2004) defend. As I understand that view, the epistemic justification one has to believe a given position is a function of one's internal states. The slogan is that in all possible worlds two people in the same internal states have precisely the same justification to believe precisely the same propositions.[11] The only way one can hold such a view consistently is to combine it with the claim that if some property of a believer gives that believer justification for believing a given proposition, then it is

---

9. The epistemic conservative takes the fact that you find yourself believing P to be itself *prima facie* evidence for P.

10. Goldman's (1979) is still the classic statement of process realibilism. There has been no shortage of attempts by externalists to deal with the new evil demon problem. See Goldman (1986), Sosa (2009), Henderson and Horgan (2007), Bergmann (2006), and Lyons (2009) for representative examples.

11. Though to be plausible this must be interpreted as a view about propositional justification. Doxastic justification replete with a basing requirement will depend on empirical factors involving the causal grounds of a belief.

a *necessary* truth that the relevant justification supervenes on that property. The view still allows (as all views should) that two equally rational people might each have views that are incompatible with what the other believes. But we will need to trace that difference in justification to a difference in their respective internal states. And I strongly suspect that once one excludes implausible candidates for the internal states that provide epistemic justification (beliefs and seemings, for example), one will rather naturally suppose that there really isn't much of a difference between the justifiers available to the theists and the justifiers available to the atheists (and the agnostics). Once again we will be forced to the conclusion that two of the three (atheists, theists, and agnostics) have epistemically irrational positions.

Much more would need to be said before one could conclude that from an internalist's perspective parties in the debate over the existence of God have essentially the same evidence at their disposal. The claim should almost certainly be restricted to relatively "idealized" parties to the disputes in natural theology—participants in the debate who are fully aware of most of the relevant literature, for example. Without such a stipulation, one would need to worry a great deal about the fact that the beliefs of ordinary people are heavily influenced by their cultural environment. That might not necessarily translate into a different *evidence* base that is relativized to those cultures, but we would do well to remember how heavily *all* of us rely on testimony (broadly construed). The fact is that most of what I believe about the world is based on what others tell me (more informally or through publications of various sorts). My own view is that testimony is not a "fundamental" source of justification. To be justified in believing P on the basis of someone else's telling you that P, you are going to need some nonquestion begging way of justifying your belief that the testifier is generally reliable. But if we are to avoid a fairly radical skepticism, we had better be able to figure out how we can get the relevant justified background beliefs. Setting aside large skeptical challenges, I'm inclined to think that someone who relies on what most people around them say has at least prima facie justification for such trust. The difficulty, of course, is that one doesn't need to be much of a cosmopolitan to realize that people are "testifying" in different ways in different cultures about religious matters. Moreover, it also doesn't take much sophistication to realize that the more esoteric and abstract the subject matter of testimony is, the more epistemically problematic it becomes. One would be ill advised, for example, to accept the testimony of "expert" philosophers regarding the truth of any philosophical thesis.

When it comes to the conceivability of at least some people having a dramatically different evidence base that bears on the plausibility for them of theism, there is the more dramatic possibility of mystical experience discussed earlier. It is, of course, far from clear what epistemic significance such experience would have. However different or psychologically compelling the experience might seem to those who form belief on its basis, it is obviously possible that the experience is hallucinatory. But then it is also possible that the mundane experiences we take to be veridical indicators of external reality are also massively misleading. In the context of this paper, I'll simply ignore this sort of putative evidence that might be available to some and unavailable to others.

EPISTEMIC DISAGREEMENT AND EPISTEMIC HUMILITY

As I indicated, I'm not sanguine about any of the above possibilities for an epistemic rapprochement between theists and atheists. Nor do I think that *either* side is particularly interested in letting the other "off the hook" when it comes to charges of epistemic irrationality. Still, we might do well to explore other reasons for what one might call epistemic humility.

There has been a lot of discussion in the last decade about the epistemic significance of disagreement. Some of the best philosophers I know have philosophical positions that are incompatible with my own. Moreover, it is tempting to suppose that these philosophers have access to roughly the same evidence as I do—they have read just as extensively as I have, they have considered roughly the same arguments as I have, they are just as skilled at logic as I am, and so on. They are, as the literature often puts it, my epistemic peers. The question then arises as to whether the discovery that these philosophers disagree with me should defeat, or seriously weaken at least, my own epistemic justification for holding my philosophical positions.[12] Of course, the situation is symmetrical (or so I would like to think). It would be nice to think that some of my philosophical opponents think of me as their epistemic peer, and should be equally worried about my considered views seriously weakening whatever justification they might otherwise have had for their philosophical views. I have tried to explain my views about the epistemic significance of disagreement elsewhere, so I won't rehearse them here. The reason I bring the issue up, is that one might wonder if this isn't yet another reason that theists and atheists might have to soften their views about each other's respective epistemic irrationality. There are surely some very good philosophers in the history of philosophy who have reached theistic conclusions, while there are some equally fine philosophers who are confirmed atheists. Might not reflection on the fact that intelligent people have reached incompatible conclusions lead one to soften at least one's confidence in one's own position (and correspondingly weaken one's confidence that the people with whom one disagrees have wildly irrational beliefs)?

At first blush, one might worry how the appropriate adjustments in epistemic attitudes should be made, even if one decides to give weight to the conclusions of one's respected peers. Agnosticism might seem a natural middle ground toward which one could move if one were a theist faced with the realization that there are intelligent and literate atheists (or an atheist faced with the realization that there are intelligent and literate theists). But what if the world contained only atheists and agnostics? Where is the epistemic Switzerland in that war of views? One response (suggested to me by my colleague Evan Fales) is to treat belief and disbelief as a continuum. If one's atheistic commitment to there being no God was a .8 on one's scale of belief and the agnostic whose intellect one respects is at a .4, one could split the difference, so to speak, and lower one's degree of confidence to .6.

12. An analogy might be helpful. If I add a long column of figures and get a number different from the one you got when you added the same column of figures, then, assuming you are my "addition peer," we probably each have just acquired fairly strong reason to doubt our original conclusion.

But worrying about how to adjust one's level of confidence in a given view to take into account the views of one's respected peers is all a bit premature. It's not clear just exactly how we are to understand the philosophical or intellectual admiration one has for those with whom one disagrees. Sometimes that respect goes hand in hand with one's conviction that the philosopher in question has a completely implausible view. David Lewis was clearly one of the brightest philosophers around, but hardly anybody takes seriously a full-blooded "actualism" about possible worlds. The marvel is that he could defend the view as well as he did given that the view is obviously false. I was once "complimented" on being able to make the most bizarre epistemological views sound plausible for roughly the duration of a talk. I take it that the kind of "praise" I'm discussing here is an admiration for something more like what Socrates derisively called sophistry—the ability to argue in a plausible way for even the most extreme of philosophical positions. In any event, the admiration can be easily divorced from any conclusion about the epistemic probability of the propositions for which skillful philosophers might argue.

I've argued elsewhere (Fumerton, 2010) that the real value of reflecting on the arguments and views of one's philosophical peers is that it often reminds us of our own epistemic fallibility. While I am a confirmed foundationalist who thinks that an ideal structure of belief will be built through legitimate inference from secure foundations, I also think it is almost obvious that that's not how many of my beliefs are actually formed. And that is particularly true of some of the more abstract philosophical positions (and here I also include theological views) for which I have, nevertheless, argued. We often take positions to see how far we can "run" with them, testing them against opposing argument, and hanging on to them until we are forced to retreat. Our opponents often do the same, and the limitations of argument being what they are, it is notoriously difficult to dislodge people from their respective positions. Over time we sometimes forget how capricious the original position was and our psychological commitment to our views far outstrips the actual epistemic justification we have for those views.

Again, none of this has any direct implication for the epistemic rationality or irrationality of any *particular* belief one has, but this kind of reflection often leads me to wonder at the degree of confidence that philosophers often seem to have over even the most esoteric of philosophical positions. Once I leave the phenomenological character of experience with which I am directly acquainted, I'm not all that sure of much of anything. I instinctively find some philosophical views more attractive than others, but it is hard for me to imagine dying in the trenches to defend trope theory over realism about the nature of properties.

Does any of this suggest that theists and atheists ought to have a healthy tolerance for each other's views and, with it, a healthy humility toward the possibility that they might be in error with respect to their own views? I'm inclined to think that it does. To be sure, in this context, we are probably going to set aside a host of skeptical challenges. As I hinted earlier, I'm not sure how we acquire epistemically satisfying justification for even mundane beliefs about bread box-sized objects in our immediate environment (when all we have to go on is fleeting, subjective appearances). But even if I suppose that we have a decent solution to the traditional problem of perception (and memory, and induction, and other minds, and reasoning to the best explanation), I am certainly not sanguine about any answers to the most fundamental questions concerning the origin and nature of the cosmos. I'm obviously not an expert in any of the relevant empirical fields, but I do try to follow the more accessible literature as best I can. And the first thing one is bound to notice is that empirical views seem to be changing over the years. Something like the Big Bang still seems to be the most common view of the origin of the cosmos (or this part of the cosmos, or the latest incarnation of this part of the cosmos), but when physicists start talking about the *creation* of time or space, or form views about the amount of time or space there is, they are clearly straddling the line between philosophy and science and, in my experience, they tend to be no better at philosophy than I am at physics.

Of course, one might insist that the empirical discoveries of science are simply irrelevant to the plausibility of theism. Of the three most influential arguments for the existence of God, two, the ontological argument and the cosmological argument, seem to be immunized from the putative discoveries of empirical science. The ontological argument purports to rely on premises, all of which are supposed to be knowable *a priori*. The premises of the cosmological argument are probably intended to be knowable *a priori* as well, though here the issue is a bit more complicated. If the critical premise is the claim that everything that has a beginning has a cause, the argument might appear to rest on a contingent empirical claim. Most proponents of the argument, however, want the stronger claim that it is metaphysically necessary that everything that has a beginning has a cause, and, if true, that arguably renders the premise at least a good candidate for *a priori* knowledge.[13] I won't attempt to evaluate either the ontological or the cosmological argument here. But neither argument has ever seemed to me even initially plausible. Valid versions of the ontological argument seem to have a question-begging premise as soon as the term "God" is used in anything other than a conditional.[14] And the cosmological argument can distinguish an eternally existing God from eternally existing matter and energy only by placing God "outside of time," a hypothesis that renders dubious the intelligibility of talk of creation.[15] In any event, I've always thought that the most intriguing argument for the existence of God is some version of the argument from design. And that argument *does* seem to rely on an empirical premise concerning the plausibility of alternative explanations of the universe as we know it.

13. At least on the assumption that necessary truths of this sort are, in principle, knowable *a priori*. I realize that post-Kripke it has become almost the received view that many necessary truths are knowable only *a priori*. I think that view is false, but in any event, it is hard to see how *this* truth, if necessary, would be discovered *a posteriori*.

14. Obviously, one could write an entire book on the ontological argument. There are all sorts of interestingly different versions of the argument, and the comment made here would rightly be viewed as hit and run. The charge of being question begging is most clearly leveled in Russell's (1905) classic.

15. Creation seems to me a causal notion and I can't make sense of causes that are atemporal. For a survey of philosophers who have argued that a God who explains the existence of contingent stuff must be outside of time (a doctrine that goes back at least to Augustine), see Lucas (1989), Craig (2001), Stump and Kretzmann (1981), and Leftow (1991).

The argument from design is interesting not just for the reason that it seems to put theism into play alongside rival scientific theories. It is also the one argument for the existence of God that seems to leave open the nature of the "designer." The argument doesn't even hint that the designer posited as the underlying explanation for the wondrous intricacies and complexity of the world is omniscient, omnipotent, or omnibenevolent. Nor does it hint at the idea that the designer is "outside" of time (whatever that could mean). One could argue that any conscious being (or beings) responsible for the cosmos should only count as a God (or Gods) if they possess the properties associated with perfection. But this is a purely semantic question. One can stipulate the meaning of an expression as one pleases. But as a purely historical observation, it is obvious that people have used the expression "God" without implying that something would count as a God only if it exemplified perfection. Indeed, that idea came into prominence only relatively late in the game. There is a huge benefit for the theist who posits a God (or Gods) who lack perfection. Such theists no longer need to worry about the problem of evil. If the creator of the universe lacked omniscience, omnipotence, or omnibenevolence, there is no reason whatsoever to suppose such a being wouldn't allow bad things to happen. But the price to pay for putting theology on the same playing field as science is that the playing field is, indeed, even. The theist needs to argue that the positing of a conscious designer is more plausible than scientific views that posit "big bangs" that "begin" the existence of matter and energy, evolution that explains how one can get from relatively homogenous stuff to the angler fish, and to creatures who watch reality TV.

I'm not sure that the theist (who embraces the appropriate humility about the nature of the God to whom he or she is committed) can't compete on that playing field. But as I suggested earlier, that's partly because I think that science at the level of abstraction of which we are talking isn't that different from philosophy. And I have already suggested that when I think carefully about my own philosophical views and the way in which they came about, it suggests to me that a great deal of "epistemic humility" is in order.

THE EVILS OF THEISM?

I suggested in the introduction to this paper that the new atheists also aggressively denounce the evils that result from theism. Not only is theism said to be *epistemically* irrational, it is also thought to be pragmatically problematic. The hypothesis that one can apply the pragmatic "ought" to beliefs is far from uncontroversial. The pragmatic "ought" might seem to imply "can" or, more plausibly, "control." And it is not clear to what extent what we believe is under our control. But when the dust settles, it does seem that we can at least indirectly affect what we end up believing. If that is so, there is no obvious connection between what one epistemically ought to believe and what one pragmatically ought to believe. I won't rehearse the traditional examples, but it isn't hard to make a powerful case for the claim that some epistemically irrational beliefs might be pragmatically useful, pragmatically problematic, or pragmatically neutral. The new atheists argue that very bad things have happened as a result of people holding religious beliefs and, for that reason, we shouldn't treat religion as a quaint and harmless relic of a superstitious past.

The first step in responding to the charge that religion has been and continues to be responsible for much evil in the world is to make distinctions. In the preceding discussion I haven't distinguished carefully a bare commitment to theism from a commitment to some organized religion. The more specific one's religious beliefs are, the more difficult it is to defend both the epistemic rationality of those beliefs and the pragmatic innocence of such beliefs. Although the interpretation of Hume is difficult, it does seem to me that in the final analysis he expressed some sympathy for the argument from design. But he carefully remained agnostic with respect to the nature of the possible designer. I must confess that it does strike me as odd to suppose that if there is a being that exemplifies enough properties to count as a God, that being would have much sympathy for the factionalization of humanity that comes from the supposition that God would endorse the *details* of some particular religion. I was raised a Catholic, but never took seriously the hypothesis that God would inspire Cardinals to select the person God wanted to be Pope. It seems almost transparently obvious that such decisions are as political as the nomination process of Republican or Democratic candidates for the U.S. presidency. And the idea (with which I was raised) that a God would condemn to eternal suffering those who refused the opportunity to convert to Catholicism seems not just incompatible with perfection, but almost perversely whimsical. But I don't want to pick on Catholicism. Most members of organized religions seem to suffer from what looks like serious hubris in their commitment to the hypothesis that God would have a decided preference for them and their beliefs over others. Therein lies at least one potential reason to worry that such beliefs might easily lead to behavior that many of us find worrisome.

Consider again, just for the purpose of illustration, the history of Roman Catholicism. If a confirmed Catholic really did think that those who fail to convert are consigned to eternal suffering and if one were a kind person who cared about others, one probably would consider the Spanish Inquisition a noble effort at saving souls. To be sure, if rational, one would worry that conversion resulting from fear of pain isn't genuine conversion, but certainly one shouldn't condemn the *motives* of those bent on bringing about that conversion. For whatever reason, most Western religions don't seem all that bent on conversion any more (or at least conversion through force or threat of force), but some segments of Islam seem to be in the mood to save the world, by violence if necessary, from the evils that will befall it should too many fail to see the light. There is really no need to detail the checkered past of deeds done in the name of religion. Surely no one will deny that much needless pain and suffering has resulted, and continues to result, from conflicts that seem to derive, at least in part, from the convictions of religious sects. And this is what the new atheists justifiably worry about when they refuse to accept the invitation to take a more "live and let live" attitude toward people who have adopted, by the lights of the new atheists, epistemically irrational beliefs.

Unfortunately, the evaluation of counterfactuals is difficult.[16] It is not obvious to me that the world really would have contained fewer conflicts if the world lacked religious sects. Organized religion might be a symptom rather than a cause of aspects of human nature that cause strife. The cynic in me suspects that people actually enjoy conflict—or at the very least enjoy forming groups that allow them to view others as importantly different (and often inferior). If people don't have religion to generate that "us against them" mentality, they invent organized sports so that people who live in Boston can hate the Yankees (and people in New York can hate the Red Sox). Furthermore, there have usually been straightforward political goals that have almost always gone hand in hand with wars of religion. The land that was occupied by heathens and now belongs to us happily makes us wealthier and more powerful.

When engaging in a discussion of the causal effects of organized religion, it is also only fair to remember that there is a flip side to harm done in the name of religion. One could easily argue that the world would have lost many of its human-made wonders had it not been for the powerful influence of religion. Colossal buildings, cathedrals, philosophy, literature and the arts thrived, at least in part, from the sponsorship by religions that enjoyed enormous power and wealth. That power and wealth might have been built on the suffering of many, but how much suffering should one trade for the thrill of seeing the pyramids or the ceiling of the Sistine chapel? As I indicated earlier, counterfactuals are never easy to evaluate—it isn't even clear that they have determinate truth values. Perhaps the cultural riches that flowed from religion might have been inspired by more secular institutions. But it isn't easy to see why individuals would have made the enormous sacrifices necessary to create great things absent the driving force of religion.

So I'm not really sure what the final pragmatic cost/benefit balance sheet is for organized religion. But it is important to recognize that neither the costs nor the benefits obviously flow from bare theistic commitment. The theist who remains agnostic about the nature and intentions of a God or Gods displays a humility that may well lead to more tolerance of the beliefs of others. That theist isn't much of a threat to anything about which we care deeply.

REFERENCES

Bergmann, Michael. 2006. *Justification Without Awareness*. Oxford: Oxford University Press.
Conee, Earl, and Feldman, Richard. 2004. *Evidentialism*. Oxford: Oxford University Press.
Craig, William 2001. *Time and Eternity: Exploring God's Relationship to Time*. Wheaton, IL: Crossway Books.
Fumerton, Richard. 2010. "You Can't Trust a Philosopher." In *Disagreement*, ed. Richard Feldman and Ted A. Warfield, 91–111. Oxford: Oxford University Press.
Chisholm, Roderick M. 1955. "Law Statements and Counterfactual Inference." *Analysis* 15: 97–105.
Goldman, Alvin. 1979. "What Is Justified Belief?" In *Justification and Knowledge*, ed. George Pappas, 1–23. Dordrecht, The Netherlands: Springer.
Goldman, Alvin. 1986. *Epistemology and Cognition*. Cambridge, MA: Harvard University Press.
Goodman, Nelson. 1955. *Fact, Fiction and Forecast*. Cambridge, MA: Harvard University Press.

16. The best discussions of the issue are still probably Goodman (1955) and Chisholm (1955).

Henderson, David, and Horgan, Terry. 2007. "The Ins and Outs of Transglobal Reliabilism." In *Internalism and Externalism in Semantics and Epistemology,* ed. Sanford C. Goldberg, 100–30. Oxford: Oxford University Press.

Huemer, Mike. 2001. *Skepticism and the Veil of Perception.* Lanham, MD: Rowman and Littlefield.

Leftow, Brian. 1991. *Time and Eternity.* Ithaca, NY: Cornell University Press.

Lucas, John R. 1989. *The Future.* Oxford: Blackwell.

Lyons, Jack. 2009. *Perception and Basic Beliefs.* Oxford: Oxford University Press.

Ruse, Michael. 2000. *Can a Darwinian Be a Christian?* Cambridge: Cambridge University Press.

———. 2010. *Science and Spirituality.* Cambridge: Cambridge University Press.

Russell, Bertrand. 1905. "On Denoting." *Mind* 14: 479–93.

Sosa, Ernest. 2009. *Reflective Knowledge,* Volume II. Oxford: Oxford University Press.

Stump, Eleonore, and Kretzmann, Norman. 1981. "Eternity." *Journal of Philosophy* 78(8): 429–58.

Affective Theism and People of Faith

JONATHAN L. KVANVIG

1. INTRODUCTION

The belittlers, as I will call them,[1] object to faith on multiple grounds, but the fundamental concern expressed is that such faith cannot survive epistemic scrutiny. Some even go so far as to say that religious faith involves, by definition, beliefs that lack epistemic warrant.[2] I hardly recognize this picture of religious faith and religious life, except in the sense that one can cease to be surprised or shocked by the neighbor who jumps naked on his trampoline after having seen it for years. But it remains alien to me, even if I've become accustomed to the characterization. This essay explains why. My goal is thus to describe an alternative perspective on faith

---

1. Including the New Atheists—Sam Harris, Christopher Hitchens, Richard Dawkins, and Daniel Dennett—but also others, having in common perhaps only their conviction that a world without religion would be a much better place.
2. And not only Mark Twain here ("Faith is believing what you know ain't so"); see, for example, Leiter (2012), "religious belief in the post-Enlightenment era involves culpable failures of epistemic warrant" (82) and "Religious beliefs, in virtue of being based on 'faith,' are insulated from ordinary standards of evidence and rational justification, the ones we employ in both common sense and in science" (33–34). Such characterizations are far from exceptional, enjoying widespread endorsement both within philosophy and in general. See other references to endorsements of such in nonacademic settings by Steven Pinker, Alexander Rosenberg, and Richard Dawkins in Howard-Snyder (2013). It is worth pointing out, in defense of such secular critics, that they are agreeing with a long line of religious thinkers who endorse a similar position, contrasting faith with doubt and insisting that true faith often involves ignoring or rejecting grounds for doubt. See Howard-Snyder (2013) for discussion of this position, which he labels "the Common View."

© 2013 Wiley Periodicals, Inc.

and one particular way in which a life of faith can arise, and then consider the charges raised by the belittlers.

It is important here to note that the task is not to defend any and every response of faith, nor to claim that there aren't lives of faith built on beliefs that involve culpable failures of epistemic warrant. For the belittlers are not on a sorting mission. Instead, their goal is to reprimand religious faith of every sort. So what I seek here is not a defense of faith or a defense of religious belief as such, but something much weaker. We seek, that is, one version of a life of faith on which its importance and value is perspicacious and which falls outside the scope of the complaints of the belittlers.

We can think of the criticisms in question, and the characterization of faith on which they rely, as inherently cognitive. Such a picture arises quite naturally from our use of the term "faith" to stand for the particular truth claims made by a given religion. There is talk of the Christian faith, the Baptist Faith and Message; talk of knowing what "we" believe and why (a phrase strangely at odds with first-person authority regarding our own mental states). Moreover, the history of religion is fairly represented by the history of Christianity, in which major differences of opinion are resolved in a way that calls down damnation on those who do not doxastically conform.[3] From this use of the language of faith, it is easy to adopt a cognitive picture of what faith involves: to be a Christian is to endorse the Christian faith, it is to believe and have faith in some vague but important subset of the truths that constitute the Christian faith.

I said above that I hardly recognize this picture of religious faith and religious life. Here, I'll try to say why, but a quick preview will help set the stage. Religious life is a matter of both head and heart, and the cognitive picture above has the head dominant. I will here reverse the order of dependence.

2. LIVES OF FAITH

We can begin with the idea that there can be both unified approaches to life and approaches that involve disunity or disconnectedness. In the latter category are lives that instance the Humean view of causation: just one damn thing after another, with no attempt on the part of the individual in question to be doing anything beyond coping with whatever comes one's way. Such patterns of life are difficult to sustain, but it is not uncommon to see lives that display it in significant temporal chunks. In contrast to such patterns of behavior are approaches that pursue unity, that aim at connecting the multiplicities in experience into some sort of plan or purpose, and the boundary of such a search involves plans, purposes, and goals that are all-encompassing. The development of plans and purposes typically arise out of conative or affective aspects of human life,[4] such as negative emotional

---

3. See, for example, the Athanasian Creed, which ends: "This is the catholic faith; which except a man believe truly and firmly, he cannot be saved."

4. I will here use the terms "conative" and "affective" interchangeably, thinking of the mental life of a person as divided into two parts. Conation is sometimes defined as one of three parts of mental function, distinguished from both cognition and affection, but I am perplexed by attempts to sort the conative from the affective, so won't abide by the strictures of this definition here.

experiences and positive emotional experiences. Among the negative emotional experiences are fear, horror, regret, guilt, worry, sorrow, shame, anger, misery, meaninglessness, and despair; among positive affective states are joy, compassion, awe, wonder, and experiences of beauty and the sublime.[5] Such aspects of human life can provoke an interest in finding meaning or in developing a plan or purpose or goal that reaches beyond merely coping with each particular episode in life as it comes. In some cases, the call of the goal is merely attractive, in other cases it takes on the guise of the mandatory. In either case, these features of human life need not prompt the kind of unification that interests me, but the possibility exists, and is often realized, of responding to such by adopting a pattern of life that involves longer-term projects, goals, and plans.

Such responses involve decisions, whether in the most self-conscious, deliberative sense, or in the hardly discernible way in which, for example, one chooses to follow one's standard route from home to work. The point is that the response counts as human behavior, motivated by the affective states and experiences in question.

It is on these affective origins of the pursuit of ideals of one sort or another that I want to focus initially, because these unifying responses, I want to suggest, are responses that involve faith of one sort or another. To adopt a longer-term project or goal or plan involves a kind of hope that success may be possible, or at least a decision not to give in to feelings of hopelessness, and a kind of self-trust and trust in the structure of the universe and the society in which one hopes to flourish, regarding the accomplishment of some plan. None of these underlying attitudes or dispositions need to be ones brought to consciousness in deliberate reflection on the experiences that prompt them, nor need they be part of any fully deliberate approach taken to the motivations for them. Ordinary human experience in response to the kinds of motivations I want to focus on range from the spontaneous to the fully deliberative. But what is important about the responses in question is that they involve a setting of a direction for the individual, one which a person may faithfully pursue.

Faith, in this sense, is an orientation of a person toward a longer-term goal, an orientation or disposition toward the retaining of the goal or plan or project in the face of difficulties in achieving it, one prompted by affections of various sorts and involving complex mental states that are fundamentally affective even if they involve cognitive dimensions as well. A plan, purpose, or goal is developed, and the culmination of this process involves a commitment by the individual to such a plan, and in following through on such a commitment the person displays the kind of faith that I am describing. People can be faithful to their commitments, or not, and when faithful, they follow through in a way that displays an orientation or

---

5. Some might think that the experiences of beauty and the sublime should be classified with the cognitive rather than the affective. Since nothing I say here turns on the issue, I'll bypass extended discussion of the issue here by simply noting the attraction of views that treat normative and evaluative experiences and judgments as essentially involving a pro-attitude or con-attitude. So by classifying these experiences with the conative and affective, my intention is to signal the way in these attitudes can function in the story of faith in much the same way as the emotions cited.

disposition toward retaining the goal or plan or project in the face of whatever difficulties are encountered.

I have avoided describing such faith in terms of the language of mental states or attitudes, since even though such faith may involve specific attitudes, it would be unwise to begin from that assumption. It is, to be sure, an orientation of the person, a disposition of the self, toward a certain ideal.[6] The metaphysics of such is messy and interesting in its own right, but I will not pursue that topic here except to caution against any assumption that all such personal features must fall into the the category of intentionality, displaying a characteristic "aboutness" whether of the *de re* or *de dicto* sort. The caution I'm voicing is that we shouldn't begin by insisting that the discussion be herded into the arena of intentionality. Perhaps some attitudes are not intentional in the required sense: perhaps a person can be angry without being angry about anything (and certainly not angry about everything),[7] just as a person can have undirected anxiety, or moments of pure joy, without there being any good answer to the question "Concerning what?" More generally, however, it is clearly possible to have dispositions or orientations that don't involve intentional aboutness at all: dispositions such as be loving or caring or miserly or mean. So, too, we should assume about the kind of faith I speak of: one can display it without it being about anything. It is an orientation of a person, a stance taken, that displays itself in a faithful pursuit of a goal or ideal. I do not rule out the possibility of some fancy story that reduces such to the level of the intentional, but we should not start there.

To return to the issue of the nature of this orientation of a person, the first lesson to note is that such faith is thoroughly mundane, and the reason for focusing on the affective features of it is that they are worn on its face, whereas whatever cognitive dimensions there might be are more variable and harder to discern. We can see these points more clearly by considering a specific example. Suppose a young Little League pitcher gives up a game-winning home run and experiences the typical despondency for having done so. One reaction is to adopt a goal of becoming a better pitcher and never having to feel that way again. Such a reaction can generate an orientation or disposition toward various efforts at becoming better, in hopes of doing so (or at least some aversion to the idea that any efforts of any sort are hopeless), and display a kind of self-trust or self-reliance and perhaps some trust of others who may be recruited to help in the project. Our youngster makes a commitment to a certain kind of future. It might be intense

---

6. I use the language of an ideal, even though the reality will be much more specific, in terms of the realization of some goal or the following of some pattern of life. What all of these have in common is an appearing under the guise of the good or a felt attraction for the object in question, and it is for this reason that I choose to use the language of ideals to describe the varieties of objects toward which a life of faith might be directed.

7. Thanks to Kris McDaniel for reminding me that defenders of Brentano's thesis that intentionality is the mark of the mental, displaying a characteristic "aboutness," have resources here. For example, undifferentiated anger can be treated in terms of being angry at the world. I won't pursue this issue here, since there are plenty of other grounds for resisting a treatment of faith in terms of intentional attitudes of a *de re* or *de dicto* sort, but will merely note that I don't find this story plausible. Being angry at the world (earth? universe?) is one thing, and simply being angry is another. I've experienced both. They aren't the same. Or so I say.

commitment or more causal in its firmness, but when he carries through on this commitment, he will be properly characterized as being faithful to it, or pursuing his goal faithfully.

Our question about such a mundane example is what kind of mental states, cognitive or affective, must all of this involve? We have already seen the affective source and sustenance of the faith; we might even characterize it as a kind of affective faith, involving an attraction toward a certain ideal and an aversion toward its alternative. These affective states not only cause the disposition or orientation toward the ideal of becoming a better pitcher, they are inherent in it. And what of cognition? What role can we find for it? Doesn't he have to have certain types of belief here, and aren't there beliefs that inhere in the faith in the same way that the affections inhere in the faith?

I doubt it. Let's consider what particular beliefs might be involved in being faithful to the ideal of becoming a better pitcher. Certainly our youngster needn't believe that he will succeed, nor that it is likely that he will succeed, or even that there is some chance that he will succeed—his commitment to the ideal and the way in which he follows through with his plan reveals some hope of success, and that is enough to make sense of the process in question. Nor need our young athlete believe that the ideal is worthy of pursuit or that achieving the ideal is a good thing.[8] Such beliefs might be present, but it is equally possible that our young athlete either hasn't formed any beliefs with such lofty axiological components and possible that the conceptual elements required of such beliefs are simply not present yet. Beliefs of the sort described may be present, but they are not constitutive of the faith in question nor necessary for it. Might we insist on a role for other beliefs, such as believing that there is such a thing as the game of baseball, that there are coaches, and teammates, and (obnoxious) parents involved in Little League?

I expect he does believe these things, though I'm not sure he has to believe them. Perhaps cases of this sort could occur in which the affective faith remains, but only dispositions to believe are present rather than occurrent or dispositional beliefs.[9] A further possibility is to be in cognitive states that differ from belief. Perhaps, for example, our young pitcher only presupposes these claims, or assumes them in such a way that his belief box remains empty of the sought items. There is, of course, the reductive project of showing that presuppositions and assumptions are kinds of belief, but reductive projects do not have an impressive track record in philosophy. Among cognitive features of human persons are not only beliefs, but expectations, assumptions, and presuppositions, as well as mental assents to certain claims without actually believing them, and a committing of the self to a viewpoint or cause, whether or not such commitment involves something like a mental state having a certain proposition as its content. One can, as it were, nail one's theses to the wall, taking one's stand on them, all the while knowing that one falls short of believing them. My point is that there is a lot of philosophical work required before we can say that, even if our Little Leaguer is properly characterized in some way

---

8. Cf. Howard-Snyder (2013) on this point.
9. See Audi (1982, 1994).

or other in terms of the claims just cited, the proper characterization must be in terms of belief.

In any case, the relevant point is elsewhere. Even if there are beliefs or other cognitive elements present, they are merely background conditions for the faith in question and not constitutive of it nor doing the work that the affective elements are doing in sustaining it. The cognitive elements were already in place prior to the emergence of the affective faith in question, and form no part of the attraction of the ideal in question or the aversion to its central contrast. They are, at most, background conditions already in place that make possible the story, no more a part of the affective faith in question than his background beliefs that he exists and has hands.

On the idea here that there is a difference between explainers and background conditions, it is correct to note that the distinction between the two is hard to characterize. This difficulty leads some to claim that there is no such distinction: there is merely what we treat as background and then what appears in the foreground as a result. Vary what we hold fixed, vary what we treat as background, and any of the features involved in the story will turn out to be an explainer.

Such skepticism overreaches. In a theory of rationality, we distinguish between conferrers of rationality and enablers: the absence of defeaters of the confirming power that some piece of information provides for a given action or belief is an enabler but not a conferrer; a belief that entails that another belief is true or that an action must be done, is a conferrer of rationality and not an enabler. A full account of rationality, however, has to include both the presence of conferrers and enablers, on pain of violating the defeasible nature of rationality. Since adequate explanations are subject to the same defeasibility feature (X can explain Y, whereas X&Z doesn't), we need both the feature that is doing the explanatory work and the features that are enabling the work to be done. In the case of the faith in question, the story is told to make this clear: what is doing the work is the affective state in question. For it to do its work, various other conditions, some cognitive in nature, are needed. None of the particular items mentioned is itself needed, perhaps—but at least one of a broad variety of enabling possibilities must be realized. But these enabling conditions are not doing the work here and do not enter into the nature of the faith in question. Only the feature present that is doing the work partially define or partially constitute the nature of that faith.

Moreover the disposition or orientation of our young pitcher has a kind of deictic element to it, pointing to the affective element central to the example. The disposition in question is not merely one of becoming a better pitcher, it is, rather, a disposition to work to become a pitcher who doesn't let *that* happen again. Of course, it is possible over time for all this to change, but that is not the kind of case we are presently considering. Our case is, instead, one where the source of the goal is embedded in, and active in sustaining, the motivation that leads to the faithful pursuit of that goal.

One last try to force a cognitive dimension here, based on the plausible idea that even affective faith involves a dimension we might characterize in terms of closure of inquiry regarding various claims surrounding the plan or goal in question. For example, consider the issue of the possibility of success. If one raises the question of what our Little Leaguer thinks about the possibility of success, and he retains the plan and his faith in it in the presence of the question, the question will get shrugged off or met with an affirmation. The question is a closed one, and will remain so as long as the plan, and the faith that undergirds it, remains in place.[10] His being closed to inquiry on the issue is a personal feature of the boy, an attitude or disposition toward the possibility of success. But we need not suppose that our young possessor of mundane faith takes some attitude toward this possibility in order to be closed to inquiry on the issue. We should thus abandon the search for cognitive dimensions of affective faith, and consider more directly what we can learn about faith from this particular kind of faith.

One thing leaps out about such faith: it is obvious that such mundane faith is often a good thing, and anyone who begrudges our youngster such faith and its effects deserves remonstrance. We owe people our full support in their pursuits of such hopes and dreams, or at least the hands-off stance of not working to undermine their efforts. Of course, if we change the example sufficiently, we get different assessments: if the goal is to become the greatest dragon-killer of all time, the unrealistic character of the goal calls for intervention of some sort. But such is not the case in our present example. Nor are the values implicit in trying to be a great pitcher sufficiently problematic to warrant concern, even for those dismissive of a culture that places inordinate value on athletic accomplishments. Even relatively unimportant projects, such as amassing the largest stamp collection in history, or surfing the largest wave on record, or growing the largest pumpkin, involve mundane faith to which opposition is generally inappropriate.

The point of this discussion, then, is to point to the tolerance and, yes, respect that such expressions of faith deserve. We should grant the indefinite variety of ways of pursuing the good life, granting the usefulness and need of such mundane faith, and refraining from chastisement except in extreme cases. The mere fact that you place no value whatsoever on being a great pitcher is irrelevant. Now, of course, if you are convinced that the goals are repulsive and disgusting, then perhaps something must be done. About you. Not the young pitching prospect.

My point is not simply to insult, but to call attention to the extreme difficulty of life without such mundane faith. One might even say, though I will not try to defend it, that there is no such thing as a good life without it. But whether or not there can be good life without such affective faith, it would be deeply mistaken to suggest faith of this type is morally, practically, or epistemically deficient. So, if the epistemic complaints of the belittlers is to be defensible at all, it must be on the basis of crucial and important contrasts between such mundane faith and religious faith. I turn, then, to the question of the relationship between the two.

3. MUNDANE FAITH AND RELIGIOUS FAITH

We can move toward an account of the kind of religious faith that I find the most interesting philosophically by first enlarging the scope of the projects, plans, and purposes that might be adopted. For mundane faith can be exhibited about the

10. For further exploration of this dimension of faith, see Buchak (2012).

most trivial of interests, and a person might clutter a life with a wide variety of such projects and plans. Such a person might do so with a metaplan in mind as well: that a life full of a variety of interests is what makes for a full and flourishing life.

So neither the presence of mundane faith, nor the presence of mundane faith attached to a metaplan is to be counted as religious faith. I will make no attempt here to give a full and complete characterization of religious faith, one that separates it from every other kind of faith, but it is important, in assessing the complaints of the belittlers, to move as close as we can toward what religious faith involves. I believe the key here is not to disallow a variety of projects and plans that might involve religious faith, but rather to see religious faith as involving an overall metaplan that structures and organizes whatever other plans one might have in terms of some ideal. Religious faith thus aims at the full integration of a life in relation to an all-encompassing ideal, even if the actual situation for a given individual falls short of that ideal (i.e., even if their faith is weak with respect to the ideal in question). The unification of the specific items of human behavior from one moment to the next in teleological terms counts as an expression of religious faith only when the ideal involved contains in its essence the goal of structuring all plans, purposes, and goals in terms of a single pursuit or ideal. It may also involve affective states under the guise of the mandatory, rendering the pursuit of the ideal nonoptional, though I suspect this is simply a quite common feature of religious faith of the affective sort under discussion here and not essential to it.

An advantage for an approach to faith that acknowledges the possibility of such affective faith[11] is that there is a ready explanation of the connection between such affective faith and salvation. It makes sense for allegiance to a cause, for fidelity to a call, to be "credited as righteousness," as in the case of Abram. Such credit, of course, is not required; but it makes sense to so credit it. But when the issue is the cognitive one, making sense of why one's eternal destiny turns on the question of what specific *beliefs* one holds, we confront a head-scratcher: why that standard? I am not claiming, of course, that defenders of more cognitive kinds of faith will have nothing to say here, but whatever they say, they have a considerable hill to climb to get past the initial incredulity such a position generates. One might even feel some suspicion that the only way to do so is to make any other kind of faith be partially constituted by affective faith.

Whatever one might say in defense of other kinds of religious faith, however, we should note that the ideal unity involved in affective faith need not involve specifically religious faith. A purely moral faith can be of this sort, as well as the philosophical faith of the sort found in the Stoics and Epicureans, and the utopian faith of certain forms of Marxism. Nor should we fail to mention the possibilities of distortions of personhood that involve a fully integrated teleology aimed at trivialities, or the corrupted expression of faith in service of the horrific, such as the promotion of the Aryan race. So the varieties of faith that satisfy this important

---

11. Stronger positions might not only acknowledge it, but insist on it. Perhaps, it is fundamental, in the sense that any other kind of faith needs to be explained in terms of it. Or perhaps all other kinds of faith are false faiths, or bad faiths, or faux faiths. Though tempted toward these stronger claims, I here resist making them.

feature of religious faith is wide indeed. But I think this essential feature provides us with enough information about how to distinguish religious faith from more mundane varieties to be in a position to consider the features of such faith and what it would take for the epistemic criticisms of the belittlers to be appropriate concerning such faith.

So, begin with a fully integrated teleological structure for a person that is not religious. For example, consider a person whose entire life is organized for the purpose of achieving a utopian ideal, or a person facing all that life brings with a single-minded devotion to experiencing quietude or tranquility and the fulfillment it brings by achieving the Stoic's apatheia. Such faith can arise in a multitude of ways: through the experience of sorrow and despair at the ways in which our social and political structures multiply suffering in the world, through an imaginative experience of the sublime character of no longer being at the whims of the turbulent sea of emotions, or through the deep admiration and adoration of another person providing an ideal representative of the way of life in question.

Our question concerns what kinds of questions and complaints might be lodged against such a person, without impropriety. Well, not quite, since human beings have a nearly infinite capacity for generating new kinds of criticisms; we are, as Ernest Sosa has pointed out, "zestfully judgmental."[12] So let's distinguish between central and important criticisms of a way of life, and all the rest (never mind that there will be no agreement on which category a given criticism falls into—I'll simply appeal to the reader's good judgment on this score). So we might criticize the Stoic for lacking a proper interest in pizza, and the Marxist for lacking a proper love of scuba diving. And both criticisms might be exactly right. They are nonetheless irrelevant. Instead, the proper response on hearing such a criticism is an eyebrow raised toward the one bringing the criticism, or at least a soft chuckle at the distortion of values required to view such a lack as important.

We thus need to focus on criticisms that focus on what truly matters, and here it is worth noting the impropriety of criticism of the affective source in question and the values involved in the faith that results. Ameliorating the amount of suffering in the world is noble and admirable, and working toward happiness and fulfillment by lessening the amount of distress caused by the proliferation of desires we are all subject to is also a good thing. Moreover, devoting one's life to the pursuit of such goals is, from an affective point of view at least, hard to criticize. Such devotion to important things is itself a thing of beauty and inspiration.

Of course, there are other commitments to a way of life, prompted by the affections, that may produce a bit more consternation. One might aim at becoming the consummate Parisian upon being overwhelmed by the beauty of the place; one might, in more ancient times, become attached to Rome because of the ideals it embodies. One might also find the beauty of nature strong enough that one devotes one's life to its preservation, or one might find science itself to be such an astounding human accomplishment that allegiances are formed with the enterprise of such strength and fervor that the life that results can only be properly characterized by the language of fidelity and faith. For each of us, some of these expressions of faith

12. Sosa (2007), 70.

that involve the full integration of a personality with teleological purposes, both first-order and higher-order, will strike us as unseemly, perplexing, and difficult to understand. But at the same time, it is a smallness of spirit to insist that the desires of the heart have to match or overlap significantly with one's own to make any sense, a failure with respect to magnanimity, and it is a failure of imagination to be unable to appreciate the vast variety within what counts as the good life (at least when we limit the topic of discussion to what happens from birth to death).

The commitment to the life of the samurai or shaman may be difficult to understand, but it is not to be classified with the commitment to a life devoted to the superiority of the Aryan race. And to have as the desire of one's heart to be a great pitcher or the greatest expert on French literature of the nineteenth century may be similarly alien to most of us, but even in the middle of this experience of the alien we can recognize the diversity of the good life and show tolerance and respect for it and its affective source.

My point here is not meant to render free from criticism every way of life involving morally neutral passional elements. We may point out, for example, that some such lives are incomplete; that they are missing out on important goods, even if organized around desires of the heart that are either neutral or good in themselves; that the ideal human life involves aspects that are being ignored in lives of such truncated dimensionality.

Note, however, the category into which these critiques fall. They are not about the cognitive dimensions of such expressions of faith, but rather about the affective dimensions involved. As such, there is no room here for talk of epistemic impropriety or defect, for such talk is only appropriate when focusing on the cognitive dimensions of a way of life. So, if we are looking for ways in which epistemic impropriety or defect might be an appropriate charge to raise against certain types of faith, we will have to identify first which cognitive commitments are involved in a life of faith of the sort being described.

Return to the cases of utopians and Stoics, let us ask how to go about identifying the cognitive elements involved in such a life of faith, in order to determine whether any such elements are epistemically inappropriate or defective. But what exactly are those cognitive aspects? What cognitive dimensions are required of our Marxist or Stoic?

A natural answer here is this: you have to believe some version of Marxism or Stoicism. So tell us which version you believe and we'll go from there.

But this response is inadequate in the present context. The goal here is to raise the possibility that the cognitive dimensions of a way of life and the faith it embodies might involve epistemic difficulties. For that purpose, it is not enough to find some expressions of such a way of life to be problematic. Instead, one must identify certain cognitive features as essential to that way of life, and then find these essential features to be epistemically troubling.

My hope is that the examples of pursuing ataraxia through apatheia, and pursuing the alleviation of human misery through a utopian construction make clear how difficult it is to say precisely which cognitive commitments such ways of life require. And to that extent, it is equally difficult to find criticisms of such ways of life that are appropriate. That is not to say that there are not appropriate criticisms of specific individuals who have embarked on such a way of life, but the issue is the way of life itself and not particular embodiments of it. Shall we say that a utopian must believe that the achievement of the utopian ideal would usher in an era in which all misery has been eliminated? That would be a silly position: why would a utopian have to be so oblivious as to think that natural disasters such as tornados, forest fires, hurricanes, and the like would either disappear or have no negative consequences for human beings were the utopian ideal achieved? Must a Stoic believe that it is possible to have no desires whatsoever? Surely not. The way of life is a path toward greater fulfillment, and the path involves the pursuit of apatheia, a pursuit that can lead to increasing levels of fulfillment even if it is impossible to achieve the absence of all desires of any sort (as well as any other affective states that might lead to the loss of tranquility).

Perhaps the criticism should be that the goals in question will not or cannot be achieved. Well, the modal claim is surely unsustainable, and the charge of the ways of life being unrealistic does not penetrate deeply. For no way of life needs to hang its respectability on likelihood of success: to insist otherwise is to miss the fundamental role that hopes and dreams play in the expressions of faith involved in the ways of life in question. Such hopes and dreams may be dashed in the end, but such is life, and it is a particular way of giving in to despair to insist on pursuing no goal that one is not likely to achieve.

4. THE COGNITIVE DIMENSIONS OF RELIGIOUS FAITH

Given this understanding of faith and what we have learned by considering non-religious expressions of it, let us now turn to the kind of religious faith I want to focus on in assessing the complaints of the belittlers. We begin, then, with the following: religious faith can be of the kind I am describing, a kind of faith that arises from the affections, as described above: perhaps it arises from the sublime and terrible experience of being thrown from a horse on the road to Damascus; it may arise from the apparent majesty and greatness of spirit found in a prophet or shaman or holy man of a particular religious tradition; it could arise from experiencing the beauty of creation and the moments of pure joy at its wonders; or it might be the darker experiences of misery and despair and misery and injustice that cry out for a ray of hope and somehow receive it. Such affective sources are surely as immune from criticism as any similar source that gives rise to secular ways of life and the kind of faith they embody.

I'll focus here on Christian faith in order to make the discussion more focused, even though much of what I say here will have wider application to most, if not all, religious faith. My point here is to insist that it is a shallow understanding of faith that does not recognize the possibility of such fundamentally affective faith, both in terms of source and sustenance. In this regard, we can think of the inadequate philosophical theology about faith as having such wide-reaching scope that our ordinary language about faith has come to identify it with a type of belief: people are counseled to just have faith, to just keep believing, to abandon their doubts and hold to the faith, and in countless other ways that presuppose a fundamentally cognitive picture of what faith involves.

Given what we have already seen, however, it should be obvious that even if there are kinds of faith that are fundamentally or predominantly cognitive, they are not the only kinds of faith. Nor should we let our philosophical theorizing be controlled by whatever features might be gleaned from ordinary language, given how easy it is for ordinary practices of thought and talk to codify the results of prior theory. What I'm interested in is the phenomena of faith itself, and the prospects of the belittlers for faith of a particular type. So, we must consider, given that criticism of a life of faith that is fundamentally affective in source and sustenance can gain no decent foothold within the passional dimensions themselves, whether there are certain unavoidable cognitive accoutrements to such an affective faith that are worthy of criticism.

By now, I'm sure many readers will be impatient: "Isn't it obvious that to be a Christian, and thus to display Christian faith, one has to believe that God exists,[13] must believe that Jesus is God's Son,[14] must believe a host of other things in order for the faith in question to be *saving faith*; so even if there is an affective faith of the sort described, it is not the faith that is essential to being a Christian?" And not only belittlers will ask such things—such language is ubiquitous among Christians themselves. So, it would seem, if the target of the belittlers is the particular doctrinal commitments that are standard fare here, the targets would seem to be fair game: they are precisely the sorts of things that even Christians themselves treat as essential.

I intend here to avoid getting bogged down in philosophical minutiae, even if of such is the life of the philosopher composed. But I need to loosen the grip of this way of thinking a bit before returning to our painting of a fundamentally affective life of faith and its cognitive dimensions. First, included in the complaint is the central point: if we assume the truth of Christianity, what kind of faith is required for salvation? And the way to determine this is to ask what, from the Christian perspective, is required for presence in heaven? Here we must confront an important second point: an appropriate answer to the first question must not be an answer that will exclude from heaven the great saints of the Hebrew Bible.

So, the issue here is both about mental state and content, with the impatient reply above focusing on certain contents of traditional Christian doctrine, with the mental state in question being that of belief. Now, there is a strong element of a focus on belief in Christian Scriptures, and we can begin to loosen the grip of the above metanarrative about Christian salvation by noting some of the unavoidable difficulties in translating various terms in Hebrew and Greek with our modern concept of belief:

> While belief now refers to a state of mind, a disposition to assent to a set of propositions, even within the early Christian intellectual tradition historically

---

13. "And without faith it is impossible to please God, because anyone who comes to him must believe that he exists and that he rewards those who earnestly seek him." (Heb. 11:6, New International Version [NIV])

14. "Whoever believes in him is not condemned, but whoever does not believe stands condemned already because he has not believed in the name of God's one and only Son." (John 3:18, NIV)

it had as much or more to do with love, loyalty, and commitments akin to pledging one's allegiance to a person as Lord or to a cause or to entering into a covenant such as marriage. The Latin word credo (apparently a compound of *cor, cordis* 'heart' and *-do, -dere,* 'to put' derived from the proto Indo-European root for placing one's heart upon something, **kred-dhē*) means 'I set my heart' upon the entity or doctrines in question. Even for scholastics such as Aquinas . . . credo meant to pledge allegiance to, to give one's self and one's loyalty. The Latin terms most closely expressing today's meaning of belief and opinion, *opinio* ('opinion, belief, supposition') and *opinor* (*opinari,* to be of the opinion, to believe) played an almost negligible role in Christian thought. (McKaughan, 2013, 107–08)

While there is some worth questioning here (e.g., belief is clearly a state of mind, but may not be a disposition to assent), I want to call attention to two important distinctions here that are useful for our discussion. The first is a distinction between intentional attitudes and kinds of actions, and the second is a distinction between cognitive attitudes and connative or affective ones. To place one's heart upon something involves some kind of internal action involving commitment, as does pledging allegiance, and the source and sustenance of such commitments is fundamentally affective. Hence, to believe, in this more ancient sense, is thus primarily about attitudes of the heart and commitments made in light of them rather than attitudes of the mind. Understood in this way, talk about belief and saving faith isn't primarily about cognitive attitudes but rather affective ones and their expression.

Given this point, we should be hesitant to endorse doxastic requirement in the impatient reply above, in spite of the fact that it is a quite common presupposition about what Christian faith involves. It is a theoretically inelegant story to focus on *belief* in its modern sense when describing Christian faith and the life of the believer. Central to the message of Jesus is that true life is found in moving away from a central concern for self and following him. Though there is much more to the story of Christianity than the paradoxes of the Kingdom,[15] these paradoxes cut to the heart of a central and basic point in the message of Jesus, and this ideal of selflessness simply isn't about belief in the modern sense. If we begin with the idea that the central essential feature of being a follower of Jesus has to do with losing one's life rather than seeking it and in terms of servanthood rather than a pursuit of power, fame, fortune, or even honor and glory, it is hard to see how to fit talk of belief in the modern sense into this picture. For the topic of discussion isn't cognitive; instead, it is about one's cares and concerns, desires and motivations. With respect to this feature of being among the faithful, even entrenched atheists can be included. For here we find, not concepts such as truth and falsity, evidence and its lack, but what we find attractive, what is beautiful, what we adore, and that for which we wish, hope, and long.

---

15. Included are claims such as these: the last shall be first and the first last, he who wishes to be great must be the servant of all, it is in dying that we live, those who find their life will lose it and those who lose their lives for Jesus's sake will find it, and so forth.

Moreover, such a description fits nicely and is the natural offspring of a fundamentally affective faith of the sort being described here. Whether the motivational source is in a sense of guilt and shame, or in an experience of overwhelming beauty and goodness in a person, the natural expression of such an experience is a commitment to the good and the right and the just, together with sense of urgency both for oneself and other people that we all not miss out on something of great importance. It is a life directed toward certain moral and religious ideals, and involves a turning away from a life directed toward the self in pursuit of fame, fortune, and the goods of this world.

The critic will be impatient again, however, this time with the failure to address the central question of the content of various cognitive states, whether or not accurately characterized in terms of our modern notion of belief. The complaint still is that there are various cognitive commitments that cannot be avoided, if one is to be among the Christian redeemed. Among those contents are those listed above: that God exists, that Jesus is God's Son, that he lived and died to secure our redemption, etc.

It is, of course, correct to point out that when someone is a follower of a certain person, they presuppose that the person being followed exists. But recall that the issue is more generic than the question of who self-identifies as a follower of Jesus. The question is rather, from the Christian point of view, when is saving faith present and when isn't it, and it is clear that one can possess saving faith and never have heard about Jesus. That is precisely the point of giving the saints of old—Abraham, Isaac, Jacob, and all the rest—their due.

Don't say here, "But central to the Christian story is that before Jesus existed there was one standard for salvation, and afterward, another." While it is true that some Christians endorse such claims, they are, we might say, making it up as they go. Most decisive here is the Scriptural record itself: St. Paul is clear that both he and Abraham are saved in precisely the same way: by faith.[16] To avoid misunderstanding, let me point out that affective faith and the way of life embodying it will always involve cognitive commitments of one sort or another—how could it not? The point, however, is that the precise nature of those cognitive commitments is quite indeterminate. There is no ready answer, in general, for the question, "What must a person believe or cognitively endorse in order to be saved?"

My point here is not, nor does it rely on, the banal point that the range of adherents of the Christian religion runs from the most conservative fundamentalism to the most liberal theologies, or even atheologies. Even from the point of view of the most right-wing, inerrantist Evangelicalism, the case can be made that there is no ready answer here.

To get a sense of the grounds for hesitance about the precise cognitive elements involved in such affective faith, a couple of distinctions will help. First, notice the relatively strong Christian tradition of doubt and unbelief even among the faithful. The disciple Thomas doubts and won't believe without empirical confirmation, but is neither reprimanded nor ostracized for his doubts. One might

---

16. The argument of the letter to the Romans could not be more clear on this point. See especially Romans 4:17–21.

think otherwise, since his stance is contrasted with those who are blessed for believing without seeing,[17] but viewing that remark as a reprimand overreaches. Students can be told that life will go better for them the earlier they start on end-of-semester projects without any negative attitude toward those who do not start until a week before the deadline. Blessed is the early bird for it will get the worm; but it is false that the normal sleeper has done something wrong.

A second example of unbelief in the Christian Scriptures is when Jesus says to the father of the boy possessed, "All things are possible to him who believes," and the father's confession of unbelief is not treated as a deal breaker. It is instead treated for what it is: an honest expression of an inability to embrace and commit to a particular level of confidence regarding the future for him and his son. So even when it is fully appropriate to treat the language of belief as involving or implying a particular mental state with particular content, there is no reason to adopt some blanket prohibition against lack of belief among those who are following Jesus.

Part of the attraction of this affective picture is that it can make sense of such. For even if it is in some sense required that one come at some point to believe certain things and to adopt a particular cognitive perspective on all there is and one's place in it, it would be a strange gospel to impose this requirement in the backtracking fashion that insists that what must be true in the end in order to be saved must be true now in order to be being saved. It is, in a phrase, a confusion between process and product, between the path and the destination.

Furthermore, it is a more fitting picture of the Christian life to think of cognitive commitments as arising through the process of being saved, rather than being imposed by religious authority from the outset. At the heart of Jesus's message about following him is an emphasis on motivation and intention rather than on product, and his initial followers had no good idea what a commitment to him would involve, either in terms of practical consequences or cognitive commitments. Why initial commitments and faithful follow-through should have changed since this is beyond me to fathom. In particular, the idea that one must believe a certain set of doctrines, independent of coming to see them as true from a love of truth, is baffling.

Even the most theologically conservative must grant this point regarding the cognitive development that occurred with Jesus's disciples during his lifetime and with the early church as it sought to sort out orthodox positions on central doctrines of the Christian faith. It shows a smallness of spirit to think that Nestorians, for example, are damned because of their beliefs. The most that could plausibly be claimed here is that there will be no Nestorians in heaven—by the time they get there, they will have seen the light. A simple version of such a point might appeal to a spiritual analogue of the slogan that ontogeny recapitulates phylogeny: one should expect the possibility of the individual maturation process to take the form of whatever process of doctrinal maturation occurred in the course of salvation history. But a more general point can be made, mirroring the failure of the slogan in question in the scientific context: the variability of individual maturation has no

---

17. Then Jesus told him, "Because you have seen me, you have believed; blessed are those who have not seen and yet have believed." (John 20:29, NIV)

particular doctrinal or cognitive boundaries, whether or not tested in course of religious history.

Seen in this way, the process in question may involve the affective faith I am focusing on, and the cognitive aspects of such ways of life may vary considerably.[18] Is there anything within this variability that is suitable as a target for the attacks of the belittlers? I turn to this question in the next section.

5. AN ALTERNATIVE STORY ABOUT THE ROLE OF THE COGNITIVE IN A LIFE OF AFFECTIVE FAITH

Begin with a central example of truly admirable faith. Consider Abram, who is told to leave Ur and go to a foreign land. He does so in commitment to a certain way of life, and it counts as an expression of saving faith. What propositional contents must he have believed in order for this story to make sense? Did he have to believe that God exists? I suppose he did so believe, but the same story could have been true if he had only been disposed to believe such, or disposed not to believe the denial, or if he had merely mentally assented to the claim and was determined to behave in accord with the assumption or presupposition that God exists. So I assume Abram was a theist, both before and after leaving Ur, but it is hard to see why that is required for the story. After all, the story is about being faithful to a perceived directive from God, and the credit that ensues is a function of this faithfulness. The contrast to faith of this type is not doubt or disbelief, but change of direction, loss of heart, and weariness of spirit, a failing to follow through on what one sees in terms of what is worth pursuing or, even stronger, what is required of one. And it is obviously possible for a person to commit to a certain way of life, fully and wholeheartedly, while finding belief beyond them–all they have is hopes and dreams and possibilities.

We must grant, of course, that such lives of faith are not the norm. The human drive of curiosity aims at systems of understanding of what there is and our place in it,[19] and the ordinary human experience is to satisfy that drive by drinking deeply

---

18. Perhaps something stronger can be affirmed, though I won't defend it here. Perhaps religious faith, or the only religious faith worth respecting, is that which arises in the contrast between the faithful pursuit of the self, through seeking honor, or glory, or fame, or riches, and the faithful pursuit of the good. In ages and places where theism can be assumed, this distinction is that between faithful pursuit of a theism as talisman, hoping for more rain and better hunting, and the ethical monotheism of the Abrahamic tradition. When theism is no longer assumed, an adequate philosophical soteriology ought to begin from the fundamental distinction between seeking the talisman and seeking the good, often involving a commitment to ideals connected in some way with the feelings of being forgiven and accepted and belonging or of being one with or in accord with something unspecifiable, and being thankful (when no particular object can be cognitively identified as intentional object of such emotions). It is for that reason that one can think of nontheists as falling under the rubric I choose: affective theism. (But this point should not be confused with a closely related point, that religious faith worth respecting is nothing more than a purely moral faith: to draw that conclusion would confuse process and state just as much as what I've accused cognitive pictures of faith of doing.)

19. For defense and explanation of this view of curiosity and the fundamental role in cognition of the goal of understanding, see Kvanvig (2013a).

from one's current culture and those who have come before. So when one fully embraces an ideal, such as becoming a follower of a certain person, and there is a long history of other people who have taken the same path, the ordinary human experience will involve adopting the traditional system of understanding developed by one's forefathers in the faith, and the human predilection for fixation of belief typically results in an adoption that takes the form of belief rather than mere assent or some lesser state of intellectual commitment. Furthermore, the historical development of Judeao-Christian theology makes the experience of injustice and the responses of faithfulness in standing against it central to the development of the central platitudes of the Christian religion concerning the fallenness of the natural order, the possibility of redemption, and the hope of a life to come. It is in the crucible of reprehensible moral monstrosities of human history that the pursuit of religious ideals come to be tested and fallenness experienced, and the development of theological perspectives emphasizing the possibility of redemption and hope of a life to come can be seen as natural cognitive responses that express the continued disposition toward a way of life that involves the affective faith in question, in opposition to the despair and despondency and loss of such faith displayed in cognitive responses that conclude that we are on our own. In the process of making sense of the totality of experience presented to us, optionality reigns in the range of experimental attitudes a person might take in the all-thing-considered rational pursuit of understanding the world and our place in it.

But belief in such a system of understanding is never to be confused with what is essential for a way of life expressing the kind of affective faith under discussion here. Such is the nature of the human experience: to approach life experimentally, sorting when to defer to one's culture and associates and when to demur. In this grand experiment to make sense of the world and our place in it, we adjust across time on what weight to give to which sources of information, and at every moment of decision regarding such, the options are wide and broad—that is the lesson of the Quine/Duhem thesis.[20] This fundamentally pragmatic process results in various changes to total cognitive state, some of which involve belief formation and change, and others of which involve intellectual commitments that need not be doxastic in character. One might, in a thoroughly experimental fashion, engage in mental assents of a strong form, perhaps with the expectation that such engagement will likely result in doxastic commitments of some form in the future. One may think such nondoxastic commitments are rare among, say, conservative Christians, but I suspect that a nuanced psychology here will find this experience rather widespread. There is the Shakespearean suspicion here that protesting too much is a useful indication that we don't have the whole story, and too much adamant bluster about various doctrinal points may be an indication of a commitment to a point of view that one doesn't quite (or fully) believe.

This possibility ought to be taken even more seriously once we note the standard metanarrative concerning the nature of faith in such conservative circles. Faith is essential to the Christian story of salvation, and the standard metanarrative

---

20. See Quine (1953); I discuss and defend this Epistemic Optionalism in Kvanvig (2011, 2012, 2013b).

concerning faith is that it is, or involves, a form of belief. So if one self-identifies as a Christian, adopting or assuming this standard narrative, one will hold oneself to the standard of having to have certain beliefs. Thus, for any claim taken to be part of the Christian story, it will be presupposed by the individual in question that this claim is among the things this individual believes and must believe. The internal psychological pressure that such a presupposition imposes can easily be imagined to yield exaggerated overt behavior when talking about such matters, since failure of belief would be, by the metanarrative in question, lack of faith.

It is, to my mind, a fundamental mistake deriving from the very earliest Church councils to insist on morphing a fundamentally affective orientation of a person into a set of cognitive requirements demanded so as to preserve the unity of the faith. The mistake here is to grasp at a mechanism to prevent schism that is fundamentally cognitive, and doxastic at that. Would that the approach had been fundamentally affective instead, in line with the Scriptural injunction to "greet each other with a holy kiss." That is, instead of demanding doxastic uniformity, the approach could have involved an affirmation that the faith involves the pursuit of a life of praxis constituted by the Johannine attitude of self-giving love, that cognitive differences were to be expected in such a grand experiment, and that the threat that such differences created were to be met with the same fundamental affective response that prompts and constitutes such a life of faith in the first place.

Moreover, the standard metanarrative on faith creates cognitive dissonance in those for whom the life of faith is a life of affective faith of the sort I'm focusing on here. For the standard, doxastic metanarrative is presupposed to such an extent that it is hardly noticed how it fails to cohere with the more natural narrative of affective faith and a story of cognitive commitments arising out of it. As a result, self-deception becomes highly likely among people of affective faith, with reaction formations against the very idea of apostasy forcing one to insist with greater and greater vehemence the standard doctrines required on the standard metanarrative. And perhaps that metanarrative, presupposed deeply enough, can have the desired effect, the effect of getting people standardly to believe what they have been told they must believe to be saved.

Regardless of how common it is for beliefs of particular kind to be present or absent, epistemic criticism of the cognitive dimension here cannot make any blanket assumptions about what the essential cognitive elements are concerning expressions of affective faith. In the process of finding ways of life compelling or attractive, it may be true that we express affective faith at least initially in ways that exemplify whatever systems of understanding are ready-to-hand, and it would be strange fruit of the tree of epistemology that found such reliance on testimony and community always and everywhere, or even typically, to be irrational.

It is worth noting the essentially pragmatic role played by the drive for understanding as well as the interest in full integration of cognition with affection. We should expect a fundamentally affective origin to yield cognitive fruit and efforts at systematic understanding that cohere with such affective features. In the process, it can be fully rational to adopt points of view that fail to pass epistemic scrutiny, much as we might find among scientists committed to a certain research program, whether a dying one or one that merely shows some promise. And all of this, without mentioning the ways in which our typical philosophical views, and especially our epistemic views on what it takes to survive suitable epistemic scrutiny, fail to measure up to the standards of knowledge in more mundane contexts.

Given this background, it becomes easy to see what kinds of opposition by belittlers would be appropriate and what kinds would not. The moral offense taken by the belittlers at much of the historical behavior of Christians[21] is an offense all should share, religious or not, and the strongest expressions of contempt for such behavior is appropriate. If affective religious faith led inexorably to such, no further criticism would be needed.

In addition, even some forms of belligerence are appropriate for the standard cognitive accouterments of typical expressions of faith, especially in the context of Christianity in America. Bobby Jindal claims that Republicans must cease being "the stupid party,"[22] and similar advice is sorely needed among conservative Christians. The belittlers are not alone in experiencing consternation at the current state of religion in America, but it is equally true that it is not a criticism of the life of faith as such to point out the utter stupidity of certain beliefs held by vast swaths of contemporary Christians.

The central point, however, is this. The critiques raised by the belittlers are orthogonal to the way of life at which they are directed. It is a fundamental misunderstanding of the life of faith, at least when involving the affective faith I'm focusing on here, to draw conclusions about the propriety or rationality or justification of religion as such or Christianity in particular on the typical grounds given by critics such as Dawkins, Dennett, Harris, and Hitchens.[23] Written in the tradition of concern over the clash of faith and reason, all such approaches think of faith as something belief-like or at least requiring quite specific cognitive commitments, so that the central question about religious faith is whether the beliefs involved can be held rationally. And then the question of whether religious faith makes any kind of sense turns into the question of whether adequate grounds can be found for religious belief. But if my description of a life of faith is where we start the discussion, there will be no specific cognitive contents that can be identified as the ones that are both epistemically problematic and essential to affective faith as such. On the picture of faith developed here, people of this kind of (religious) faith might include various kinds of skeptics and agnostics regarding the existence of God and any or all of the central claims of the major world religions. That is, one can commit to a certain ideal, even to being an unconditional follower of Jesus or Mohammed or whatever, without any of the standard cognitive attitudes of ordinary folk on such paths, and still be a person of faith—on the straight and narrow—in spite of one's cognitive uncertainties and confusions. The faith in question is a function of the depth of commitment to the chosen path and the disposition or orientation that leads to following through on such an unconditional commitment. As such, epistemic criticisms that attempt universal destruction of the rationality of people

---

21. See in particular Hitchens (2007).
22. January 26, 2013 at the Republican National Committee retreat in Charlotte, North Carolina.
23. See especially Dawkins (2006), Dennett (2006), Harris (2004), Hitchens (2007).

of faith cannot succeed. There will, instead, only be piecemeal criticisms to be raised about particular cognitive and affective combinations, and no such criticisms could possibly sustain such blanket judgments as that religion poisons everything.

6. CONCLUSION

The view I have been characterizing and defending allows for quite a wide variety of cognitive stances compatible with Christian faith. One can almost say that the account here resists the cognitive picture by accusing it of a scope fallacy. The affective picture allows that for every instance of Christian faith, there will be, or come to be, beliefs or other cognitive commitments of some type and intensity present; but that it is false that there are some types of belief of some intensity which are present in every instance of Christian faith. Once this new picture of faith is in place, the belligerence of the belittlers is hard to fathom. Against particular lives of faith and the particular beliefs held, criticism, including epistemic criticism, is certainly warranted. Here I'm on the side of the belittlers. But in any kind of sweeping, general way, there could be no epistemic grounds for rejecting the very idea of religious faith, anymore than their could be for rejecting the very idea of mundane faith.

REFERENCES

Audi, Robert. 1982. "Believing and Affirming." *Mind* XCI(361): 115–20.
———. 1994. "Dispositional Beliefs and Dispositions to Believe." *Noûs* 28(4): 419–34.
Buchak, Lara. 2012. "Can It Be Rational to Have Faith?" In *Probability in the Philosophy of Religion*, ed. Jake Chandler and Victoria S. Harrison, 225–46. Oxford: Oxford University Press.
Dawkins, Richard. 2006. *The God Delusion*. London: Bantam Press.
Dennett, Daniel. 2006. *Breaking the Spell: Religion as a Natural Phenomenon*. New York: Viking Penguin.
Harris, Sam. 2004. *The End of Faith: Religion, Terror, and the Future of Reason*. New York: W. W. Norton.
Hitchens, Christopher. 2007. *God Is Not Great: How Religion Poisons Everything*. New York: Twelve.
Howard-Snyder, Daniel. 2013 (forthcoming). "Propositional Faith: What It Is and What It Is Not." *American Philosophical Quarterly* 50(4).
Kvanvig, Jonathan L. 2011. "The Rational Significance of Reflective Ascent." In *Evidentialism and Its Critics*, ed. Trent Dougherty, 34–54. Oxford: Oxford University Press.
——— 2012. "Perspectivalism and Reflective Ascent." In *The Epistemology of Disagreement*, ed. David Christensen and Jennifer Lackey, 223–43. Oxford: Oxford University Press.
——— 2013a (forthcoming). "Curiosity and a Response-Dependent Account of the Value of Understanding." In *Knowledge, Virtue, and Action*, ed. Timothy Henning and David Schweikard. London: Routledge.
——— 2013b (forthcoming). "Epistemic Normativity." In *Epistemic Normativity*, ed. John Turri and Clayton Littlejohn. Oxford: Oxford University Press.
Leiter, Brian. 2012. *Why Tolerate Religion?* Princeton, NJ: Princeton University Press.
McKaughan, Daniel J. 2013. "Authentic Faith and Acknowledged Risk: Dissolving the Problem of Faith and Reason." *Religious Studies* 49: 101–24.
Quine, Willard V. O. 1953. "Two Dogmas of Empiricism." In W. V. O. Quine, *From a Logical Point of View*, 2–46. New York: Harper Torchbooks.
Sosa, Ernest. 2007. *A Virtue Epistemology*. Oxford: Oxford University Press.

Discreditable Origins and the Significance of Natural Theology

GREGG TEN ELSHOF

STAGE SETTING

For nearly as long as there have been "new atheists," folks have been wondering what's new about their contribution to the perennial discussion of religion and religious belief. Many, failing to find anything new in the new atheists' contribution to the discussion of the *rationality* of religious belief, have focused instead on the suggestion (ubiquitous in the new atheism literature) that religion is not only irrational but also positively harmful to the society. I doubt that this latter claim has much more going for it by way of novelty than does the suggestion that religious belief is irrational. Whatever the case, in what follows I wish to discuss what appears to me to be one genuine development of the past decade or so in the contemporary discussion of the *rationality* of religious belief—a development owing (in some measure anyway) to the new atheists.

To begin, consider something that has *not* changed. One thing that is not new about the new atheistic platform is that it has, as a crucial plank, a naturalistic account of the origins of religious belief. The idea that religious belief can be discredited by explaining its origins found repeated expression in the nineteenth and twentieth centuries. One thinks here of the accounts offered by Hegel, Marx, Feuerbach, Russell, Freud, and others. These older attempts to discredit religious belief by appeal to its origins, though, were not terribly impressive. They were, it's tempting to say, merely just-so stories with little going for them beyond their capacity to capture the imagination of naïve would-be skeptics.

© 2013 Wiley Periodicals, Inc.

John O'Leary-Hawthorn's assessment of these older attempts in 1999 (before the rise of the new atheism) is characteristic:

> Criticisms of religion based on accounts of psychological origin hold little sway among professional philosophers. It is all too easy to come up with speculative psychologies concerning the origin of this or that belief. But the process of arriving at such speculations seems to me and many like me altogether too undisciplined to be worthy of serious respect.[1]

Since these early psychological accounts were speculative and lacking in scholarly discipline, they could be summarily dismissed and posed no credible threat to the rationality of religious belief. The new atheism, by contrast, draws on an impressive and growing body of disciplined research in cognitive psychology, anthropology, evolutionary biology, and other fields.

Gone are the days when psychological explanations of religious belief could be dismissed for being undisciplined, speculative, and unscientific. Instead of outright dismissal (or, at least, rejection), many theistic philosophers seem to be favoring a response that accommodates these attempts to explain the origins of religious belief. These theists (I'll call them the new theists) are responding (each in their own way) with the claim that these accounts pose no threat to religious belief, not because the accounts can be rationally rejected, but because they don't have any negative evidential bearing on the truth or rationality of the beliefs they purport to explain.[2] The basic idea is that one (or a combination) of these accounts can be adopted and incorporated into a larger supernaturalistic framework, according to which it is God who orchestrates (or allows to come about) the circumstances under which theistic belief arises.

In what follows, I wish to explore the implications of this accommodating response to recent deliverances of cognitive psychology (and related fields). In particular, I will suggest that the accommodating response creates for the project of defending the rationality of religious belief greater dependence on the success of natural theology.

---

1. John O'Leary-Hawthorn, "Arguments for Atheism" in *Reason for the Hope Within*, ed. Michael J. Murray (Grand Rapids, MI: Eerdmans, 1999), 134.

2. See, for example, Michael Murray, "Evolutionary Explanations of Religion," in *God is Great, God is Good: Why Believing in God is Reasonable and Responsible*, ed. William Lane Craig and Chad Meister (Downers Grove, IL: InterVarsity Press, 2009), 91–106, and "Scientific Explanations of Religion and the Justification of Religious Belief," in *The Believing Primate*, ed. Jeffrey Schloss and Michael J. Murray (New York: Oxford University Press, 2009), 168–78; Peter Van Inwagen, "Explaining Belief in the Supernatural: Some Thoughts on Paul Bloom's 'Religious Belief as an Evolutionary Accident'," in *The Believing Primate*, ed. Jeffrey Schloss and Michael J. Murray (New York: Oxford University Press, 2009), 127–38; John F. Haught, *God and the New Atheism: A Critical Response to Dawkins, Harris, and Hitchens* (Louisville, KY: Westminster John Knox Press, 2008); Kelly James Clark and Dani Rabinowitz, "Knowledge and the Objection to Religious Belief from Cognitive Science," *European Journal for Philosophy of Religion* 3 (2011): 67–81; Gregory R. Peterson, "Are Evolutionary/Cognitive Theories of Religion Relevant for Philosophy of Religion?," *Zygon* 45(3) (2010): 545–57; Gregory E. Ganssle, *A Reasonable God: Engaging the New Face of Atheism* (Waco, TX: Baylor University Press, 2009).

THE CASES

My exploration of the implications of the accommodation response will focus on the relationship between two cases and a particular account of religious belief that comes to us from contemporary cognitive science. It falls beyond the scope of my project here to survey the various naturalistic accounts of religious belief currently on offer.[3] It will help, though, to have one before us for the sake of what follows. Justin Barrett's explanation of religious belief as rooted in a hypersensitive agency detector will do nicely to represent the field of options.

Barrett's HADD[4]

That we have religious belief is largely to be explained by the activity of a hypersensitive agency detection device (HADD). This device, when confronted by apparently purposive phenomena in the environment, causes it to seem to the subject as though there is an agent causing the phenomena. It, then, is the mechanism responsible for the production of beliefs to the effect that agents are present in our environment even while unseen. Since sensitivity to potential predators is a priority item on the things-needed-to-survive list, it's not surprising from an evolutionary perspective that creatures should evolve with agency detection devices. And it's further to be expected that these devices would evolve in such a way as to err on the side of delivering a lot of false positives since the cost of a false negative could be fatal (hence, HADD's hypersensitivity).[5]

Barrett's account of religious belief as a product of HADD is characteristic of the field in that it resists dismissal on grounds like those cited by O'Leary-Hawthorn. It must be dealt with as a serious deliverance of contemporary scientific scholarship (whether or not it is, at the end of the day, true that HADD is responsible for religious belief). It is also characteristic in that it is silent on the *truth* of religious belief. It is consistent both with theism and atheism. It is its silence on the truth of HADD-produced religious belief that both (1) motivates the new atheists to think that it discredits religious belief and (2) makes possible the accommodation response of the new theists.

As to (1), new atheists trade on something like the following principle: If the best explanation for my believing that P is indifferent to the truth of P (and I know it), that spells trouble of some kind for my belief that P.[6] As to (2), new theists are

---

3. For a nice survey of the kinds of explanations being explored, see Jeffrey Schloss, "Evolutionary Theories of Religion: Science Unfettered or Naturalism Run Wild?" in *The Believing Primate*, ed. Jeffrey Schloss and Michael J. Murray (New York: Oxford University Press, 2009), 1–25.

4. In what follows, I'll use the expression "Barrett's HADD" as shorthand for the account which explains our having religious beliefs by appeal to HADD.

5. See Justin Barrett, *Why Would Anyone Believe in God?* (Lanham, MD: AltaMira Press, 2004).

6. We needn't settle the precise nature of the trouble to get hold of the basic intuition here. Different versions of the principle will presumably refer to trouble of different sorts (e.g., trouble for justification, warrant, rationality, knowledge, etc.). Jeffry Schloss, for example, calls the following an uncontroversial scientific principle: "If our best theory of why people believe P does not require that P is true, then there are no grounds to believe P is true" (Schloss 2009, 19).

quick to point out that there is no contradiction whatever in the suggestion that it is God who orchestrates the evolution of creatures with HADD precisely in order that they might believe (truly) that God exists. So the question of God's existence, while interesting and important, does not turn in the slightest on the question of the adequacy of Barrett's HADD to explain religious belief.

I turn now to two cases, reflection on which will, I hope, make clear the implications of the accommodation response.

Murray's HAND[7]

Michael Murray invites us to imagine the following case, which might be thought to parallel the epistemic situation we're in with respect to religious belief should religious belief be explainable in terms of Barrett's HADD. An agent is sitting in a psychology lab staring at her hand. She has the belief that her hand is in front of her face. Unbeknownst to her, however, the hand belief is being caused by a researcher's device aimed in her direction emitting radiation that causes subjects both to go blind and to have a belief that there is a hand in front of their face.[8]

For Murray, the hand belief's being caused in this way precludes its being justified since the subject would have the hand belief *even if there were no hand there*.[9] Does HADD, if true, similarly undermine the justification of religious belief? No, according to Murray, since HADD does *not* have as an implication that we would have religious belief *even if there were no God*. It could have that implication only were it to rule out the suggestion that the universe owes its existence to God. And it surely doesn't do anything so grand as that. The God case and the hand case, says Murray, are not analogous at all.[10]

van Inwagen's Bat Urine

Peter van Inwagen invites us to imagine the following: A statue of the Virgin in an Italian church appears to weep. The weeping statue is taken to be a sign of God's special favor on the church. It is eventually discovered, however, that the apparent tears are the urine from bats that have made their home in the dim recesses of the church ceiling.[11]

For van Inwagen, discovering the bats would spell trouble for the belief that God intended to communicate his special favor for the church by means of the "weeping" statue. As he puts it, the bat urine account "*resists* being incorporated into a larger supernaturalistic explanation—it strongly suggests that there's

---

7. Once again, I'll use the expression "Murray's HAND" to refer to the case Murray gives us.
8. See Murray and Schloss (2009), 174, and Craig and Meister, eds., (2009), 103.
9. According to Murray, this implication holds only on an externalist account of justification by which he means one according to which a justified belief bears a certain relationship to facts in the external world.
10. Craig and Meister, eds., (2009), 103.
11. Schloss and Murray, eds., (2009), 134–35.

'nothing more to it' than ordinary causes and chance."[12] One could, of course, coherently propose that the bat urine was God's chosen instrument by which to bring about the apparent tears and the (true) belief that God's special favor rests on the church. But this attempt to incorporate the bat urine explanation is, by van Inwagen's lights, unreasonable, contrived, artificial, and desperate. Older accounts of the origin of religious belief (e.g., those of Feuerbach, Marx, and Freud), according to van Inwagen, similarly resist rational incorporation into a supernaturalistic account. On the other hand, evolutionary explanations of religious belief (e.g., Barrett's HADD), according to van Inwagen, do not so resist. van Inwagen does not find it contrived to suggest that God, knowing that a mechanism like HADD would eventually deliver up theistic belief and desiring for there to be creatures with theistic belief, allowed the evolution of HADD to be the cause of those beliefs.

Both Murray and van Inwagen, then, give us cases that appear to parallel the situation we're in with respect to an explanation of religious belief in terms of HADD. Since these apparently parallel cases make trouble for their respective target beliefs, it appears as though religious belief is similarly in trouble. Both argue, however, that the appearance of a parallel is illusory—that the epistemic situation we're in with respect to HADD and religious belief is relevantly different. I'll argue, on the other hand, that these three cases are analogous with respect to the epistemic concerns at hand. The conditions under which one would be justified in retaining theistic belief parallel the conditions under which one would be justified in retaining the hand belief or the special favor belief, and this has interesting implications for religious epistemology generally.

DRAWING THE CASES TOGETHER

Consider again Murray's HAND. Suppose Murray's right to point out that Barrett's HADD does not imply that we'd have religious belief even were there no God.[13] Even so, neither does Murray's HAND imply that the subject would have her hand belief even were she not holding her hand in front of her face. This is because the case is silent on the conditions under which the researcher shoots radiation at the subjects in the lab. For all we've been told, it may be that the researcher shoots radiation at subjects when (and only when) the belief induced by the radiation is true. Neither case has as an implication that the target belief would arise whether or not it were true. If, as Murray suggests, this is sufficient to show that Barrett's HADD (all on its own) makes no trouble for religious belief, then Murray's HAND (all on its own) ought not to make trouble for the subject's hand belief.

But surely Murray's HAND (all on its own) *does* make trouble for the subject's hand belief. Suppose *I* am the subject of the experiment in Murray's

12. Ibid., 135.
13. Whether or not he *is* right turns on interesting questions about how to assess the relevant counterfactuals. Which atheistic world is closest to ours? One in which there is no life at all? Or one in which there are human beings just like us with (false) theistic beliefs? For my purposes here, I grant that the counterfactuals work themselves out in the way Murray suggests.

HAND and I come to know as much.[14] Will this not negatively affect the justificatory status of my hand belief? If I learn that my hand belief is caused by a dose of radiation that has rendered me blind and caused in me a belief that my hand is in front of my face, I'm surely failing to satisfy some epistemic desideratum or other if I blithely carry on believing—this despite the fact that the explanation of the hand belief I've accepted is silent on the question whether I would have the belief were it false (since it is silent on the intentions of the researcher). Of course, if I've got *independent* reasons for thinking that the researcher intends to shoot me with radiation when (and only when) my hand belief is true, then I may be justified in retaining my hand belief even upon having accepted Murray's HAND. But merely recognizing the *possibility* that the researcher has those intentions won't do the job. I'll need positive reasons for thinking that my belief is reliably tied to the truth—reasons independent of the belief itself (or the perceptual seeming that gives rise to it) if my belief is to be justified.

The same is true with respect to HADD and religious belief. If I accept Barrett's HADD as the explanation of my religious belief, then I'm in exactly the same situation I would be in were I to accept Murray's HAND as the explanation of my hand belief. HADD does not rule out the possibility that the evolutionary process is guided by God in such a way as to (eventually) kick up true religious belief. But I'll need reasons independent of my belief itself (or whatever seeming gives rise to it) for thinking that God exists if I'm to be justified in believing that he does. Prior to having accepted HADD, its seeming to me that theism is true *may* have been sufficient to justify theism.[15] But having accepted an explanation of its seeming to me that theism is true, which severs the connection between the seeming and the truth of the belief, I now stand in need of independent reasons for thinking that the seeming is, in fact, reliably tied to the truth. Absent such reasons, my belief is unjustified. Again, the conditions under which I would be justified in retaining my hand belief, having accepted Murray's HAND, parallel the conditions under which I would be justified in retaining theistic belief having accepted Barrett's HADD.

Consider now van Inwagen's bat urine. van Inwagen thinks it contrived (not to mention unreasonable, artificial, and desperate) to incorporate the bat urine explanation into a larger supernaturalistic framework. Attempts to incorporate older psychological accounts of religious belief (e.g., those of Freud, Marx, et al.) are deemed similarly contrived. Not so, though, the incorporation of an account like Barrett's HADD into a supernaturalistic framework. Why not? Because, says van Inwagen, God, knowing that HADD would eventually kick up religious belief and desiring as much, might well have allowed HADD to do the relevant causal work.

---

14. Note that I'm not merely recognizing the *possibility* that I'm the subject of such an experiment as I might when I consider standard skeptical arguments. Rather, I'm accepting it as the actual explanation of my belief that I'm the subject of such an experiment.

15. Whether or not the seeming is sufficient for justification will, of course, turn on questions about whether and in what form Foundationalism can be cogently defended. Here, I grant that its seeming to S that P can do justificatory work for S *vis-à-vis* the proposition that P.

But surely God, knowing that the bat urine would cause the belief that God's favor rests on the church and desiring as much, might well have allowed the bat urine to do the relevant causal work. Similarly, God, knowing that the human tendency to project its inner nature would eventuate in a belief that God exists and desiring as much, might well have allowed the projection tendencies described by Feuerbach to do the relevant causal work. There is simply no difference in the cases along the lines suggested by van Inwagen.

To be fair, van Inwagen doesn't take himself to be in possession of an *argument* for the claim that the incorporation of HADD into a supernaturalistic framework is natural while the incorporation of these other explanations is contrived. The test for contrivance, as he understands it, has more to do with whether or not unbiased observers will recognize it as such. We know it when we see it. I suspect (although not much turns on this point) that the degree to which the incorporation of an explanation seems contrived will have much to do with the initial familiarity of the kind of explanation in question. Incorporation of evolutionary explanations is less likely to appear contrived because we've grown accustomed to them. Bat urine explanations and explanations having to do with the projection of our inner nature are far less familiar, and so their incorporation into a larger framework (even if perfectly coherent) may, for some, have the appearance of contrivance. For my part, I simply report that I do not detect what van Inwagen reports himself as detecting—viz. contrivance in the incorporation of the bat urine explanation and the older psychological explanations of a sort not on display in the incorporation of explanations like Barrett's HADD into a supernaturalistic framework. Either they're all contrived or none of them are.

But are they contrived? Is it unreasonable to incorporate these explanations into a larger supernaturalistic framework? The answer to that question, I think, depends on whether or not there are independent reasons for thinking that the larger supernaturalistic picture is true.

Consider again the bat urine explanation. Is it a contrivance to think that God used the nesting of the bats in the church ceiling (and their subsequent urination) to bring about the belief that God's special favor rests on the church? It seems so if there is no independent reason for thinking that God's special favor rests on the church. But suppose the discovery of the bats occurred in a context replete with evidence of God's special favor for this church. Suppose something like the weeping statue was happening every week at the church. Last week, it was the sudden appearance of what looked like blood stains on the hands of the Jesus mural. The week prior, an audible voice from nowhere interrupted worship and proclaimed God's special favor on this church. And so on for weeks and weeks on end. Against a certain background of independent evidence for God's special favor on the church, it would not be unreasonable whatever to think that God had used the nesting of these bats to communicate as much. And this would be true whether or not anyone ever believed that the "weeping" was anything other than the urination of bats. Against a certain backdrop of evidence, I might rationally conclude that God was communicating his favor on the church by means of the "weeping" statue even if I recognized from the start that the apparent tears were, in fact, bat urine.[16]

Is it a contrivance to think that God used the messy and long evolutionary process eventuating in creatures with HADD to bring about the belief that God exists? It seems so if there is no independent reason for thinking that God exists. But suppose the discovery of HADD occurred in a context replete with evidence of God's existence. Against such a background of independent evidence, it would not be unreasonable whatever to think that it was through the evolution of mechanisms like HADD that God chose to have belief in God's existence arises. Once again, the cases parallel one another. The conditions under which the incorporation of the bat urine explanation is contrived parallel the conditions under which the incorporation of HADD is contrived.

IMPLICATIONS

I've been arguing that theistic belief in the context of having accepting Barrett's HADD is on all fours with hand belief in the context of having accepted Murray's HAND, and belief that God's special favor rests on the church in the context of having accepted the bat urine explanation. In each case, the target belief is in danger of being rendered unjustified by the acceptance of an explanation that severs the connection between the belief and its being true. In each case, however, justification can be retained if there are independent reasons justifying the incorporation of the explanation into a larger framework that reestablishes the connection between the belief and its truth.

Of course, natural theologians in the Christian tradition (not to mention theistic traditions of other varieties) have long been about the business of developing independent reasons of just the sort in view—reasons for believing that God exists that float free of *my* belief that God exists or its seeming to me that God exists. If Barrett's HADD parallels Murray's HAND and van Inwagen's bat urine in the ways I've been suggesting, then this natural theology project is more central to the defense of the rationality of theism than would be the case were it not for the increasing plausibility of HADD-like explanations of religious belief. This conclusion would be of little interest if all were agreed that the rationality of religious belief stands or falls with the success of natural theology. But not all are so agreed. Increasingly popular over the past few decades has been the suggestion that, although there may or may not be good arguments for God's existence, the rationality of belief in God doesn't depend on them. Belief in God is (or can be anyway) properly basic. Niceties aside, the suggestion is that my belief in God, like my belief that there is a hand in front of my face, does not depend for its rationality on there

---

16. Of course, there is room here for reasonable disagreement (I'm grateful to Doug Geivett, in particular, for disagreeing reasonably in correspondence about this). Maybe it's beneath God to bring about beliefs by means of the urination of bats. I'm not sure. The crucial point for my purposes is that the incorporation fails to be contrived *only if* there are independent grounds for thinking that God's favor rests on the church. Independent grounds are necessary for rational incorporation. It seems to me that they're also sufficient in a case like this. But maybe not. What matters for the larger aims of this paper is that they're necessary.

being *reasons* independent of my belief (or the seeming that gives rise to it) for thinking it true. Maybe that's right. But accepting Murray's HAND would give rise to the need for independent reasons supporting my hand belief where previously there had been none. Likewise, even if theistic belief can be properly basic (in the way that my hand belief is properly basic), accepting Barrett's HADD gives rise to the need for independent reasons supporting theistic belief where previously there had been none.

The accommodation response to HADD-like accounts of religious belief, then, has as an implication that the stakes are higher in the debate over the success of natural theology.[17]

A NOD TO BAYESIAN CONFIRMATION THEORY

According to one very sensible way of assessing the epistemic situation, the questions I've been addressing all turn on whether or not Barrett's HADD functions as disconfirming evidence of theism for the theist who has no evidence for theism independent of its seeming truth.

Let "G" be the proposition that God exists. Let "SG" be the proposition that it seems that God exists. And let "H" be Barrett's HADD. Our question, then, comes to this:

$Pr(H/G\&SG) < Pr(H/\text{-}G\&SG)?$[18]

And the answer to that question will turn on whether or not the theist for whom it seems that God exists should be any more surprised to observe Barrett's HADD than should be the atheist for whom it seems that God exists. And, one might argue, the theist should not be surprised in the slightest to learn that God brought about theistic belief via HADD. After all, there are innumerable ways in which God could have brought about theistic belief in humans, and we're in no position to discern *a priori* which of these ways God would prefer. So there's no cause for surprise should the empirical data support the conclusion that God brought about theistic belief by means of HADD. But then the answer to our question will be no. And Barrett's HADD will not function as disconfirming evidence of theism.

Does this Bayesian analysis explain away any initial appearance of trouble from Barrett's HADD for the rationality of religious belief? For a couple of reasons, I don't think so.

First, if this line of response makes possible a theistic accommodation of Barrett's HADD, it should also make possible a theistic accommodation of any number of other explanations of religious belief. One should be able to accommo-

---

17. Here, I use "natural theology" as a catch-all term for evidence independent of my belief that God exists (or its seeming to me that God exists). Some have offered evidence of the relevant sort and have suggested that it falls outside the scope of natural theology properly understood. See, for example, Paul Moser, *The Elusive God* (Cambridge: Cambridge University Press, 2009).

18. I'm grateful to Tom Crisp for the suggestion that the disagreement between myself and the new theists may come finally to a difference in our intuitive response to this question.

date the suggestion, for example, that theism owes to wish fulfillment. In the absence of any conviction about how it is that God might choose to bring about theistic belief, why be surprised should it turn out that wish fulfillment was his preferred method? But to accept an account of theistic belief as arising via wish fulfillment and to persist in theistic belief (in the absence of independent evidence for its truth) seems like a bad epistemic business. So this response is too permissive.

This won't convince everyone, of course. Plantinga, for one, is ready to countenance the possibility that warranted Christian belief may have come about in exactly this way.[19] Here, I must confess that I'm at the end of argument. It seems to me that a belief that has nothing to recommend its truth beyond its wish fulfillment-induced seeming truth is in a bad epistemic way. This is not to say that God couldn't have intended for the belief in question to be produced in just that way. And if he did so intend, then the belief would be in keeping with the design plan that gave rise to it—a, no doubt, laudable condition for a belief to be in. But unless we've got some independent reason for thinking that God *did* so intend, a discovery to the effect that the belief is the product of wish fulfillment is a significant mark against it.

Second, *should* the theist be more surprised to observe Barrett's HADD? The answer to our question is yes. The theist for whom theism seems true should be surprised to learn that the mechanism responsible for its seeming to her that God exists has a long history of unreliability (remember that HADD is hypersensitive—that it has, historically, delivered up a lot of false positives). But the atheist for whom it seems that God exists will have every reason to expect that the mechanism responsible for its seeming to her that God exists is unreliable (since, *qua* atheist, she'll already be convinced that, in this case, the mechanism is getting it wrong). In general, if you think that a current seeming gets it right, you should be surprised to learn that it's the deliverance of a mechanism with a history of unreliability. But if you think a current seeming is illusory, you should be less surprised to learn that it's the deliverance of a mechanism with a history of unreliability. In fact, perhaps you should expect as much.

INTRINSIC DEFEATER-DEFEATERS TO THE RESCUE?

I've argued that the accommodation response, while not implausible, does not come for free. It renders more central to the case for the rationality of theism some degree of success for natural theology.[20]

But what about Plantinga's suggestion that a proposition can sometimes have justification sufficient to defeat its own defeaters? Suppose p is a basic belief for me, and I acquire some justification for q that threatens to defeat p. Need I

---

19. Alvin Plantinga, *Warranted Christian Belief* (New York: Oxford University Press, 2000), 197ff.

20. Questions about what would count as success along these lines fall beyond the scope of this paper. Presumably, though, a limiting case would be the existence of one good independent reason for thinking that God exists.

always come up with some independent reason for rejecting q or for persisting in my belief that p? No. In some cases, p *itself* can function as a defeater of would-be defeaters. Recall Plantinga's example:

> I am applying to the National Endowment for the Humanities for a fellowship; I write a letter to a colleague, trying to bribe him to write the Endowment a glowing letter on my behalf; he indignantly refuses and sends the letter to my chairman. The letter disappears from the chairman's office under mysterious circumstances. I have a motive for stealing it; I have the opportunity to do so; and I have been known to do such things in the past. Furthermore an extremely reliable member of the department claims to have seen me furtively entering the chairman's office at about the time when the letter must have been stolen. The evidence against me is very strong; my colleagues reproach me for such underhanded behavior and treat me with evident distaste. The facts of the matter, however, are that I didn't steal the letter and in fact spent the entire afternoon in question on a solitary walk in the woods; furthermore I clearly remember spending that afternoon walking in the woods.[21]

In this case, argues Plantinga, I am rational to continue in my belief that I did not steal the letter on grounds that I clearly remember walking in the park at the time of the theft—this despite the fact that there is a compelling body of evidence in support of the proposition that I stole the letter. My colleagues are aware of this body of evidence and conclude (rationally) that I did, indeed, steal the letter. I know everything they know, and I don't so conclude. Moreover, I've no grounds *independent of the belief in question* for drawing *my* conclusion instead of the conclusion of my colleagues. The belief that I didn't steal the letter, grounded in clear memorial experience as it is, suffices to defeat its own potential defeaters.

Might not the same move be available here? Might not theism, itself, function as an intrinsic defeater of HADD-like defeaters for theistic belief? I don't think so. There is an important difference between Plantinga's NEH letter case and the cases we've been considering. In the NEH letter case, I am rational to persist in my belief that I didn't steal the letter since that proposition derives from its origin in clear memory more justification than is enjoyed by its potential defeater. The latter enjoys whatever justification it does on the basis of the evidence I share with my colleagues.

But the NEH letter case is very different from Barrett's HADD and Murray's HAND. Imagine the subject of HAND persisting in her hand belief after having accepted an explanation of its seeming to her that her hand is in front of her face in terms of the researcher's device. Can she appeal to the strength of the justification she enjoys for her hand belief—grounded as it is in clear perceptual experience—to defeat the justification-defeating potential of Murray's HAND? No. Murray's HAND, if accepted, renders the perceptual seeming incapable of doing its ordinary justificatory work since it explains the perceptual seeming

21. Alvin Plantinga, "The Foundations of Theism: A Reply," *Faith and Philosophy* 3(3) (1986): 310.

without appeal to the alleged object of appearance. Nothing in Plantinga's NEH letter case functions similarly to render the memorial experience incapable of doing its ordinary justificatory work. So the memorial belief is capable of functioning as an intrinsic defeater-defeater, while the hand belief is not.

Consider an embellishment of Plantinga's NEH letter case as follows. Convinced as they are that I've stolen the letter and frustrated that I've not been willing to join them in this conclusion, my colleagues probe deeper into the events of that day. They wonder how I could have the memorial experience that I do have since (as they're convinced) I was not in the woods but in my colleague's office stealing the letter. Finally, they hypothesize that the orange juice I drank that morning was laced with a time-delayed hallucinatory element that implants seeming memories of just the sort I report having. They pose this to me and not as a *mere* possibility—a just-so story. Instead, they present me with compelling evidence for the claim that my memorial experience was, in fact, caused by just such a hallucinatory element in my orange juice. Suppose I accept this explanation of my memorial experience. Could I then rationally persist in my belief that I did not steal the letter on the memorial grounds earlier cited? I don't think so. If I accept the explanation on offer of my seeming memory, then the memorial belief loses its capacity to function as an intrinsic defeater-defeater. And this will be true even if, as a matter of fact, my seeming memory gets it right—even if, that is, I was strolling in the woods and not stealing the letter at the time of the theft.

Return finally to Barrett's HADD. If I accept Barrett's HADD as the explanation of my theistic belief, then I'm not in a position like the one depicted by Plantinga's NEH letter case. I'm in a position like the one depicted by Murray's HAND and by my embellished NEH letter case. In these latter cases, the target belief loses its capacity to function as an intrinsic defeater-defeater because the explanation undermines the nonpropositional grounds upon which the target belief's justification rests. And if those grounds no longer confer justification on the target belief, it can't have justification sufficient to outweigh its potential defeaters.

But wait a minute, one might say, mightn't there be some beliefs the rationality of which is impervious to defeat from an explanation of their origins—beliefs it would be rational to retain come-what-may with respect to what we learn about how they arose?

Descartes famously thought so. But, equally famously, he thought that the class of beliefs so describable was a limited one indeed. Even beliefs so obvious as that $2 + 2 = 4$, that I have a body, and that there are other minds were excluded. Perhaps the belief in my own existence qualifies, or the belief that I'm currently having thus-and-so experience. There's no logical incoherence that I can see in the suggestion that belief in God is among these cogito-like beliefs that it's rational to retain come-what-may with respect to an explanation of their origins. But many (including many who think that belief in God is properly basic) have stopped well short of claiming anything so impressive as cogito-like status for theistic belief.[22]

---

22. My response here resembles Philip Quinn's response to Plantinga's suggestion that theistic belief could be an intrinsic defeater-defeater. See Philip Quinn, "The Foundations of Theism Again: A Rejoinder to Plantinga," in *Rational Faith: Catholic Responses to Reformed*

So there is this bit of novelty in the new atheistic platform. Speculative naturalistic accounts of the origins of religious belief, easily dismissed by theistic philosophers, have been replaced by careful scientific naturalistic accounts that make accommodation the more tempting response. But accommodating these accounts complicates the suggestion that the rationality of theism floats free of the success of natural theology. From a certain theistic perspective, that's not such a bad thing. For millennia, theists who thought that much depends on the success of natural theology have labored with considerable benefit to themselves and the church at the development of arguments for the existence of God. The new atheists, perhaps, are to be thanked for helping us recover the urgency of that project.[23]

Epistemology, ed. Linda Zagzebski (Notre Dame, IN: University of Notre Dame Press, 1993), 14–47. Quinn there responded to Plantinga's suggestion that theistic belief may parallel clear memorial beliefs (or other beliefs for which we have compelling nonpropositional evidence) in its capacity to serve as an intrinsic defeater-defeater. Quinn wondered whether or not there were very many folks for whom theism presented itself with the kind of vivacity and force as do, say, our perceptual beliefs or our beliefs grounded in clear memory. In this new dialectical context, though, even memorial and perceptual beliefs fail to have what it takes to function as intrinsic defeater-defeaters. Even if Quinn underestimated the number of people for whom theism presents itself with the same kind of obviousness as do memorial beliefs, it's surely a stretch to think that theism presents itself with cogito-like force to very many theists at all.

23. Even those who cannot be appropriately thanked for the *development* of these accounts can be thanked, perhaps, for forcing attention to them by pushing the reductionist line. Beyond the new atheists, I wish also to thank the following friends and colleagues for helpful conversation and critical feedback on earlier drafts of this paper: Robin Collins, Thomas Crisp, Douglas Geivett, Stewart Goetz, JP Moreland, Michael Murray, Jason Runyan, Kevin Seybold, and Dan Speak.

New Atheism and the Scientistic Turn in the Atheism Movement

MASSIMO PIGLIUCCI

I

The so-called "New Atheism" is a relatively well-defined, very recent, still unfolding cultural phenomenon with import for public understanding of both science and philosophy. Arguably, the opening salvo of the New Atheists was *The End of Faith* by Sam Harris, published in 2004, followed in rapid succession by a number of other titles penned by Harris himself, Richard Dawkins, Daniel Dennett, Victor Stenger, and Christopher Hitchens.[1]

After this initial burst, which was triggered (according to Harris himself) by the terrorist attacks on September 11, 2001, a number of other authors have been associated with the New Atheism, even though their contributions sometimes were in the form of newspapers and magazine articles or blog posts, perhaps most prominent among them evolutionary biologists and bloggers Jerry Coyne and P. Z. Myers. Still others have published and continue to publish books on atheism, some of which have had reasonable success, probably because of the interest generated by the first wave. This second wave, however, often includes authors that explicitly

---

1. Sam Harris, *The End of Faith: Religion, Terror, and the Future of Reason* (New York: W. W. Norton, 2004); Sam Harris, *Letter to a Christian Nation* (New York: Vintage, 2006); Richard Dawkins, *The God Delusion* (Boston: Houghton Mifflin Harcourt, 2006); Daniel C. Dennett, *Breaking the Spell: Religion as a Natural Phenomenon* (New York: Viking Press, 2006); Victor J. Stenger, *God: The Failed Hypothesis: How Science Shows That God Does Not Exist* (Amherst, NY: Prometheus, 2007); Christopher Hitchens, *God Is Not Great: How Religion Poisons Everything* (New York: Twelve Books, 2007).

© 2013 Wiley Periodicals, Inc.

distance themselves from the tone and some of the specific arguments of the New Atheists, most prominently Alain De Botton and A. C. Grayling.[2] Finally, we have follow up entries in the literature by some of the original New Atheists, especially Harris, but also Hitchens.[3]

My goal in this paper is to analyze the new Atheist "movement" from a particular angle: what I see as a clear, and truly novel, though not at all positive, "scientistic" turn that it marks for atheism in general. To do so, I will begin in the next section with a brief discussion of what I think constitutes New Atheism broadly construed, as well as what counts as scientism. I will then present a brief historical overview of atheism in the Western world (to which the impact of the New Atheism seems to be largely confined), to make clear how classical Atheism differs from the new variety. The following section will then explore some examples of what I term the "scientific turn" that has characterized some (but not all) New Atheist writers (and most of their supporters, from what one can glean from the relevant social networks). The next to the last section will summarize the problems with scientism, and I will then conclude by proposing a new middle way between classical and New Atheism as more sound from both the scientific and philosophical standpoints.

II

Before proceeding, we need to have a clearer idea of what the New Atheism and scientism amount to. I shall therefore provide a brief conceptual outline of both, eschewing the often fallacious demand for clear-cut, precise definitions. With Wittgenstein, I simply do not believe that most interesting concepts are amenable to such definitions anyway.[4]

There has been much discussion about exactly what is "new" in the New Atheism. The novelty is not to be found in public advocacy of atheism, which at the very least dates to some of the figures of the Enlightenment, such as the Baron d'Holbach and Denis Diderot. Nor does there there appear to be anything particularly new from a philosophical standpoint, as the standard arguments advanced by the New Atheists against religion are just about the same that have been put forth by well-known atheist or agnostic philosophers from David Hume to

---

2. Alain De Botton, *Religion for Atheists: A Non-Believer's Guide to the Uses of Religion* (New York: Vintage Books, 2012); Anthony C. Grayling, *The God Argument: The Case against Religion and for Humanism* (London: Bloomsbury, 2013).

3. Sam Harris, *The Moral Landscape: How Science Can Determine Human Values* (New York: Free Press, 2010); Sam Harris, *Free Will* (New York: Free Press, 2012); Christopher Hitchens, *The Portable Atheist: Essential Readings for the Nonbeliever* (Cambridge, MA: Da Capo Press, 2009).

4. "I can give the concept 'number' rigid limits . . . that is, use the word 'number' for a rigidly limited concept, but I can also use it so that the extension of the concept is not closed by a frontier. And this is how we do use the word 'game'. For how is the concept of a game bounded? What still counts as a game and what no longer does? Can you give the boundary? No. You can draw one; for none has so far been drawn. (But that never troubled you before when you used the word 'game'.)" (Ludwig Wittgenstein, *Philosophical Investigations*, §68)

Bertrand Russell.[5] Indeed, not even the noticeably more aggressive than usual tone often adopted by the New Atheists, and for which they are often criticized even by other secularists, is actually new. Just think of the legendary abrasiveness of American Atheists founder Madalyn Murray O'Hair.

Rather, it seems to me that two characteristics stand out as defining New Atheism apart from what I refer to as classical Atheism, one extrinsic, the other intrinsic. The extrinsic character of the New Atheism is to be found in the indisputably popular character of the movement. All books produced by the chief New Atheists mentioned above have been worldwide best sellers, in the case of Dawkins's *God Delusion*, for instance, remaining for a whopping 51 weeks on the *New York Times* best-seller list. While previous volumes criticizing religion had received wide popular reception (especially the classic critique of Christianity by Bertrand Russell), nothing like that had happened before in the annals of Western literature. The search for the reasons explaining such an unprecedented level of popularity is best left to sociologists, and at any rate is not really relevant to my aims here. It is likely, though, that the New Atheism qua popular movement is a direct result of the complex effects of the 9/11 terrorist attacks. We have seen that the first book in the series, by Sam Harris, was written explicitly in reaction to those events, and I suspect that careful sociological analysis will reveal that that is also what accounts for Harris et al.'s success.

The second reason is intrinsic, and close to the core of my argument in this paper: the New Atheism approach to criticizing religion relies much more forcefully on science than on philosophy. Indeed, a good number of New Atheists (the notable exception being, of course, Daniel Dennett) is on record explicitly belittling philosophy as a source of knowledge or insight. Dawkins says that the "God hypothesis" should be treated as a falsifiable scientific hypothesis; Stenger explicitly—in the very subtitle of his book—states that "Science shows that God does *not* exist" (my emphasis); and Harris later on writes a whole book in which he pointedly ignores two and a half millennia of moral philosophy in an attempt to convince his readers that moral questions are best answered by science (more on this below). All of these are, to my way of seeing things, standard examples of scientism. Scientism here is defined as a totalizing attitude that regards science as the ultimate standard and arbiter of all interesting questions; or alternatively that seeks to expand the very definition and scope of science to encompass all aspects of human knowledge and understanding.

Interestingly, it used to be that the term "scientistic" was meant only and explicitly as derogatory, as indicating a simplistic and indefensible view of science itself. But after the success of the New Atheism, even some philosophers have come to embrace the label in a defiantly positive fashion,[6] perhaps in an attempt to complete the process of relinquishing their own field to the natural sciences, something that arguably began with W. V. O. Quine during the middle part of the

---

5. See, for instance: David Hume, *Dialogues Concerning Natural Religion* (1779), <http://www.gutenberg.org/ebooks/4583>; Bertrand Russell, *Why I Am Not a Christian and Other Essays on Religion and Related Subjects* (New York: Touchstone, 1967).

6. For example, Alex Rosenberg, *The Atheist's Guide to Reality: Enjoying Life without Illusions* (New York: W. W. Norton, 2011).

twentieth century.[7] As I hope it will become clear during the rest of this paper, however, this isn't a simple issue of turf wars between science and philosophy, but rather an attempt to clarify the differences—as well as overlap and mutual reinforcement—between the two fields, broadly construed.

III

After having developed a clearer conception of both the New Atheism and of scientism, we need to briefly consider, in very broad strokes, the history of classical Atheism within Western culture,[8] to prepare the terrain for a more thorough examination of how classical and New Atheism differ from each other, and why that difference hinges on the resurgence of scientism.

The word atheist comes, of course, from the Greek *atheos*, meaning "denying the gods, or ungodly," and the philosophical concept of atheism traces its roots to at the least the fifth century BCE. Despite this, it is often not easy to discern exactly what the ancient Greek philosophers thought of the matter. Socrates was put to death for "impiety," but it is clear from various Platonic dialogues that he was not an atheist. Epicurus—often portrayed as a kindred spirit by modern-day atheists—was explicit about his belief in god, although it was a god with no contact whatsoever with the human, or indeed, physical universe; and it is of course important to remember that Epicureans were vehemently against organized religion, which they identified as a major source of unhappiness among fellow humans, and a chief obstacle to the goal of ataraxia.[9] The first materialistic philosophers were atomists like Democritus and Leucippus, and we can find explicitly atheistic pronouncements in the works of playwrights such as Aristophanes and Euripides. Diagoras of Melos (fifth century BCE) is sometimes referred to as "the first atheist," and we can probably count the later Theodorus of Cyrene in the same group.

Be that as it may, explicit atheism took a philosophical nose dive during the Middle Ages, for obvious reasons. It reemerged during the Renaissance, with the term appearing for the first time in the English language in 1566, courtesy of John Martiall (who did not use it in a complimentary fashion). The first well-characterized public defense of atheism was published (posthumously) by Jean Meslier in 1729. As far as the Enlightenment goes, Denis Diderot was accused of

---

7. This is obviously not the place for an extensive consideration of Quine's work and its impact on contemporary philosophy (but see <http://plato.stanford.edu/entries/quine/%20for%20an%20overview>). It is clear, however, that Quine's reaction to the excesses of logical positivism led him to an arguably equally excessive scientist position famously stating, among other things, that epistemology is just a branch of psychology (although see Robert T. Fogelin, "Quine's Limited Naturalism," *The Journal of Philosophy* 94 (1997): 543–63, for a view of how Quine's naturalism may turn out to be less scientific than Quine himself might have realized).

8. I will limit my discussion to the Western philosophical tradition for a couple of reasons. First, it is significantly more difficult to trace explicitly atheistic or strongly agnostic positions within Eastern and Middle Eastern philosophies; second, and more importantly, the New Atheism is a quintessential Western—indeed mostly Anglo-Saxon—phenomenon.

9. See *The Philosophy of Epicurus: Letters, Doctrines, and Parallel Passages from Lucretius*, translated with an introduction and commentary by George K. Strodach (Evanston, IL: Northwestern University Press, 1963).

atheism, and the Baron D'Holbach was openly atheist, a position that his friend David Hume did not quite embrace, despite the latter's scathing writings on miracles and religion. Notwithstanding his popularity among modern-day atheists, Voltaire was a deist (and thought that atheism is actually pernicious for society). Things changed remarkably at the onset of the following century, when Percy Bysshe Shelley published (anonymously) *The Necessity of Atheism* in 1811. The door was open for some of the most remarkable—philosophically based—rejections of religion, from Marx to Nietzsche, just to mention two of the most prominent examples.

Even in the twentieth century, that is, before the early twenty-first century advent of New Atheism, the ball was still firmly in the philosophical park when it came to defense of or apologia for atheism: just consider the writings of A. J. Ayer, John Dewey, and, naturally, Bertrand Russell. Atheism had certainly been informed by science, arguably as far back as the materialistic take of the pre-Socratic atomists, but the recognizable arguments, both against the existence of specific kinds of gods (mostly the Abrahamic one) and in favor of secular materialism, were philosophical in nature. This, of course, changed dramatically—and, I would add, controversially—with the New Atheist authors, particularly Dawkins, Harris, and Stenger.

IV

When considering New Atheism's scientific turn, we need to distinguish among a gradation of attitudes characterizing the various major proponents of New Atheism (and, of course, also a number of secondary authors that I do not have space to explicitly consider here). I will therefore focus on Christopher Hitchens, Daniel Dennett, Richard Dawkins, Victor Stenger, and Sam Harris as an ensemble that has both played a major role in the New Atheism movement and that is well representative of the spectrum of attitudes toward science among the New Atheists themselves.

Beginning with Hitchens, there is actually relatively little to say. His *God is Not Great* is a straightforward anti-religious polemic, something at which the author notoriously excelled throughout his career, whether in defense of Trotskyism or of the Bush administration's invasion of Iraq. The book is simply not about science per se, focusing mostly on philosophical (if not original) and historical arguments against both the general idea of the existence of god and the specific scriptures of the Judeo-Christian-Islamic tradition.

Things become more complex with Daniel Dennett's *Breaking the Spell*, which is very much about science, but in a distinctive (and, I argue, more sophisticated) sense than that shared by the majority of the New Atheists. The major thrust of the book is to turn the table on the standard take concerning the science–religion controversies, putting forth in some detail the idea that religion itself can (and should) be the target of scientific investigation. Religion, as Dennett puts it, not only cannot make a coherent case for the supernatural, but is itself a natural phenomenon, something that a particular species of large-brained social primates invented for a variety of reasons (it helps with prosocial behavior, it validates structural hierarchies of power, it plays on human beings' innate tendency to overinterpret patterns in the world and to project agency onto the world). Although I disagree with some of Dennett's specific ideas (e.g., I am still baffled by why he takes the concept of "memes" seriously), this is no exercise in scientism. Indeed, whether there is a supernatural realm or not, much of what Dennett says about scientific investigations into the human cultural phenomenon of religion still applies.

Things change dramatically, for the purposes of this paper, when we consider the Dawkins–Stenger–Harris trio, in whose books the scientist turn of New Atheism is particularly evident and problematic.[10] The most impactful of this subset of New Atheist works is surely Dawkins's *The God Delusion*, which has been criticized on different grounds, ranging from a failure to engage with serious theology (assuming there is such thing) or at least philosophy of religion, to caricaturing its target into a hardly recognizable straw man, to eschewing counter-criticism aimed at highlighting the carnage that has historically been brought about by secular-atheistic regimes during the twentieth century.

While *The God Delusion* is all over the map, covering for instance material common to both Hitchens (critique of Judeo-Christian-Islamic scriptures) and Dennett (sketching hypotheses about the cultural evolution of religion), the topics that are most germane to our discussions are: (1) Dawkins's revisitation of the standard arguments for the existence of god; (2) his discussion about the possibility of morality without gods; and of course (3) the centerpiece of his book: the idea that "the god hypothesis" is sufficiently akin to a scientific hypothesis so that science-based evidence becomes the major reason to reject it.

Concerning (1), Dawkins here is simply rehashing a number of well-known philosophical objections to a particular idea of god (again, the Judeo-Christian-Islamic one). Not only do several such objections not apply to a number of other concepts of gods (especially the more rarefied, deistic, flavor), but they are neither new nor do they have much to do with science per se. In (2), Dawkins discusses the possible naturalistic origins of gods and religions and then addresses the question of why being moral without gods. Besides the fact that his treatment of various hypotheses for the cultural evolution of religion is somewhat superficial (and slanted: Dawkins really dislikes even the possibility of group selective explanations), that part of the discussion is of course irrelevant to the main purpose of the book: it may very well turn out that human beings have evolved religions and their concepts of gods because of their biological–cultural makeup, and yet that gods or a supernatural realm actually do exist, in some form or another. When it comes to the issue of why being moral, however, Dawkins shows most clearly his limitations. For instance, he seems to be unaware of what many philosophers consider by far the most powerful argument in favor of the idea that gods and morality are entirely logically independent issues: the so-called Euthyphro dilemma posed by Plato in

10. Interestingly, and I do not think at all coincidentally, these three authors are the chief New Atheists with science backgrounds (and to this list we could easily add evolutionary biologist Jerry Coyne and developmental biologist P. Z. Myers, as mentioned previously), though Stenger has long since retired from physics, Dawkins has not put out technical works in decades, and Harris has turned to a career as a full-time author after completing his PhD in neuroscience.

the homonymous dialogue from 24 centuries ago.[11] Moreover, of course, the positive argument in favor of secular morality has been made forcefully and comprehensively by a number of philosophers throughout the past two millennia, from Socrates in *The Republic* to Immanuel Kant and John Stuart Mill. Science here is simply not needed, and its role is largely confined to the—again completely distinct—question of how a sense of morality may have evolved biologically, as opposed to how morality itself is justified logically.

Finally, let us turn to point (3), the part of the book devoted to a scientific examination of "the god hypothesis." Here Dawkins does manage to reasonably bring up scientific notions that, for instance, make ideas like a young earth, or the slightly more sophisticated concept of "irreducible complexity" championed by Intelligent Design proponents, clearly untenable. Nonetheless, in the end he has to resort to philosophical aid, what he refers to as his "argument from improbability," which is essentially an invocation of Occam's razor. That is not a problem in and of itself, since after all Occam's razor—as much as it is clearly an extra-empirical criterion—is routinely invoked within scientific practice. The real issue is that Dawkins (and most if not all of the New Atheists) does not seem to appreciate the fact that there is no coherent or sensible way in which the idea of god can possibly be considered a "hypothesis" in any sense remotely resembling the scientific sense of the term. The problem is that the supernatural, by its own (human) nature, is simply too swishy to be pinpointed precisely enough. For instance, while of course the notion of a planet earth that is only a few thousand years old is scientifically laughable and contradicts much that we think we know about how the universe works, young earth creationists are largely unfazed by what should be an insurmountable obstacle. That's because they (think they) have a plethora of options at their disposal, ranging from rejecting "materialistic" science altogether to my favorite, a doctrine sometimes referred to as "Last Thursdaysm," according to which it simply looks like the universe is billions of years old and the geological column abundant with fossils, but in reality the whole thing was created *ex nihilo* last Thursday to make it look that way and test our faith. It is germane to note that Last Thursdaysm is both ridiculous on the face of it and absolutely impregnable by scientific analysis. It does, however, have nasty theological consequences that any graduate student in the philosophy of religion would quickly be able to point out.

To recap, then, what is considered to be perhaps the quintessential text of the New Atheism is an odd mishmash of scientific speculation (on the origins of religion), historically badly informed polemic, and rehashing of philosophical arguments. Yet Dawkins and his followers present *The God Delusion* as a shining example of how science has dealt a fatal blow to the idea of gods.

My treatment of Victor Stenger's contributions will be shorter insofar as this author makes the same mistake as Dawkins, only in the realm of physics rather than biology. Stenger's primary contribution in this area came out in 2007, the year after *The God Delusion*, and the title pretty much summarizes the author's intent and approach: *God: The Failed Hypothesis; How Science Shows That God Does Not Exist*. Just like Dawkin's volume, Stenger's is an odd mix of standard arguments

---

11. See <http://classics.mit.edu/Plato/euthyfro.html>

against the existence of god, comments on how morality is possible without gods, and actual treatment of the relevant scientific evidence for the alleged "hypothesis." Besides the obvious fact that one can genuinely be puzzled by what exactly qualifies Stenger (or Dawkins) to authoritatively comment on the straightforward philosophical matters that make up most of their books, the basic problem with Stenger is precisely the same as Dawkins: he treats the "god hypothesis" as if it were formulated precisely and coherently enough to qualify as a scientific hypothesis, which it manifestly isn't, for the reasons already explained. It is, of course, this very insistence on the part of Dawkins, Stenger, and others that provides the bulk of the evidence for the conclusion that the New Atheism movement has a markedly scientific flavor which was missing from its historical predecessors.

The last example I will consider here is somewhat different: Sam Harris's *The Moral Landscape: How Science Can Determine Human Values*. This book is not part of the early "canon" of New Atheism, and in fact it is not directly about atheism at all. But it is by one of the major proponents of the movement, has been well received, and is another spectacular example of scientism on the part of the New Atheists. Harris's project is as ambitious as it is misguided: he doesn't just make the (rather uncontroversial) claim that empirical evidence ("science," very broadly construed) is relevant to moral reasoning. No serious philosopher, I hope, would disagree with that. His project, rather, as clearly stated in the subtitle of the book, is to bypass philosophy altogether and provide a scientific determination of moral values.

Harris is motivated here by the same basic goals shared by all New Atheists: to wrestle a significant sphere of human concern—in this case morality—from the nefarious grips of religion. Harris, like Dawkins, is also worried about postmodern moral relativism, which he sees as prevalent within the academic left, and considers to be just as pernicious as religion's claim to be the source of morality. It is this second worry that seems to motivate much of Harris's acrimony toward (and dismissal of) philosophy. The irony, I think, is that the best answers to both of those concerns come from serious philosophy, not from science.

But let us consider Harris's approach in some more detail.[12] Harris undermines his own project right off the bat, in two notes that appear in the opening pages, but are conveniently tucked in at the back of his book. In the second note to the Introduction, he acknowledges that he "do[es] not intend to make a hard distinction between 'science' and other intellectual contexts in which we discuss 'facts.' " If that is the case, if we get to define "science" as any type of rational–empirical inquiry into "facts" (the scare quotes are his), then we are talking about something that is not at all what most readers are likely to understand when they pick up a book with a subtitle that says How *Science* Can Determine Human Values (my emphasis). One can reasonably smell a bait and switch here. Second, in the first footnote to chapter 1, Harris says: "Many of my critics fault me for not engaging more directly with the academic literature on moral philosophy . . . [but] I am convinced that every appearance of terms like 'metaethics,' 'deontology,' . . .

---

12. Part of what follows is adapted from a book review of Harris's volume that appeared in *Skeptic* magazine.

directly increases the amount of boredom in the universe." This is so mind-boggling that I had to reread it several times: Harris is saying that the whole of the only field other than religion that has ever dealt with ethics is to be dismissed because he personally finds it boring. Is that a fact or a value judgment, I wonder?

As I said, Harris wants to deliver moral decision making to science because he wants to defeat the evil (if oddly paired) twins of religious fanaticism and leftist moral relativism. Despite the fact that I think he grossly overestimates the pervasiveness of the latter, we are together on this. Except of course that the best arguments against both positions are philosophical, not scientific. The most convincing reason why gods cannot possibly have anything to do with morality was presented 24 centuries ago by Plato, in the already mentioned (in the context of Dawkins's book) *Euthyphro* dialogue, and which goes, predictably, entirely unmentioned in *The Moral Landscape*. Needless to say, moral relativism, too, has been the focus of sustained and devastating attack in philosophy, for instance by thinkers such as Peter Singer and Simon Blackburn, and this is all to be found in the large ethical and metaethical literature that Harris finds so increases the degree of boredom in the universe.

Harris's chief claim throughout the book is that moral judgments are a kind of fact, and that as such they are amenable to scientific inquiry. First of all, the second statement does not at all follow from the first. Surely we can agree that the properties of triangles in Euclidean geometry are "facts," in the sense that nobody who understands Euclidean geometry can opine that the sum of the angles in a triangle is not 180° and get away with it. But we do not use science, or any kind of empirical evidence at all, to arrive at agreement about such facts. At the very least, and without wanting to push an argument for moral realism, this makes the point that "facts" is too heterogeneous a category, and that Harris needs to be much more careful on how to handle it.

Harris wants science—and particularly neuroscience (which just happens to be his own specialty)—to help us out of our moral quandaries. But the reader will await in vain throughout the book to find a single example of new moral insights that science provides us with. Harris, for instance, tells us that genital mutilation of young girls is wrong. I agree, but certainly we have no need of fMRI scans to tell us why: the fact that certain regions of the brain are involved in pain and suffering, and that we might be able to measure exactly the degree of those emotions doesn't add anything at all to the conclusion that genital mutilation is wrong because it violates an individual's right to physical integrity and to avoid pain unless absolutely necessary (e.g., during a surgical operation to save one's life, if no anesthetic is available).

Indeed, at some point Harris' argument becomes puzzling to the point of absurdity: on page 121 and the immediately following text Harris observes that the medial prefrontal cortex of the brain shows a similar pattern of activity when people are asked about their mathematical beliefs and when they were queried about their ethical beliefs. From this, he concludes: "This suggests that the physiology of belief may be the same regardless of a proposition's intent. It also suggests that the division between facts and values does not make much sense in terms of underlying brain function.... This finding of content-independence challenges the fact/value distinction very directly: for if, from the point of view of the brain, believing 'the sun is a star' is importantly similar to believing 'cruelty is wrong,' how can we say that scientific and ethical judgments have nothing in common?" I will leave it to the reader to work out why this is a colossal nonsequitur, and arguably the silliest thing written by any of the New Atheists to date.

V

I have argued throughout this paper that what really characterizes the New Atheism, as distinct from previous versions of atheism, is its marked turn toward scientism. This move has been accompanied—almost by definition—by an overt hostility to philosophy, even by philosophers like Daniel Dennett and especially Alex Rosenberg. My position is not just descriptive, however, but prescriptive: I maintain—as a scientist and philosopher—that such a move has been a bad one for public atheism, for three reasons:

1. *Scientism is philosophically unsound.* This is because a scientistic attitude is one of unduly expanding the reach of science into areas where either it does not belong (e.g., determining human values, *à la* Harris) or it can only play a supportive role (e.g., providing empirical evidence against supernaturalistic claims, *à la* Dawkins and Stenger). I am not here engaging in a parochial defense of philosophical turf, as I see both science and philosophy as crucial to atheism in particular, and to human understanding in general. Nor am I endorsing a simple demarcation criterion between science and philosophy (or science and anything else, for that matter).[13] Science is best conceived as a family, in the Wittgensteinian sense, of activities having a variety of threads in common, including but not limited to the systematic carrying out of observations and/or experiments, the testing of hypotheses, the construction of general theories about the functioning of the world, the operation of a system of pre- and postpublication peer review, and the existence of a variety of public and private funding sources for projects deemed to be worthwhile.

What I do object to is the tendency, found among many New Atheists, to expand the definition of science to pretty much encompassing anything that deals with "facts," loosely conceived. So broadened, the concept of science loses meaning and it becomes indistinguishable from just about any other human activity. One might as well define "philosophy" as the discipline that deals with thinking and then claim that everything we do, including of course science itself, properly belongs to philosophy. It would be a puerile and useless exercise, and yet it is not far from the attitude prevalent among the New Atheists.

---

13. Indeed, I coedited an entire collection on the demarcation problem which is meant to provide a nuanced approach to this difficult epistemological issue: *Philosophy of Pseudoscience: Reconsidering the Demarcation Problem*, ed. Massimo Pigliucci and Maarten Boudry (Chicago: University of Chicago Press, 2013).

Moreover, it seems clear to me that most of the New Atheists (except for the professional philosophers among them) pontificate about philosophy very likely without having read a single professional paper in that field. If they had, they would have no trouble recognizing philosophy as a distinct (and, I maintain, useful) academic discipline from science: read side by side, science and philosophy papers have precious little to do with each other, in terms not just of style, but of structure, scope, and range of concerns. I would actually go so far as to charge many of the leaders of the New Atheism movement (and, by implication, a good number of their followers) with anti-intellectualism, one mark of which is a lack of respect for the proper significance, value, and methods of another field of intellectual endeavor.

2. *Scientism does a disservice to science.* Despite representing a strong attempt to expand the intellectual territory, as well as prestige, of science, I think that scientism is detrimental to science in at least two ways: internally to the discipline itself, because it represents a misunderstanding of what science is and how it works, which is unlikely to serve well either practicing scientists or graduate students as scientists-in-training; externally because it has the potential of undermining public understanding and damaging the reputation of science.

Take the United States as a quintessential example of the culture wars within Western countries. Scientists enjoy a very high degree of respect among the American public,[14] and yet certain scientific notions, like evolution[15] and climate change,[16] are under constant attack and are rejected by about half of the population. Scientists in the United States, therefore, have been threading for a while in a cultural environment that displays a somewhat disjointed attitude toward their profession. The last thing they need is to project an aura of arrogance where they pretend to single-handedly settle delicate issues such as the existence of gods or the foundations of morality—especially when science is not, in fact, well equipped to do so anyway.

3. *Scientism does a disservice to atheism.* Finally, I maintain that a scientistic turn does not do much good to atheism as a serious philosophical position to begin with, contra the obvious explicit belief of many if not all of the New Atheists. This—it should be clear by now, but perhaps bears repetition—is most certainly not because science is irrelevant to atheism. On the contrary, atheism makes increasingly more sense the more science succeeds in explaining the nature of the world in naturalistic terms. After all, Hume's arguments against intelligent design were devastating, but he lacked an alternative explanation for the appearance of design in nature, and it was Darwin that provided it. Indeed, I think the Hume–Darwin

---

14. <http://www.people-press.org/2009/07/09/public-praises-science-scientists-fault-public-media/>

15. <http://www.pewforum.org/science-and-bioethics/public-opinion-on-religion-and-science-in-the-united-states.aspx>

16. <http://www.usclimatenetwork.org/hot-topics/climate-polling>

joint dispatching of ID is an excellent example of how naturalism—qua philosophical position—is the result of the inextricable link between sound philosophy and good science.

But what the New Atheists seem to be aiming at is a replacement of philosophy by science, or at the very least a significant demotion of the former with respect to the latter. And this appears to be the case even among the philosophers who count themselves as New Atheists, Dennett and Rosenberg chief among them. This ends up diminishing the case for atheism and allied positions about gods, as they lose some of the the strong intellectual ground that has been their hallmark since the Greek atomists.

VI

Assuming my critique of what is actually new about the New Atheism hits the mark, one can still pose the reasonable question of what might be the most constructive way for atheists of the new generations to look upon their metaphysical position, and in particular upon how it relates to both sound philosophical and scientific notions. I think that atheists need to seriously reconsider how they think of human knowledge in general, perhaps arching back to the classic concept of "scientia," the Latin word from which "science" derives, but that has a broader connotation of (rationally arrived at) knowledge. Scientia includes science *sensu stricto*, philosophy, mathematics, and logic—that is, all the reliable sources of third-person knowledge that humanity has successfully experimented with so far. In turn, when scientia is combined with input from other humanistic disciplines, the arts, and first-person experience it yields understanding.[17]

What the atheist movement needs, therefore, is not a brute force turn toward science at the expense of everything else, but rather a more nuanced, comprehensive embracing of all the varied ways—intellectual as well as experiential—in which human beings acquire knowledge and develop understanding of their world. A healthy respect for, and cooperation with, other disciplines should be the hallmark of the twenty-first century atheist, and this is precisely the direction toward which some post–New Atheism writers, such as De Botton and Grayling (not at all coincidentally, both philosophers) have been pushing most recently. That path, rather than the one attempted by the New Atheists, is the one that I think has the most potential to lead to a long-standing rational and persuasive case for atheism.

---

17. I expand on this idea here: <http://www.aeonmagazine.com/world-views/massimo-pigliucci-on-consilience/>

The New Atheists and the Cosmological Argument

EDWARD FESER

Cosmological arguments for the existence of God purport to show that the world exists only because it is caused to exist by a First Uncaused Cause. They have, in the history of Western philosophy and theology, been the central sort of philosophical argument for God's existence. The basic idea was developed in various ways by Plato, Aristotle, and the Neoplatonic tradition; Muslim thinkers like Al-Ghazali, Avicenna, and Averroes; Jewish philosophers like Maimonides; Christian Scholastic thinkers such as Bonaventure, Aquinas, Scotus, and Suarez; rationalist metaphysicians like Leibniz and Clarke; and empiricists like Locke and Berkeley. Even Anselm, better known for the ontological argument for the existence of God, also defended a version of the cosmological argument. Twentieth-century Thomist writers such as Reginald Garrigou-Lagrange, Jacques Maritain, Etienne Gilson, and Mortimer Adler defended it. In recent philosophy, versions of the argument have been defended by Bruce Reichenbach, Richard Taylor, Richard Swinburne, Robert Koons, Richard Gale and Alexander Pruss, John Haldane, Christopher Martin, David Oderberg, Brian Davies, William Lane Craig, and others.[1]

---

1. For this recent work, see for example, Bruce Reichenbach, *The Cosmological Argument: A Reassessment* (Springfield, IL: Charles C. Thomas, 1972); Richard Taylor, *Metaphysics*, 4th ed. (Englewood Cliffs, NJ: Prentice-Hall, 1992); Richard Swinburne, *The Existence of God* (Oxford: Clarendon Press, 1979); Robert C. Koons, "A New Look at the Cosmological Argument," *American Philosophical Quarterly* 34 (1997): 193–211; Richard M. Gale and Alexander R. Pruss, "A New Cosmological Argument," in *The Existence of God*, ed. Richard M. Gale and Alexander R. Pruss (Burlington, VT: Ashgate, 2003); J. J. C. Smart and J. J. Haldane, *Atheism and Theism* (Oxford:

© 2013 Wiley Periodicals, Inc.

The writers whose best-sellers inaugurated the "New Atheist" movement include, most famously, Richard Dawkins, Christopher Hitchens, Sam Harris, and Daniel C. Dennett.[2] Other writers who have contributed to the New Atheist literature include Victor J. Stenger, Lawrence M. Krauss, and Alex Rosenberg.[3] Some recent works of popular science from Peter Atkins and Stephen Hawking and Leonard Mlodinow also evince something like a New Atheist attitude toward religion.[4] Among the elements which make the atheism of these writers "new" is the easy confidence with which they suppose that the traditional arguments for God's existence can, at least at this point in history, be dismissed out of hand as unworthy of any further serious consideration. Hitchens avers that "we [will] never again have to confront the impressive faith of an Aquinas or a Maimonides" insofar as "[r]eligion comes from the period of human prehistory where nobody . . . had the smallest idea what was going on" whereas "[t]oday the least educated of my children knows much more about the natural order than any of the founders of religion."[5] Science, in short, has put religion, including philosophy of religion, out of business for good. Dawkins assures his readers that Aquinas's Five Ways (which include several versions of the cosmological argument) are "easily . . . exposed as vacuous."[6] Rosenberg thinks such exposure is not even worth the effort, telling his own book's readers that:

> [W]e won't treat theism as a serious alternative that stills [sic] needs to be refuted. This book's intended readers have moved past that point. We know the truth.[7]

That the self-confidence of the New Atheists is massively out of proportion to their knowledge and understanding of the actual arguments of theologians and philosophers of religion has by now been established by their critics many times

---

Blackwell, 1996); Christopher F. J. Martin, *Thomas Aquinas: God and Explanations* (Edinburgh: Edinburgh University Press, 1997); David S. Oderberg, "Traversal of the Infinite, the 'Big Bang' and the Kalam Cosmological Argument," *Philosophia Christi* 4 (2002): 305–34; Brian Davies, *The Reality of God and the Problem of Evil* (London: Continuum, 2006); and William Lane Craig, *The Kalām Cosmological Argument* (New York: Barnes and Noble, 1979).

2. See Richard Dawkins, *The God Delusion* (New York: Houghton Mifflin, 2006); Christopher Hitchens, *God Is Not Great* (New York: Twelve, 2007); Sam Harris, *The End of Faith* (New York: Norton, 2004); Sam Harris, *Letter to a Christian Nation* (New York: Alfred A. Knopf, 2006); and Daniel C. Dennett, *Breaking the Spell: Religion as a Natural Phenomenon* (New York: Viking, 2006).

3. See for example, Victor J. Stenger, *God: The Failed Hypothesis* (Amherst, NY: Prometheus Books, 2008); Victor J. Stenger, *God and the Folly of Faith* (Amherst, NY: Prometheus Books, 2012); Lawrence M. Krauss, *A Universe from Nothing* (New York: Free Press, 2012); and Alex Rosenberg, *The Atheist's Guide to Reality* (New York: W. W. Norton, 2011).

4. Peter Atkins, *On Being* (Oxford: Oxford University Press, 2011); Stephen Hawking and Leonard Mlodinow, *The Grand Design* (New York: Bantam Books, 2010).

5. Hitchens, *God Is Not Great*, pp. 63–64.

6. Dawkins, *The God Delusion*, p. 77.

7. Rosenberg, *The Atheist's Guide to Reality*, p. xii.

over.[8] My aim in what follows is to show in a more systematic way than has perhaps been done before how, in the particular case of the cosmological argument—which has, again, historically been the central argument for the existence of God—the objections raised by the New Atheists draw no blood. There are two reasons why these objections are worth answering, despite their philosophical shallowness. The first is that the New Atheists have many readers who are philosophically unsophisticated, and who will for that reason falsely suppose that their objections carry weight. The second is that—as is evidenced by the fact that Dennett and Rosenberg are to be numbered among the New Atheists—even many professional philosophers who are not experts in the philosophy of religion are prone to endorse some of the same superficial objections. To debunk New Atheist criticisms of the cosmological argument is, sad to say, to debunk much of what passes for the conventional wisdom on the subject in academic philosophy (again, at least outside the circles of professional philosophers of religion).

Much of the superficiality that surrounds criticism of the argument derives from the fact that the criticism is commonly directed at a nearly omnipresent straw man—an argument that is widely regarded as representing the basic thrust of the cosmological argument, but which in fact bears no interesting relationship to what any of the defenders of the argument referred to above have ever actually said. In the next section of this paper, I will identify this straw man in the hope that the otherwise unwary reader will be forewarned not to presuppose either that defenders of the cosmological argument are committed to it, or that objections to the straw man have any tendency to cast doubt on what defenders of the cosmological argument actually do say. In the subsequent section I will summarize four representative approaches that actually have been taken historically to spelling out a cosmological argument, which I call the *act/potency approach*, the *simplicity/composition approach*, the *necessity/contingency approach*, and the *kalām approach*. In the final section, I will survey the objections against the cosmological argument raised by New Atheist writers, and show that whether or not they have force against the straw man version of the argument, they completely fail as refutations of any the approaches actually taken by the argument's defenders.

I hasten to emphasize that I do not pretend that what I have to say in this paper suffices to show, all by itself, that the cosmological argument ultimately succeeds (though my own view is that at least some versions of it do succeed). To

---

8. I have criticized the four original New Atheists at length in *The Last Superstition: A Refutation of the New Atheism* (South Bend, IN: St. Augustine's Press, 2008). I reviewed Rosenberg's and Krauss's books in *First Things* magazine, in the November 2011 and June/July 2012 issues, respectively. I reviewed Hawking and Mlodinow's book in the November 29, 2010 issue of *National Review*, and Atkins's book in the Winter 2011/2012 issue of *The Claremont Review of Books*. Among the great many other critiques of the New Atheists are David Berlinksi, *The Devil's Delusion: Atheism and Its Scientific Pretensions* (New York: Crown Forum, 2008); Terry Eagleton, *Reason, Faith, and Revolution: Reflections on the God Debate* (New Haven, CT: Yale University Press, 2009); David Bentley Hart, *Atheist Delusions: The Christian Revolution and Its Fashionable Enemies* (New Haven, CT: Yale University Press, 2009); Alvin Plantinga, *Where the Conflict Really Lies: Science, Religion, and Naturalism* (Oxford: Oxford University Press, 2011); and Keith Ward, *Why There Almost Certainly Is a God: Doubting Dawkins* (Oxford: Lion UK, 2008).

make that case would require a book. What I do claim to show is that the criticisms raised by the New Atheists are intellectually unserious.

WHAT THE COSMOLOGICAL ARGUMENT DOES NOT SAY

Dennett begins the single paragraph he devotes to the cosmological argument as follows:

> The Cosmological Argument ... in its simplest form states that since everything must have a cause the universe must have a cause—namely, God ...[9]

The assumption that this is the basic thrust of the cosmological argument is, as I say, by no means confined to New Atheist polemical literature. It can be found not only in purportedly neutral works of pop philosophy but even in at least one book by someone who specializes in the philosophy of religion. Robin Le Poidevin summarizes what he calls "the basic cosmological argument," of which at least some other versions are "modifications," this way:

1. Anything that exists has a cause of its existence.
2. Nothing can be the cause of its own existence.
3. The universe exists.

Therefore: The universe has a cause of its existence which lies outside the universe.[10]

Examples of similar summaries of the argument could easily be multiplied.[11] The standard next move of those presenting these summaries is, of course, to suggest that the argument founders on the obvious retort: If everything has a cause, then what caused God? If the response is that nothing caused God, then, the critic maintains, we might as well say that nothing caused the universe. The critics also sometimes suggest that the argument gratuitously assumes that the universe had a beginning, whereas if we suppose instead that it did not, the pressure to look for a first cause of any sort disappears. More complex versions of the cosmological argument are then sometimes treated as if they were desperate and doomed attempts to patch up the glaring holes in this "basic cosmological argument."

The problem is this: *Not one of the many prominent defenders of the cosmological argument referred to above ever actually put forward anything like this*

---

9. Dennett, *Breaking the Spell*, p. 242.
10. Robin Le Poidevin, *Arguing for Atheism: An Introduction to the Philosophy of Religion* (London: Routledge, 1996), p. 4.
11. Further examples taken mostly just from books lying around my study would be Michael Martin, *Atheism: A Philosophical Justification* (Philadelphia: Temple University Press, 1990), at p. 96; Graham Priest, *Logic: A Very Short Introduction* (Oxford: Oxford University Press, 2000), at pp. 21–22; Bertrand Russell, *Why I Am Not a Christian* (New York: Simon and Schuster, 1957), at p. 6; Jenny Teichman and Katherine C. Evans, *Philosophy: A Beginner's Guide*, 2nd ed. (Blackwell, 1995), at p. 22; Nigel Warburton, *Philosophy: The Basics*, 4th ed. (London: Routledge, 2004), at p. 17; and Rebecca Newberger Goldstein's philosophical novel *36 Arguments for the Existence of God: A Work of Fiction* (New York: Pantheon, 2010), at p. 348.

so-called "basic cosmological argument." In particular—and to hammer the point home—you will not find such an argument in Plato, Aristotle, Plotinus, Al-Ghazali, Avicenna, Averroes, Maimonides, Anselm, Bonaventure, Aquinas, Scotus, Suarez, Leibniz, Clarke, Locke, Berkeley, Garrigou-Lagrange, Maritain, Gilson, Adler, Reichenbach, Taylor, Swinburne, Koons, Gale, Pruss, Haldane, Martin, Oderberg, Davies, Craig, or, as far as I know, in any other philosopher who has defended the cosmological argument. Indeed, Le Poidevin (who, as a philosopher of religion, is better informed about the subject than the other critics quoted above) admits as much, writing that "no-one has defended a cosmological argument of precisely this form."[12] He just thinks it "provides a useful stepping-stone to the other, more sophisticated, versions" of the argument.

This is, when you think about it, extremely odd. Suppose "Intelligent Design" theorists routinely characterized "the basic Darwinian thesis" as the claim that at some point in the distant past a monkey gave birth to a human baby. Suppose they never cited any sources for this claim (which, of course, they couldn't do, since no Darwinian has ever said such a thing) and even admitted that no one has ever defended it. But suppose that they nevertheless suggested that it "provides a useful stepping-stone to the other, more sophisticated, versions" of Darwinism. Darwinians would rightly be outraged, objecting that such a procedure gets the whole discussion off on the wrong foot, and in particular conveys the false impression that anything Darwinians have to say about human origins is really just a desperate exercise in patching up a manifestly absurd position. Yet it is precisely that sort of false impression that is conveyed by the insinuation that the thinkers cited above, however complex their arguments, are all ultimately in the business of trying to salvage or "modify" something that at bottom amounts to what Le Poidevin characterizes as "the basic cosmological argument."

Nor could it honestly be suggested by anyone familiar with the work of defenders of the cosmological argument that they are at least *implicitly* committed to the so-called "basic cosmological argument." For one thing, none of the thinkers in question actually appeals to the premise that "everything has a cause." Indeed, some of them either explicitly or implicitly *deny* that everything has a cause! For another thing, none of the defenders of the argument cited above *assumes* that the universe had a beginning, and only one version of the argument (the *kalām* approach) is even concerned to try to *show* that it did. Indeed, many versions do not even require as a premise any claim about the universe *as a whole* in the first place.

But if defenders of the cosmological argument not only do not assume, but in fact often deny, that everything has a cause; if most of them not only do not assume that the universe had a beginning but are not even interested in the question of whether it did; and if many of them are not even arguing in the first place from any premise about the universe considered as a whole; then it is, to say the very least, highly misleading to begin a discussion of the cosmological argument the way Dennett and so many others do.

---

12. Le Poidevin, *Arguing for Atheism*, p. 4.

WHAT THE COSMOLOGICAL ARGUMENT DOES SAY

So, as we turn to an exposition of the main approaches to developing a cosmological argument, readers who are used to looking at the argument through the lens of what Le Poidevin calls the "basic" argument are asked to put that straw man out of their minds and to try to see the issue with fresh eyes. Let's consider each approach in turn.

The Act/Potency Approach

Aristotle's argument for an Unmoved Mover of the world was grounded in his theory of act and potency, which was developed in response to the claim of Parmenides and other Eleatic philosophers that change is an illusion. Parmenides had argued that change would have to involve *being* arising from *nonbeing*, which is impossible given that nonbeing is just nothing, and from nothing nothing can arise. What Parmenides failed to see, in Aristotle's view, is that between complete being or *actuality* on the one hand and nonbeing or sheer nothingness on the other hand, there is a middle ground of *potency* or potential being. For example, we might say of a certain rubber ball that it is actually red in color, solid, spherical, and sitting motionless in a drawer; and we might note as well that it is in no way a stone, a squirrel, or a Buick Skylark. But while it is actually solid and spherical while not being even potentially a squirrel, it *is* at least potentially flat and squishy (if you melt it, say). Its potency or potential for being flat and squishy is real—it is not nothing or nonbeing, even though the flatness and squishiness are not actual. And change, for Aristotle, does not involve being, full stop, arising from nonbeing, but rather "being in act" or *actual* being arising from "being in potency" or *potential* being. Change is the actualization of a potency, where the potency is something real even before it is actualized.

While the jargon of act and potency might seem archaic to many contemporary philosophers, the notions to which they refer are by no means outdated. On the contrary, the debate in contemporary metaphysics over causal powers, capacities, and categorical versus dispositional properties is essentially a revival of concerns that would have been familiar to any Aristotelian Scholastic philosopher—"powers," "dispositions," and "capacities" being more or less what the Aristotelian would call "potencies," and "categorical properties" being more or less what the Aristotelian would call "actualities." Indeed, that realism about causal powers and/or dispositions amounts to a revival of Aristotelian and Scholastic notions is now fairly widely recognized by those involved in the debate.[13]

When the theory of causation of which the theory of act and potency is the core is worked out, the Aristotelian arrives at two further notions relevant to the

---

13. For a useful brief survey of the recent debate, see Stephen Mumford, "Causal Powers and Capacities," in Helen Beebee, Christopher Hitchcock, and Peter Menzies, eds., *The Oxford Handbook of Causation* (Oxford: Oxford University Press, 2009). For a book-length survey, see Brian Ellis, *The Philosophy of Nature: A Guide to the New Essentialism* (Chesham, UK: Acumen, 2002). For a collection of articles, see John Greco and Ruth Groff, eds., *Powers and Capacities in Philosophy: The New Aristotelianism* (London: Routledge, 2013).

argument for the Unmoved Mover. The first is that *a potential can be actualized only by something already actual.* This is a version of what Scholastic writers called the "principle of causality," and it is important to take note of what it does and does not imply. It *does* imply that the actualization of a potential always has a cause; when, for instance, the rubber ball becomes flat and squishy, that is only because something already actual (the heat of a microwave oven, say) caused that to happen. For the potential flatness and squishiness, precisely because it is *merely* potential, cannot have actualized itself. The principle does *not* imply, however, that *everything* has a cause. Indeed, the Aristotelian would *deny* that everything requires a cause. A potency or potential cannot actualize itself because it is, again, merely potential and not actual, and only what is actual can do anything. That is why it needs a cause. But what is already actual does not need a cause, precisely because it is already actual. Now in general things are mixtures of actuality and potentiality—actual in some respects, potential in others—and thus while they do not require causes in some respects, they do require them in others. But suppose there were something that was *pure actuality*, with no potentials in need of actualization. Then it would be something that not only does not in any respect have a cause, but could not in principle have had one or needed one.

The other relevant further notion is the distinction between *accidentally ordered* series of causes on the one hand, and *essentially ordered* series on the other hand. The stock example of the former is a series consisting of a father who begets a son, who in turn begets another, who in turn begets another. The stock example of the latter is a hand which pushes a stick which in turn pushes a stone. The key difference is that in the former case each member of the series has *independent* causal power, while in the latter the members have *derivative* causal power. Once begotten, a son has the power to beget further sons of his own even in the absence of his father. This power is "built in," as it were. But the stick has no power on its own to move the stone. It derives its causal power to push the stone from the hand that uses it to push the stone. The hand's continual action is essential to the existence of the causal series in a way that a father's continued action is not essential to the existence of the series of begetters.

Now on analysis, the Aristotelian holds, it turns out that any essentially ordered series of causes must terminate in a first member. But it is absolutely crucial to understand that "first" here does not mean "first in a temporal sequence," and it doesn't even mean "first in the sense of coming before the second, third, fourth, etc. members of a finitely long series." Rather, what is meant by a "first cause" in this context is "a cause which can impart causal power without having to derive it." The stone's potential for movement is actualized by the stick, but the stick can *actualize* that potential only insofar its own potential for movement is in turn *being actualized* by the hand. Unless this series terminated in something that can actualize without being actualized in the same respect—as I can move the stick without someone in turn picking me up and moving me as I do so—then we would have a vicious regress, a series of causes that have *derivative* causal power without anything *from which to derive it*. The situation would be comparable to a mirror which reflects the image of a face present in another mirror, which in turn reflects the image of a face present in another, and so on *ad infinitum*, with only mirror images and never any actual face. Notice that the *length* of the series is not what is at issue here. Even if there could be an infinitely long series of mirrors each reflecting the image of a face present in the next mirror in the series, there would still have to be something outside this infinite series—the face itself—which could impart the content of the image without having to derive it. Similarly, even if the stick that moves the stone was being moved by another stick, which was in turn moved by another, and so on *ad infinitum*, there would have to be something outside the series of sticks which imparted to them the power to move things, since sticks by themselves have no such power, however many of them you add together.

Now though in examples like the one in question a thing might be a "first cause" in one respect—as I can move the stick without anyone moving me in turn—there are other respects in which it will not be "first," but depend on other things. Most crucially, any material thing will depend on other things for its *existence* at any moment. There are different ways in which this dependence might be understood. For the Aristotelian, natural substances like stones, plants, and animals are to be understood as composites of *prime matter* and *substantial form*, where prime matter is purely potential until informed by a substantial form, and substantial form is a mere abstraction apart from its instantiation in prime matter. This hylemorphic analysis of substances opens the door to an argument to the effect that no material substance can continue in existence even for an instant "under its own steam." For since the prime matter of a material substance depends for its concrete existence on the substance's substantial form, and the substantial form depends for its concrete existence on being realized in prime matter, we would have an explanatory vicious circle unless there were something outside the form-matter composite which actualizes it or keeps it in being.

Alternatively, we could hold (contrary to the standard Aristotelian story) that material substances like stones, plants, and animals are really just aggregates of simpler substances—that they are, say, "nothing but" molecules arranged in such-and-such a way. In that case, too, a material thing will depend for its existence at any moment on something other than it. It will depend, say, on its molecules being arranged in just such-and-such a way; these molecules will in turn depend for their existence at any moment on their atoms being arranged in just such-and-such a way; and so forth.

What we will have either way is a kind of *essentially* ordered causal series, with the potential existence one level of reality actualized by the potential existence of another, which can in turn do this actualizing only insofar as *its* potential existence is actualized by yet another level. For instance, the water in a certain cup will exist at any moment only insofar as a certain potential of its atoms—to constitute water, specifically, rather than (say) separate quantities of oxygen and hydrogen—is actualized; this will in turn depend on the subatomic particles being combined in one specific way rather than another, at that very same moment, which also involves a certain potential being actualized; and so on.

Now since what is being caused in this case is the *existence* of a thing, the only way to end the regress of causes is with something which can impart existence without having to derive it from anything else. That will have to be something whose existence does not in any respect have to be actualized, but just is, already, fully actual—a *purely actual actualizer*, which is, given the analysis of change as the actualization of potency, essentially what Aristotle meant by an unmovable mover ("motion" being understood by Aristotle as synonymous with change).

To be sure, Aristotle himself, as commonly interpreted, was concerned only to explain the change that things exhibit, rather than the existence of the things that change. But some later Aristotelians (and in particular, some Thomistic philosophers) have argued that the basic thrust of the Aristotelian argument can and ought to be extended to an account of the existence of things, as I have done. This, together with the other elements of the Aristotelian position I've sketched out, suggests the following possible summary of a broadly Aristotelian cosmological argument:

1. That the actualization of potency is a real feature of the world follows from the occurrence of the events we know of via sensory experience.
2. The occurrence of any event E presupposes the operation of a substance.
3. The existence of any natural substance S at any given moment presupposes the concurrent actualization of a potency.
4. No mere potency can actualize a potency; only something actual can do so.
5. So any actualizer A of S's current existence must itself be actual.
6. A's own existence at the moment it actualizes S itself presupposes either (a) the concurrent actualization of a further potency or (b) A's being purely actual.
7. If A's existence at the moment it actualizes S presupposes the concurrent actualization of a further potency, then there exists a regress of concurrent actualizers that is either infinite or terminates in a purely actual actualizer.
8. But such a regress of concurrent actualizers would constitute an essentially ordered causal series, and such a series cannot regress infinitely.
9. So either A itself is purely actual or there is a purely actual actualizer which terminates the regress of concurrent actualizers.
10. So the occurrence of E and thus the existence of S at any given moment presupposes the existence of a purely actual actualizer.

Notice a few things about this argument. First, as I have already emphasized, it does not rest on the premise that "everything has a cause"; what it says is that what actualizes a potency must itself be actual (which leaves it open that there is something whose action or existence does not involve the actualization of a potency, and thus does not require a cause). Second, it does not involve tracing a series of accidentally ordered causes backward in time to a cause which is first in a temporal sense, but rather tracing a series of essentially ordered causes existing here and now to a cause which is first in the sense of having its causal power in a nonderivative way. Indeed, most Aristotelians hold that the former sort of series, precisely because it is accidentally ordered, cannot be demonstrated to have a first member, and so they don't bother arguing for a first temporal cause when giving a cosmological argument. Third, the argument does not rest on any premise about the universe as a whole. The conclusion can be arrived at from premises that make reference only to *some natural substance or other*, the hand which moves the stick or whatever. To be sure, any defender of such an argument would go on to say that the purely actual actualizer would in fact be the cause of every other natural substance, and thus of the universe as a whole. But that would be a *consequence* of the argument rather than part of the argument itself.

The reason it would be a consequence of the argument is that there can be only one purely actual actualizer, or so proponents of this sort of argument typically argue. For there is, so the argument goes, no way to make sense of there being more than one instance of a kind of thing other than by attributing to each instance some potency or potentiality. For example, two trees differ because they are made up of different parcels of matter, occupy different regions of space, may also differ in height or color, and so forth. All of that involves potency in various ways; for instance, being material involves potency insofar as matter is always capable of taking on various forms, being at one point in space involves having the potency for being at another, and so on. But what is purely actual has no potency or potentiality. So there is no way to make sense of there being more than one thing that is purely actual. Thus, it is to one and the same purely actual actualizer that we have to trace the existence of everything whose existence needs to be actualized.

Defenders of this sort of argument typically argue that the purely actual actualizer can be shown to have many other attributes as well. Aquinas, for example, who in the first of his Five Ways puts forward a version of the Aristotelian approach to the cosmological argument, goes on later in the *Summa Theologiae* (and in several other works) to argue that a purely actual cause of things would have to be immaterial, immutable, eternal, perfect, omnipotent, omniscient, and so forth. Some of the arguments for these attributes appeal to further theses in general Aristotelian-Thomistic metaphysics. Naturally, that metaphysical system would itself need to be defended, and various possible objections answered, for a successful defense of what I am calling the Aristotelian approach to developing a cosmological argument. But what has been said suffices for the purposes of the present paper, which is to examine the specific objections raised by the New Atheists, to which we will turn after looking at the other main approaches to the cosmological argument.[14]

---

14. I have defended the Aristotelian approach, and Aquinas's First Way in particular, in several places. See *The Last Superstition* for a polemical and semi-popular treatment, and my book *Aquinas* (Oxford: Oneworld Publications, 2009) for a more detailed and academic treatment. I have defended specific aspects of the argument in "Existential Inertia and the Five Ways," *American Catholic Philosophical Quarterly* 85 (2011): 237–67, and "Motion in Aristotle, Newton, and Einstein," in Edward Feser, ed., *Aristotle on Method and Metaphysics* (Basingstoke, UK: Palgrave Macmillan, 2013). For other recent defenses of the Aristotelian approach to the cosmological argument, see chapter 9 of Martin, *Thomas Aquinas: God and Explanations*; chapter 2 of Smart and Haldane, *Atheism and Theism*; chapter 2 of David Conway, *The Rediscovery of Wisdom* (Basingstoke, UK: Macmillan, 2000); and David S. Oderberg, " 'Whatever is Changing is Being Changed by Something Else': A Reappraisal of Premise One of the First Way," in J. Cottingham and P. Hacker, eds., *Mind, Method and Morality: Essays in Honour of Anthony Kenny* (Oxford: Oxford University Press, 2010).

The Simplicity/Composition Approach

Whereas the Aristotelian tradition in natural theology emphasizes that whatever is a mixture of act and potency must ultimately be explained by reference to that which is pure actuality, the Neoplatonic tradition emphasizes that whatever is in any way composite or made up of parts (whether physical or metaphysical parts) must ultimately be explained by reference to that which is utterly noncomposite or metaphysically simple. The idea is that whatever has parts is metaphysically less fundamental than the parts themselves and whatever principle accounts for their combination. The *ultimate* explanation of anything would therefore have to be without parts, otherwise it would not be ultimate but would require a cause of its own.

Lloyd Gerson argues that something like a cosmological argument developing this basic theme is at least implicit in Plotinus.[15] My own outline of Gerson's reconstruction is as follows:

1. There must be a first principle of all if there is to be an explanation of the orderly existing world, or why anything at all exists rather than nothing.
2. If the first principle of all were composed of parts, then those parts would be ontologically prior to it.
3. But in that case it would not be the first principle of all.
4. So the first principle is not composed of parts, but is absolutely simple.
5. If there were a distinction between *what* the first principle is and the fact *that* it is, then there could be more than one first principle.
6. But in order for there to be more than one, there would have to be some attribute that distinguished them.
7. But since a first principle is absolutely simple, there can be no such attribute.
8. So there cannot be more than one first principle.
9. So there is no distinction in the first principle between *what* it is and the fact *that* it is.
10. So the first principle is not only absolutely simple but utterly unique, what Plotinus called "the One."

Let's walk through the argument step by step. (The comments that follow to some extent go beyond what Gerson himself says.) What is meant by a "first principle" in step (1) is, essentially, a bottom-level explanation of things, something that explains everything else without needing an explanation itself. One could reasonably take this premise to be at least implicitly accepted by many atheists no less than by the theist, at least insofar as the atheist regards scientific explanations as terminating in a most fundamental level of physical laws that determine all the rest—whether this takes the form of a "Theory of everything" or instead a conjunction of several physical theories left unreduced to some such single theory. The

---

15. See chapter 1 of Lloyd P. Gerson, *Plotinus* (London: Routledge, 1994) and Gerson's paper "Neoplatonism," in Christopher Shields, ed., *The Blackwell Guide to Ancient Philosophy* (Oxford: Blackwell, 2003).

dispute between Plotinus and such atheists, then, would not be over the *existence* of a "first principle," but rather over its *character*.

Of course, when the attributes of Plotinus's first principle are unpacked—and he goes on to argue that the One must have necessity, infinity, power, omnipresence, goodness, life, and so forth—the atheist might decide to reject premise (1) if that is where it will lead him. He might suggest that the existence of composite things is ultimately inexplicable, a brute fact. But as Gerson notes, this will not do:

> The possibility that the existence of a composite depends on nothing or that it is inexplicable is not considered as a serious one by Plotinus. If this possibility amounts to the claim that it is impossible that there should be an explanation of the existence of a composite, it is difficult not to share Plotinus's diffidence. How could such a thing be shown? If, however, the claim merely amounts to the assertion that, though it is possible that there should be an explanation, there is in fact none, then Plotinus' obvious reply is that he has an explanation at hand and its adequacy needs to be addressed, not by saying that there is no explanation but by showing why his explanation is not satisfactory.[16]

The "parts" referred to in step (2) of the argument are, as I have indicated, parts of any sort, whether material or metaphysical. Again, the idea here is that if a thing is composed of parts, then the parts are more fundamental than it is. Moreover, those parts would need to be combined in order for the thing to exist. (This is true even if the thing has always existed—for there would in that case still have to be something that accounts for why the parts have always been conjoined.) A purported "first principle" with parts just wouldn't be a bottom-level explanation or first principle at all, then—it would in that case need explanation itself, as step (3) says. With step (4), then, we arrive at the simplicity of the first principle of all. But when Plotinus refers to this principle as "the One," he does not mean merely that it has no parts but also that it is utterly unique—that the sort of theism his argument leads us to is necessarily a *mono*theism. That is part of what the next stage of the argument seeks to establish.

It also seeks to establish a thesis that is usually thought to be distinctive of later, Scholastic philosophical theology. The distinction in step (5) between *what* a thing is and *that* it is is, as Gerson says, an anticipation of the famous medieval distinction between a thing's *essence* and its *existence*. In things whose essence and existence are distinct—which, for a Scholastic like Aquinas, is everything other than God—the essence entails a general category under which distinct instances might fall. There is, for example, the essence *human being*, under which Socrates and Plotinus both fall as particular instances, each with its own "act of existing." Similarly, if the essence of the first principle of all were distinct from its existence, there might be *this* "first principle of all" with its act of existing, *that* "first principle of all" with its own act of existing, and so forth.

16. Gerson, *Plotinus*, p. 13.

But for that to be possible, there would, step (6) tells us, have to be some attribute that one "first principle of all" had that the other lacked. And that, Plotinus holds, makes no sense. For then it would be what they did *not* differ with respect to—what they had in *common*—that would be the true first principle of all, since it would be that which ultimately makes each of them the kind of thing it is. That is to say, one "first principle of all" and a second "first principle of all" would each be what it is only because each instantiates the same essence; and in that case it would be the common essence itself, and neither of the individual instances, which (as the explanation of these instances) would be the true first principle. Moreover, we would have in this case a distinction between a first principle and its attributes, which conflicts with the simplicity arrived at in (4). Hence there can be no such attribute (step (7)), and thus no way in principle to distinguish one first principle of all from another (step (8)), and thus no difference between the essence of a first principle and its existence (step (9)). The first principle of all is thus "simple" or without any parts in the strongest possible sense.

Once again we have an argument which raises many questions, but for present purposes I want to emphasize the following points. First, notice that this argument does not rest on the premise that "everything has a cause." What it says is that *what is composite* must have a cause, but of course it also goes on to say that there is something that is *not* composite. Second, the argument is also not concerned to argue for a *temporally* first principle but rather for a principle that is "first" in the sense of being ontologically absolutely fundamental. Third, though Gerson takes Plotinus to be offering an explanation of the universe, it seems that the argument doesn't *need* to start with the universe as its *explanandum*. It could start with *any* composite thing, and argue that *its* ultimate explanation would have to be the One. Naturally, given what Plotinus says, the One would be the explanation of everything other than itself, and thus his position entails that the One is the explanation of the entire universe. But that is an *implication* of the completed argument. The argument need not appeal to any *premise* about the universe as a whole.

The Necessity/Contingency Approach

A third kind of cosmological argument holds that only a necessary being can be the ultimate cause of the contingent things of our experience. Avicenna defended this sort of argument, as did Aquinas in the Third Way. In modern philosophy, however, it is best known from the versions defended by rationalist metaphysicians like Leibniz and Clarke. One way to understand their approach is as an attempt to show how we can get to the sort of conclusion Aristotelians, Neoplatonists, and Thomists arrived at, but without having to commit to their metaphysical premises. In place of the Aristotelian principle that *the actualization of any potential requires a cause* and the Neoplatonic principle that *anything composite requires a cause*—both of which are variations on what is sometimes called "the principle of causality"—the modern rationalist puts the Principle of Sufficient Reason (PSR), according to which there must be a sufficient reason (i.e. an adequate explanation) for why anything exists, any event occurs, or any truth obtains.

There are three key, related differences between the two principles. First, causality is a *metaphysical* notion, whereas PSR makes reference instead to explanation, which is a *logical and epistemological* notion. Second, for that reason, whereas the principle of causality is a statement about mind-independent reality as such, PSR is more along the lines of a "law of thought," a statement about how we have to *think about* mind-independent reality. Of course, for the rationalist, since the structure of reality can be read off from the structure of thought, PSR purports to tell us something about mind-independent reality as well. But it does so less directly, as it were, than the principle of causality does. Third, whereas proponents of the principle of causality typically hold that nothing can cause itself, proponents of PSR typically hold that something can explain itself. (Of course, some philosophers have held that there can be such a thing as a *causa sui* or self-causing being, but it is not clear that this is or coherently could be anything more than a colorful way of talking about a self-*explanatory* being.)

David Blumenfeld reconstructs Leibniz's PSR-based version of the cosmological argument as follows[17]:

1. If anything exists, there must be a sufficient reason why it exists.
2. But this world exists and it is a series of contingent beings.
3. Therefore, there must be a sufficient reason why this series of contingent beings exists.
4. But nothing contingent—and, in particular, neither the existing series as a whole nor any of its members—can contain a sufficient reason why this series exists.
5. A sufficient reason for any existing thing can only be in an existing thing, which is itself either necessary or contingent.
6. Therefore, a sufficient reason why this series exists must be in a necessary being that lies outside the world.
7. Therefore, there is a necessary being that lies outside the world.

The idea behind step (4) of this argument is that since anything contingent could have failed to exist, there is nothing in its nature that can explain why it exists, so that it requires an explanation outside itself. This is as true of a collection of contingent things as it is of a given individual contingent thing, since there is no good reason to suppose that a collection of two contingent things is any less contingent than one of them is taken individually, or that three are any less contingent than two, four any less contingent than three, and so on. It might be suggested that this inference commits a fallacy of composition, but on reflection it is hard to see how. Part-to-whole reasoning is, after all, not per se fallacious. It all depends on what property we are attributing to the whole on the basis of the parts. If I infer from the fact that each individual component of a computer weighs less than a pound that the computer as a whole weighs less than a pound, then I commit a fallacy of composition. But if I infer from the fact that every Lego block that has

---

17. David Blumenfeld, "Leibniz's Ontological and Cosmological Arguments," in Nicholas Jolley, ed., *The Cambridge Companion to Leibniz* (Cambridge: Cambridge University Press, 1995), at p. 367.

gone into constructing a certain wall is red to the conclusion that the wall itself is red, then I have committed no fallacy. And it seems at the very least highly plausible to say that contingency is in this respect more like redness than it is like weight.

Like Aristotle, Plotinus, and Aquinas, Leibniz argues that this ultimate cause of things that he's arrived at can, on analysis, be shown to have various other attributes—which include, Leibniz argues, understanding, will, power, infinity, and unity.

As before, there are various questions and objections that might be raised, some of which we will turn to in a moment, but for now let us note the following. First, yet again we see no commitment to the premise that "everything has a cause." We *do* see a commitment to the claim that everything has an *explanation*, but as we have noted, the notion of an explanation (an epistemological and logical notion) is not the same thing as the notion of a cause (which is a metaphysical notion). Furthermore, there is no exception here to the claim that everything has an explanation. In particular, the rationalist does not say that everything has an explanation except God—which might invite the retort that maybe the world lacks an explanation as well. Rather, the rationalist says that God, too, has an explanation. The difference between God and the world is that God, qua necessary being, is self-explanatory, whereas the world, qua contingent, is not. This entails that the *world* has a cause insofar as it requires an explanation external to it, but it does not entail that God has a cause, and indeed entails that he could not have had one. For as a necessary being, he could not have failed to exist in the first place, so that there would be nothing for a would-be cause to do. If the rationalist cosmological argument is committed to a version of the principle of causality, then, we might formulate it as the claim that *whatever is contingent requires a cause*.

A second point to note is that, once again, we do not have an argument that either assumes or argues that the world had a beginning. The rationalist view is that even if the universe of contingent things had no beginning in time, it would qua contingent still require a cause outside itself.

The Kalām Approach

The *kalām* cosmological argument, named for the *kalām* tradition in medieval Islamic thought that championed it and in recent years famously defended by William Lane Craig, is, among the main versions of the cosmological argument, the only one concerned to show that the universe had a beginning. In this connection Craig has made use of arguments from modern scientific cosmology, but his metaphysically oriented arguments, which are the ones that most clearly echo the *kalām* tradition, are intended to be decisive whatever the empirical facts turn out to be. Their aim is to show that the notion of an actually infinitely large collection (as opposed to a merely potentially infinite collection, that is, a finite collection to which we could always add another member) reduces to absurdity, and that since a beginningless series of events in time would constitute such a collection, we should conclude that such a series is not possible. To this end Craig deploys paradoxes like Hilbert's Infinite Hotel paradox. We might summarize the *kalām* approach as follows:

1. There cannot be an actually infinitely large collection (as paradoxes like Hilbert's Infinite Hotel paradox show).
2. But a universe without a beginning would constitute an actually infinitely large collection (of moments of time).
3. So the universe must have had a beginning.
4. But whatever begins to exist has a cause.
5. So the universe has a cause.

As with the other approaches to the cosmological argument, defenders of the *kalām* approach go on to argue that the cause of the world whose existence they claim to have established must have various divine attributes. Craig argues that the cause must be timeless, spaceless, changeless, beginningless, immaterial, uncaused, powerful, unique, and personal.[18] Obviously, all this raises questions, but we can note for present purposes, first, that while we have in this case an argument that does make a claim about the universe as a whole, and a claim to the effect that it must have had a beginning, it does indeed *argue* for this claim rather than merely assuming it. Second, we nevertheless have here yet another argument that does not rest on the premise that "everything has a cause." The claim instead is that *that which begins to exist* must have a cause.

NEW ATHEIST OBJECTIONS TO THE COSMOLOGICAL ARGUMENT

With these summaries of the main versions of the cosmological argument in hand, we can turn to the New Atheist criticisms of the argument. We will see that the objections are not merely weak, but for the most part miss the entire point of the cosmological argument. Let's consider them in turn:

If Everything Has a Cause, Then What Caused God?

This objection is raised in various ways by Dawkins, Dennett, Harris, Hawking and Mlodinow, Hitchens, Krauss, and Stenger.[19] As I have indicated, it is, even outside New Atheist literature, perhaps the most common objection to the cosmological argument. But it is also the least intellectually serious. For one thing, as has already been emphasized, *not a single* prominent proponent of the cosmological argument actually appeals to the premise that "everything has a cause," and some of them explicitly deny that everything has a cause. For that reason alone, the suggestion that the proponent of the cosmological argument is contradicting himself or making an arbitrary exception to his own rule is simply directed at a straw man.

---

18. Craig's views about God's relationship to time are more complicated than this indicates, but the complications are irrelevant for present purposes.
19. Dawkins, *The God Delusion*, p. 77; Dennett, *Breaking the Spell*, p. 242; Harris, *Letter to a Christian Nation*, pp. 72–73; Hawking and Mlodinow, *The Grand Design*, p. 172; Hitchens, *God Is Not Great*, p. 71; Krauss, *A Universe from Nothing*, p. xii; Stenger, *God and the Folly of Faith*, pp. 215 and 323–24.

But rhetorically to ask "What caused God?" is a bad objection even apart from the fact that the cosmological argument does not rest on the premise in question. For it is not as if the defender of the argument has given no reason why God does not need a cause even if other things do. On the contrary, part of the point of the argument is to establish that there must be something that not only lacks a cause but could not even in principle have had one, precisely because it lacks the very feature that makes other things in need of a cause.

The Aristotelian argument holds that other things require a cause because they are mixtures of actual and potential, and any potential, precisely because it is merely potential, cannot actualize itself. By contrast, what is purely actual, precisely because it lacks any potentiality, not only need not have a cause but could not have had one. The Neoplatonist argument holds that composite things require a cause because there must be some principle outside them that accounts for the composition of their parts. But what is utterly simple or noncomposite has no parts to be put together in the first place, not even an act of existence distinct from its essence. Hence it not only need not have been caused but could not have been caused. The Leibnizian argument entails that contingent things require a cause precisely because they are contingent and could have been otherwise, but what is necessary, and thus could not have been otherwise, neither need have nor could have had a cause. The *kalām* argument, since it appeals only to the notion that what has a temporal beginning requires a cause, is in no way arbitrary in denying that what has no such beginning requires a cause.

So, to ask "What caused God?", far from being the devastating retort the New Atheist supposes it to be, is in fact painfully inept. When interpreted in light of what the various approaches to the cosmological argument actually *mean* by "cause" and "God," it really amounts to asking "What caused the thing that cannot in principle have had a cause?" In particular, it amounts to asking "What actualized the potentials in that thing which is pure actuality and thus never had any potentials of any sort needing to be actualized in the first place?"; or "What principle accounts for the composition of the parts in that which has no parts but is absolutely simple or non-composite?"; or "What imparted a sufficient reason for existence to that thing which has its sufficient reason for existence within itself and did not derive it from something else?"; or "What gave a temporal beginning to that which has no temporal beginning?" And none of these questions makes any sense.

Of course, a New Atheist might say that he isn't convinced that any version of the cosmological argument succeeds in showing that there really is something that could not in principle have had a cause—something that is purely actual, or absolutely simple, or which has a sufficient reason for its existence within itself, or which lacks a temporal beginning. He might even try to argue that there is some sort of hidden incoherence in these notions. But *merely* to ask "What caused God?"—as if the defender of the cosmological argument had overlooked the most obvious of objections—simply misses the whole point. A serious critic has to grapple with the details of the arguments. He cannot short-circuit them with a single smarmy question.

Maybe the Universe Itself (or the Big Bang, or the Multiverse, or Indeterministic Quantum Events, or the Laws of Physics) is the Uncaused, Self-Explanatory, or Necessary Being

This objection, often concomitant with the first, is raised in various forms by Dawkins, Dennett, Krauss, Rosenberg, and Stenger.[20] And like the first objection, it completely misses the point of each of the versions of the cosmological argument we've considered. As we have seen, whatever one thinks of those arguments, there is no arbitrariness or special pleading in their denying that God requires a cause while insisting that everything other than God does. The difference is in each case a principled one. And the principle in each case gives an answer to the question why the universe, the Big Bang, and so forth, cannot be the terminus of explanation.

For the Aristotelian, any actualization of a potency requires a cause, while what is pure actuality, and only what is pure actuality, does not. But the universe is a mixture of actuality and potentiality, and the Big Bang involved the actualization of a potential, as would each stage in the evolution of a multiverse and each quantum event (indeterminism being irrelevant). The laws of physics are also by themselves merely potential insofar as they could have been other than they are. Hence none of these could be self-explanatory, necessary, or "uncaused" in the relevant sense of being the sort of thing that need not and could not have a cause.

Similarly, for the Neoplatonist neither the universe nor a multiverse could be uncaused, necessary, or self-explanatory, precisely because they are composite. Quantum events and laws of physics also lack the metaphysical simplicity that the Neoplatonist argues we must attribute to the first principle of all. Their contingency is one indication of this, insofar as the fact that they could have been other than they are entails a distinction between essence and existence. Leibniz, of course, would point out that the universe, Big Bang, quantum events, and laws of nature are all contingent rather than necessary and thus could not provide an ultimate explanation; while the defender of the *kalām* argument would point out that since his claim is precisely that the Big Bang and everything that came into being with it—the universe along with the laws of physics, including the laws of quantum mechanics, that govern it—require a cause, it simply begs the question against him to claim that any of these things might be the terminus of explanation.

Much more could be said. In particular, the metaphysical status of laws of nature is itself so vexed an issue that it is amazing that anyone could think a glib reference to the laws of physics might settle anything in this context. What is a law of nature? How does it have any efficacy? Is a law of nature merely a statement to the effect that such-and-such a regularity exists? In that case it isn't an *explanation* of anything but merely a *description* of the very thing that needs to be explained. Is a law of nature a kind of Platonic entity? In that case we need an account of how the world comes to participate in such a law, and why it participates in the specific laws it does rather than others. And in that case, too, laws cannot be *ultimate*

---

20. Dawkins, *The God Delusion*, p. 78; Dennett, *Breaking the Spell*, p. 242; Krauss, *A Universe from Nothing*, p. xii; Rosenberg, *The Atheist's Guide to Reality*, pp. 36–39; Stenger, *God and the Folly of Faith*, p. 215.

explanations. Is a law of nature a shorthand description of the way a natural substance will tend to behave given its nature or essence? In that case the existence of laws is parasitic on the existence of the substances themselves, and again cannot then be an ultimate explanation.[21]

Naturally the New Atheist might reject any of these views of laws of nature, along with the Aristotelian, Neoplatonic, Leibnizian, or *kalām* accounts of why the universe cannot be an uncaused cause or self-explanatory or necessary being. The point, however, is that the New Atheist has given *no reason* whatsoever to reject any of this. *Merely* to suggest that the universe, Big bang, and so forth, might be the terminus of explanation is simply to *ignore* the cosmological argument, not to *answer* it.

It Is False to Suppose in the First Place that Everything Has a Cause or an Explanation

In putting forward this objection, Stenger cites Hume's famous views on causality, and attributes some events to "chance" rather than causation.[22] Dennett and Rosenberg suggest that quantum mechanics shows that events can occur without a cause.[23]

Leave aside the point that no version of the argument actually rests on the premise that everything has a cause. None of these objections has force even against the causal principles to which the various approaches to the cosmological argument *are* committed. Take Stenger's objection, which is directed at a straw man. Naturally, no proponent of the cosmological argument denies that chance events occur. But there is simply nothing about chance that rules out causality. On the contrary, chance *presupposes* nonchance causal regularities. To take a stock example, when a farmer plowing a field comes across buried treasure, that is a chance event. But it occurs only because of the convergence of two nonchance lines of causality: the farmer's decision to plow in a certain direction that day, and someone else's decision to bury treasure at precisely that spot. Similarly, that following an earthquake, tumbling boulder A shattered boulder B, specifically, is a chance event. But it occurs only because of causal regularities like the ones involved in plate tectonics, gravitational attraction, the solidity of boulders, and so on.

Quantum physics shows at most that some events do not have a *deterministic* cause or explanation, but there is nothing in either the principle of causality or PSR per se that requires that *sort* of cause or explanation, specifically. Furthermore, quantum events occur even in a nondeterministic way only *given* the laws of quantum mechanics, which (the proponent of the cosmological argument would say) are contingent and by themselves merely potential until a universe that follows them is actualized. So it either misses the point or begs the question to

---

21. For a useful account of recent debate over this issue, see Stephen Mumford, *Laws in Nature* (London: Routledge, 2004). For an Aristotelian-Thomistic defense of the view that laws of nature are summaries of the ways natural substances tend to operate given their natures, see David S. Oderberg, *Real Essentialism* (London: Routledge, 2007), pp. 143–51.

22. Stenger, *God and the Folly of Faith*, p. 97.

23 Dennett, *Breaking the Spell*, p. 242; Rosenberg, *The Atheist's Guide to Reality*, pp. 38–39.

appeal to quantum mechanics, since that is itself part of what the cosmological argument claims stands in need of explanation.

Hoary though the Humean argument is, there are three reasons why it simply will not do to pretend, as Stenger does, that the mere mention of it constitutes a devastating response to theistic arguments. First, no working physicist, chemist, biologist, or neuroscientist would for a moment take seriously the suggestion that perhaps there simply is no cause or explanation when investigating some specific physical, chemical, biological, or neurological phenomenon. The critic of the cosmological argument thus owes us an explanation of how *his* appeal to such a suggestion in the current context is anything less than special pleading. And as Gerson points out, the fact that the cosmological argument is *itself* a proposed explanation suffices to show that it is no good to say "Maybe there's no explanation in this case." The cosmological argument has just *given* one. Therefore if the critic wants to avoid accepting it, he has to find some reason other than the bare suggestion that there might not be an explanation.

A second problem with the Humean move is that it is simply fallacious to infer from the premise that we can conceive of effects independently of causes to the conclusion that some event might in fact not have a cause. We can conceive of what it is to be a triangle without conceiving what it is to be a trilateral, but it doesn't follow that there could be a triangle which is not a trilateral. We can conceive of a man without conceiving of how tall he is, but it doesn't follow that any man could exist without having some specific height or other. And so forth.

A third problem is one identified by Elizabeth Anscombe.[24] Hume claims that it is conceivable that something could come into being without a cause, and he evidently has in mind something like conceiving of an object suddenly appearing, out of the blue as it were, where nothing had been a moment before. But what is it about this exercise in conception that makes it a case of conceiving something coming into being *without a cause*—as opposed, say, to coming into being with an *unseen* cause, or being *transported* from somewhere else in an unknown or unusual manner (by teleportation, perhaps)? The trouble is that the Humean scenario is underdescribed. We need to add something to our exercise in conception in order to make it what Hume needs it to be in order to make his point. Yet it is hard to see what we can add to it that wouldn't involve bringing causation back into the picture and therefore undermining the whole point of the example. For instance, it is hard to see how to distinguish something's coming into being as opposed to being transported unless it is by reference to its having a generating rather than a transporting cause.

Of course, perhaps the atheist can respond to these various objections. The point, however, is that the appeal to Hume is at most something which might, with considerable work, be *turned into* a serious criticism of the cosmological argument.

---

24. G. E. M. Anscombe, " 'Whatever Has a Beginning of Existence Must Have a Cause': Hume's Argument Exposed," in G. E. M. Anscombe, *Collected Philosophical Papers*, Volume I (Oxford: Blackwell, 1981). Cf. the discussion in Brian Davies, *An Introduction to the Philosophy of Religion*, 3rd ed. (Oxford: Oxford University Press, 2004), pp. 50–51.

By itself it is very far from being a serious criticism, much less the decisive one Stenger and others suppose it to be.

Why Assume that the Universe Had a Beginning or that a Regress of Causes Must Terminate?

Rosenberg and Krauss put forward something like this sort of objection when they propose that the multiverse hypothesis—according to which the Big Bang that gave rise to our universe involved a branching off from a preexisting universe, which in turn is part of a beginningless series of universes—eliminates the need for a divine cause. Krauss, citing Richard Feynman, also suggests that for all we know there might always be deeper and deeper layers of laws of physics which we can probe until we get bored.[25]

One problem with this is that as we have seen, most versions of the cosmological argument are not concerned in the first place with the question of whether the universe had a beginning. They are concerned instead to argue that even if the universe (or multiverse for that matter) had no beginning, it would require a divine cause to sustain it in existence perpetually and/or to explain why it exists at all, even beginninglessly. And the one approach that is concerned with the question of whether the universe had a beginning, the *kalām* approach, offers a metaphysical argument purporting to show that there could not in principle be a beginningless universe, or multiverse, if there is one. Craig has also raised scientific criticisms of the multiverse hypothesis. Hence, appealing to the multiverse hypothesis as if it undermined the cosmological argument either misses the point or begs the question.

I have already explained why it is no good glibly to appeal to laws of nature as if they could be the ultimate explanation of things, and the point holds true however many layers of laws of nature there are. Note also that level upon level of laws of nature would constitute an essentially ordered series—laws at one level would hold only as a special case of laws at a deeper level, which would in turn hold only as a special case of yet deeper laws—and we have seen why Aristotelians would hold that such a series cannot fail to have a first member in the sense of something which can impart causal power without deriving it. Nothing Krauss or any other of the New Atheists have to say even addresses this argument, much less undermines it.

Even if There Were a First Cause, There Is No Reason to Think It Would Be Omnipotent, Omniscient, Perfectly Good, etc.

Like "What caused God?", this is commonly put forward as a devastating objection to the cosmological argument. And like "What caused God?", it is in fact embarrassingly inept. Dawkins assures his readers that there is "absolutely no reason" to

---

25. Krauss, *A Universe from Nothing*, p. 177.

attribute omnipotence, omniscience, etc., to a first cause.[26] Krauss makes a similar claim.[27]

In fact, as I've already indicated, the proponents of each version of the cosmological argument put forward a series of arguments claiming to show that the cause of the world whose existence they've argued for must have the key divine attributes. Aquinas devotes around a hundred double-column pages of dense argumentation in Part I of the *Summa Theologiae* alone—just after presenting the Five Ways—to showing that to the cause of the world we must attribute simplicity, goodness, infinity, immutability, unity, knowledge, life, will, power, and the like. About 200 pages of argumentation in Book I the *Summa Contra Gentiles* are devoted to this topic. Much argumentation along these lines can also be found in Aquinas's other works, such as *De potentia* and *De veritate*. Much of Samuel Clarke's book *A Demonstration of the Being and Attributes of God* is, as anyone who has read just the title will discover, devoted to arguing for various divine attributes—infinity, omnipresence, unity, intelligence, free choice, power, wisdom, and goodness. I have already indicated that Plotinus, Leibniz, and Craig argue for various divine attributes. Further examples could easily be given.

Dawkins, Krauss, and the other New Atheist writers offer no response at all to these arguments. In fact it seems that they are entirely unaware that the arguments even exist.

The Cosmological Argument Proposes a "God of the Gaps" in Order to Explain Something which in Fact Either Is, or Eventually Will Be, Better Explained via a Naturalistic Scientific Theory

This is, I think it is fair to say, the central conceit of the entire New Atheist project. In the view of the New Atheists, if something is going to be explained at all, it is going to be explained via the methods of science. Therefore (so the argument goes) the appeal to God can at best be a kind of quasi-scientific hypothesis, and the problem is that it is not a good one. For Hitchens, it violates Ockham's razor.[28] Similarly, Dawkins suggests that "it is more parsimonious to conjure up, say, a 'big bang singularity', or some other physical concept as yet unknown."[29] Harris thinks that at least at the moment we can't say much more than this, opining that "[t]he truth is that no one knows how or why the universe came into being."[30] Krauss and Hawking and Mlodinow, by contrast, think that science has already given us a complete nontheistic explanation of the existence of the world, or near enough. "Because there is a law like gravity," Hawking and Mlodinow write, "the universe can and will create itself from nothing."[31] Krauss's *A Universe from Nothing* is a book-length attempt to make this sort of view plausible.

26. Dawkins, *The God Delusion*, p. 77.
27. Krauss, *A Universe from Nothing*, p. 173.
28. Hitchens, *God Is Not Great*, pp. 70–71.
29. Dawkins, *The God Delusion*, p. 78.
30. Harris, *Letter to a Christian Nation*, p. 73.
31. Hawking and Mlodinow, *The Grand Design*, p. 180.

There are two basic problems with all of this. The first is that the characterization of the question of how to explain the existence of the universe as a matter for empirical science rather than philosophical theology to settle either completely misses the point or simply begs the question. For one thing, whether or not one thinks any of them ultimately succeeds, the versions of the cosmological argument sketched above are simply *not* "god of the gaps" explanations. A "god of the gaps" explanation is one on which it is at least possible in principle that some nondivine explanation might be correct, and the claim is at most that the theistic explanation is more probable than these alternatives. The versions of the cosmological argument we've looked at, by contrast, are all attempts at *strict metaphysical demonstration*. They claim that there is no way *in principle* to account for what they set out to explain other than a purely actual cause, or an absolutely simple or noncomposite cause, or a necessary being, or a cause that is timeless and spaceless. Whether or not these claims are correct, the arguments do not stand or fall by the standards by which empirical hypotheses are evaluated—parsimony, fit with existing well-confirmed empirical theories, etc.

For another thing, the starting points of these attempts at metaphysical demonstration are not matters about which empirical scientific theory has anything to say in the first place. Rather, they have to do with what any possible empirical theory must itself take for granted. That is to say, their starting points are *metaphysical* rather than physical. Whatever the empirical facts turn out to be, they will at some level involve the actualization of potency, or so the Aristotelian will argue; they will involve composite beings, or so the Neoplatonist will argue; they will all be contingent, or so the defender of the contingency approach will argue; and they will all exist within a universe (or perhaps multiverse) that will itself require a temporal beginning, or so the defender of the *kalām* approach will argue.

Simply to assert that any explanation worth taking seriously will have to be an empirical scientific theory rather than an exercise in philosophical theology is merely to *assume* that all of this is mistaken. It is not to *show* that it is mistaken.

The second problem is that the nontheistic scientific explanation of the existence of the universe proposed by Krauss and Hawking and Mlodinow is manifestly a nonstarter. "A law like gravity" is not *nothing*; hence an explanation of the existence of the universe that makes reference to such a law is rather obviously *not*, contrary to what Hawking and Mlodinow suggest, an account of how the universe might arise from nothing. Krauss's book is notoriously shameless in committing the same basic fallacy.[32] In 185 pages purporting boldly to show how the universe can arise from nothing, Krauss spends the first 152 arguing that the universe arose from empty space endowed with energy and governed by physical law, all of which he admits does not count as "nothing." By page 170 he tries to take all of this down to just the laws of quantum gravity, but admits that this does not

---

32. I say "notoriously" because Krauss's position has been widely and harshly criticized even by philosophers with no theological ax to grind. Probably the best-known critique is that of philosopher of physics David Albert, who reviewed Krauss's book in the March 23, 2012 *New York Times* book review section.

really count as "nothing" either. At page 177 he finally resorts to suggesting that perhaps there is just layer upon layer of laws.

What is never explained is how any of this counts as explaining how the universe arose from *nothing*. There is some obfuscatory chin-pulling about "possible candidates for nothingness," and "what 'nothing' might actually comprise," along with an insistence that any "definition" of nothingness must ultimately be "based on empirical evidence" and that " 'nothing' is every bit as physical as 'something' "—as if "nothingness" were a highly unusual kind of stuff that is more difficult to observe or measure than other things are. But of course "nothing" is not a kind of stuff (physical or otherwise), nor anything that is terribly difficult to define (empirically or otherwise), nor something that "comprises" anything, nor anything particularly mysterious or worth pulling one's chin over. It is just the absence of anything. Moreover, Krauss himself seems well aware of this insofar as he ends up acknowledging that his main "candidates for nothingness" are not really *nothing* after all. And what he's left with—a basic level of physical laws or layers of laws—is not only not nothing, but cannot be the ultimate explanation of the world, for the reasons given earlier.

In the history of Western thought, the cosmological argument has not only been the central argument for the existence of God, but the fundamental approach to the question of ultimate explanation. New Atheist writers have claimed to be able to refute the argument "easily." They also purport to offer a superior approach to questions of ultimate explanation. They have, manifestly for those who know the relevant subject matter, failed miserably on both counts. The intrinsic value (or lack thereof) of their arguments does not merit them even the critical attention they have received. But the acclaim they have received in some quarters makes such attention necessary. They also offer an object lesson in intellectual hubris that all philosophers ought to heed.[33]

---

33. For helpful comments on an earlier draft of this paper, I thank Howard Wettstein and an anonymous referee.

Evidence, Theory, and Interpretation: The "New Atheism" and the Philosophy of Science

ALISTER E. MCGRATH

The term "New Atheism" was coined in 2006 to refer to a clutch of works by writers such as Richard Dawkins, Daniel Dennett, and Sam Harris, characterized as much by the aggressiveness of their rhetoric as the substance of their ideas.[1] Although given an enthusiastic welcome on its appearance, particularly in the United States, the passing of time has seen the emergence of more critical and negative attitudes toward the movement, particularly in relation to its philosophical underpinnings.

Perhaps the most important development has been the growing recognition of the quasi-religious nature of the movement.[2] As has often been observed, there are uncomfortable parallels between the "New Atheism" and religious fundamentalism—such as the conviction that they are in sole possession of truth; a somewhat disconcerting absence of tolerance for the views of their critics (Dawkins unwisely compared creationists to Holocaust deniers); their simplistic one-dimensional reduction of religion; and their overwhelming sense that they

---

1. For the original three, see Sam Harris, *The End of Faith: Religion, Terror, and the Future of Reason* (New York: W. W. Norton, 2004); Daniel C. Dennett, *Breaking the Spell: Religion as a Natural Phenomenon* (New York: Viking Penguin, 2006); Richard Dawkins, *The God Delusion* (London: Bantam, 2006). Other works of importance could be added to this list, including Christopher Hitchens, *God Is Not Great: How Religion Poisons Everything* (New York: Twelve, 2007); Victor J. Stenger, *God: The Failed Hypothesis: How Science Shows That God Does Not Exist* (Amherst, NY: Prometheus Books, 2008).
2. Chris Hedges, *When Atheism Becomes Religion: America's New Fundamentalists* (New York: Free Press, 2009).

© 2013 Wiley Periodicals, Inc.

have been oppressed and marginalized within Western society, and are entitled to cultural privilege on account of their rationalist credentials.[3] And feminist writers have noted that, like religious fundamentalism, the New Atheism is dominated by white middle-class males.[4]

Ideologies—both religious and anti-religious—regularly make use of "legitimating myths," which provide (often questionable) intellectual justification for their own claims to intellectual privilege and social dominance.[5] The "New Atheism" presents itself as standing at the cutting edge of a progressive rationalist movement that will necessarily triumph. Its failure to persuade is thus to be attributed, not to its own failures, but to the embedded power of religious ideas and institutions. Challenging such "legitimating myths"—or showing that there are others of equal or greater validity—often generates both insecurity and anger on the part of "New Atheist" apologists.

Perhaps unsurprisingly, most mainline atheists have distanced themselves from the "New Atheism," disliking both the shrill tone of its rhetoric, and its failure to take the intellectual and social aspects of religion seriously. It is therefore important not to extrapolate judgments made about the "New Atheism" to the wider atheism intellectual community. The "New Atheism" is best seen as a populist splinter movement within atheism as a whole, characterized by methods and attitudes that are not representative of the wider movement. To some, it will seem to be of questionable value to consider their philosophical arguments, precisely because these are stated in such rhetorically exaggerated and intellectually simplified forms.

It is, however, legitimate to focus on the "New Atheism," partly because its recent high media profile, and partly because some of its distinguishing features are of wider cultural interest, mapping onto other philosophical and cultural debates. One of the most distinct features of the movement that has come to be known as the "New Atheism" is its privileging of scientific discourse in the debate about God.[6] This is of interest in several respects, especially in connection with contemporary reflections on the cultural authority of science.[7] Yet it is also of philosophical interest, in that it raises the question of how the "New Atheism" uses ideas and methods drawn from the natural sciences in their polemic against religion.[8]

---

3. See, for example, Terry Eagleton, *Reason, Faith, and Revolution: Reflections on the God Debate* (New Haven, CT: Yale University Press, 2009); David Bentley Hart, *Atheist Delusions: The Christian Revolution and Its Fashionable Enemies* (New Haven, CT: Yale University Press, 2009); Amarnath Amarasingam, ed., *Religion and the New Atheism: A Critical Appraisal* (Leiden: Brill, 2010); Ian S. Markham, *Against Atheism: Why Dawkins, Hitchens, and Harris Are Fundamentally Wrong* (Malden, MA: Wiley-Blackwell, 2010). These criticisms reflect cultural, sociological, philosophical, and theological concerns.

4. Tina Beattie, *The New Atheists: The Twilight of Reason and the War on Religion* (London: Darton, Longman and Todd, 2007), 9.

5. Jim Sidanius and Felicia Pratto, *Social Dominance: An Intergroup Theory of Social Hierarchy and Oppression* (Cambridge: Cambridge University Press, 1999).

6. Neil Ormerod, "Theology and the New Atheism: Science, Religion, and Metaphysics," *Theology* 116 (2013), 187–94.

7. Harold W. Attridge and Ronald L. Numbers, eds., *The Religion and Science Debate: Why Does It Continue?* (New Haven, CT: Yale University Press, 2009).

8. See especially Karl Giberson and Mariano Artigas, *Oracles of Science: Celebrity Scientists Versus God and Religion* (New York: Oxford University Press, 2009).

It is not my intention here to discuss the historical question of the deeply problematic "warfare" model of the interaction of science and religion, which has been severely criticized both in terms of its historical reliability and its unacceptable tendency to "essentialize" both science and religion.[9] Richard Dawkins's *God Delusion* is characterized by its construction of a narrative, based on the "warfare" model, which treats science and religion as locked in mortal combat, from which only science can emerge victorious. History is thus about the relentless advance of "reason and science," and the retreat of "superstition and religion." Scientists who are interested in—or inexplicably committed to—religion are thus cast as "collaborators" or "traitors." It is one of the most widely criticized aspects of Dawkins's polemic against religion, which can be tracked back to his earlier writings.[10]

In what follows, we can consider the implicit philosophy of science within the writings of the leading "New Atheists," and correlate these with wider trends within the discipline. In preparing to engage with these issues, it is important to indicate that the degree of simplification entailed by the popularizing approach characteristic of the leading manifestoes of the "New Atheism" often leads to inadequate accounts of serious philosophical issues—such as the classic arguments for the existence of God.[11] As we shall see, this same lack of depth is often encountered in their somewhat lightweight accounts of issues concerning both the history and philosophy of science.

EVIDENCE AND THEORY

One of the central assertions of Dawkins's *God Delusion* is that beliefs should be proved with reference to evidence. Religious belief is often treated as an evidence-free zone, meriting the accolade of "blind faith." So what is meant by "evidence"? Dawkins does not appear to appreciate that an observation only becomes evidence when placed within, and assessed against, a theoretical framework. An observation can thus function as evidence for several possible theories.[12] A core assumption of Dawkins's polemic against theism is that observations can be treated as "brute," in that they ultimately have only one proper, unequivocal meaning.

This is deeply problematic. Unsurprisingly, the work of Thomas Kuhn does not feature prominently in Dawkins's writings. Kuhn rightly observed that any supposedly "univocal" observations (or methods) in science were interpreted in

---

9. See John Hedley Brooke and Geoffrey Cantor, *Reconstructing Nature: The Engagement of Science and Religion* (Edinburgh: T & T Clark, 1998); John Brooke and Ian Maclean, ed., *Heterodoxy in Early Modern Science and Religion* (Oxford: Oxford University Press, 2005).

10. Alister E. McGrath, *Dawkins' God: Genes, Memes and the Meaning of Life* (Malden, MA: Blackwell, 2004), 119–37. More recent discussions about the hijacking of biology for ideological purposes should be noted here: see especially Denis Alexander and Ronald L. Numbers, ed. *Biology and Ideology from Descartes to Dawkins* (Chicago: University of Chicago Press, 2010).

11. See the very inadequate account in Dennett, *Breaking the Spell*, 240–46.

12. As noted by John Earman, "Underdetermination, Realism, and Reason," *Midwest Studies in Philosophy* 18 (1994): 19–38. For a criticism of this position, see Igor Deuven and Leon Horsten, "Earman on Underdetermination and Empirical Indistinguishability," *Erkenntnis* 49 (1998): 303–20.

the light of the dominant paradigm of interpretation at that time, or within that community of interpretation.[13] On the relatively few occasions when Dawkins does refer to Kuhn, it is as a "truth-heckler," someone who resists Dawkins's scientific positivism in the name of covert sociological agendas.[14] The physicist Victor Stenger notes Kuhn's views, but fails to engage them.[15] It is not difficult to understand this omission: the epistemological simplicity of "evidential univocality" is seriously undermined by Kuhn's historical and philosophical analysis, which simply cannot be ignored in this situation.

Dawkins's account of the scientific method, which he subsequently applies to religion, asserts that evidence forces us to draw certain conclusions. This is entirely reasonable; the point at debate, however, is how this evidence is to be assessed. Dawkins fails to make the significant and necessary distinction between a "logic of discovery" and a "logic of verification." The manner in which a scientific theory or hypothesis is derived has little bearing on its truth. As Charles S. Pierce pointed out, a theory might emerge through an act of inspiration. Yet once formulated, a theory must be tested against observation.[16] Dawkins's understanding of this process leaves something to be desired. Its most rigorous formulation is found in one of his earliest writings, *The Selfish Gene* (1976)[17]:

> [Faith] is a state of mind that leads people to believe something—it doesn't matter what—in the total absence of supporting evidence. If there were good supporting evidence, then faith would be superfluous, for the evidence would compel us to believe it anyway.

This is a deeply problematic view of the relation of evidence and belief in the natural sciences, which fails to make the critical distinction between the "total absence of supporting evidence" and the "absence of totally supporting evidence."

In his more popular writings, Dawkins tends to the view that science proves its theories through evidence. Others within his camp take a similar position. For example, Stenger argues that incorrect theories are defeated "by calling upon empirical observations as the final judge."[18] Yet this is clearly inadequate as an account of the historical development of science, or philosophical reflection on its methods and tasks. Observations are open to multiple interpretations. These must be judged against epistemic virtues—such as simplicity, elegance, comprehensiveness, and fecundity—in order to make a judgment about which such interpretation

---

13. Thomas S. Kuhn, *The Structure of Scientific Revolutions*, 2nd ed. (Chicago: University of Chicago Press, 1970). See further Jose Diéz, "Falsificationism and the Structure of Theories: The Popper–Kuhn Controversy About the Rationality of Normal Science," *Studies in History and Philosophy of Science* 38 (2007): 543–54.
14. Richard Dawkins, *A Devil's Chaplain* (Boston: Houghton Mifflin, 2003), 16.
15. Stenger, *God: The Failed Hypothesis*, 35.
16. Christiane Chauviré, "Peirce, Popper, Abduction, and the Idea of Logic of Discovery," *Semiotica* 153 (2005): 209–21.
17. Richard Dawkins, *The Selfish Gene* (Oxford: Oxford University Press, 1976), 330.
18. Stenger, *God: The Failed Hypothesis*, 34.

is the "best" such explanation.[19] Where Dawkins and Stenger think in terms of observations proving things, the dominant view is that one is forced to make defensible, yet often unprovable *judgments* about which constitutes the "best explanation" of a set of observations.[20]

For example, consider the current debate within cosmology over whether the primordial "big bang" gave rise to a single universe, or a series of universes (the so-called "multiverse").[21] The same observations may be accommodated, with varying degrees of conviction, within two quite different theoretical frameworks, leaving the question of which is the "better" explanation wide open.

Charles Darwin's *Origin of Species* (1859), a landmark in scientific history, is fundamentally an exercise in finding the "best explanation" for his biological observations. New Atheist websites often assert that Darwin *proved* his theories, contrasting this unfavorably with the "blind faith" of religion. Darwin himself believed that his theory of "natural selection" provided the most elegant and persuasive explanation of biological life forms. But he knew he could not prove it.[22] There was no unambiguous evidence which would conclusively and incontrovertibly compel people to accept his theory. Everything that was known about the natural world could be accommodated by rival theories, such as various forms of transformism.[23] Furthermore, there were serious scientific objections and difficulties to his theory, which made many scientists of his day believe it was unacceptable.[24] The most significant of these was probably the problem of genetic dilution.[25] Darwin lacked a viable theory of genetics to explain how inherited characteristics were transmitted to subsequent generations.

Yet despite such difficulties, Darwin believed that his theory was right, and would one day be shown to be right. How, he asked, could a theory be wrong when it made so much sense of what he observed? Yes, there were loose ends everywhere, and a large number of problems. But his core idea seemed to him to be correct—despite the fact it could not be proved[26]:

> A crowd of difficulties will have occurred to the reader. Some of them are so grave that to this day I can never reflect on them without being staggered;

---

19. For the issues, see David H. Glass, "Coherence Measures and Inference to the Best Explanation," *Synthese* 157 (2007): 275–96; Stathis Psillos, "The Fine Structure of Inference to the Best Explanation," *Philosophy and Phenomenological Research* 74 (2007): 441–48.
20. Peter Lipton, *Inference to the Best Explanation*, 2nd ed. (London: Routledge, 2004).
21. Bernard Carr, ed., *Universe or Multiverse?* (Cambridge: Cambridge University Press, 2007).
22. See his famous comments on F. W. Hutton's concerns about his theory: F. Darwin, ed., *The Life and Letters of Charles Darwin*, 3 vols. (London: John Murray, 1887), vol. 2, 155.
23. Pietro Corsi, "Before Darwin: Transformist Concepts in European Natural History," *Journal of the History of Biology* 38 (2005): 67–83.
24. For a discussion of these difficulties, see Abigail J. Lustig, "Darwin's Difficulties," in *The Cambridge Companion to the Origin of Species*, ed. Michael Ruse and Robert J. Richards (Cambridge: Cambridge University Press, 2009), 109–28.
25. See here Michael Bulmer, "Did Jenkins's Swamping Argument Invalidate Darwin's Theory of Natural Selection?," *British Journal for the History of Science* 37 (2004): 281–97.
26. Charles Darwin, *Origin of Species* (London: John Murray, 1859), 171.

but, to the best of my judgment, the greater number are only apparent, and those that are real are not, I think, fatal to my theory.

The importance of these observations to contemporary debates about the existence of God will be clear. The approach of the "New Atheism," grounded on the axiom—we might even say "dogma"—of evidentiary univocity, holds that there is "no evidence for God." But this notion of evidence is unsustainable. The real issue concerns which framework of interpretation offers the best explanation of observations. It is perhaps unsurprising that recent theistic apologetics has increasingly focused on inductive or abductive approaches to the existence of God, arguing that this provides the "best explanation" of what is observed in the world.[27]

NATURALIST ACCOUNTS OF RELIGION: THE MEME

One of the most distinctive features of the criticism of religion mounted by Dawkins and Dennett is the appeal to the notion of the "meme" as a reductive explanation of belief in God. This idea was introduced in 1976 by Dawkins as part of his argument that both biological and cultural evolution could be accounted for by "units of replication" or "units of transmission."[28] Dawkins suggests that a Darwinian account of cultural evolution needs replicators analogous to genes, and posits the meme as a result of his prior conviction that cultural evolution is an essentially Darwinian process.[29]

Even in 1976, Dawkins suggested that a "God-meme" was an adequate explanation of belief in God. This approach was developed further in his *God Delusion*, which sets out the idea of the "meme" as if it were established scientific orthodoxy, making no mention of the markedly skeptical attitude toward the notion within the mainstream scientific community. Dawkins presents the "meme" as if it were an actually existing entity, capable of offering a persuasive reductive explanation of the origins of religion. Belief in God is to be attributed to a well-adapted meme. Dawkins further posits, without evidence, a meme for "blind faith,"[30] opening himself to the charge that such a belief in memes is itself a form of "blind faith."

Daniel Dennett takes a similar view in *Breaking the Spell*, arguing that human brains provide shelter for "toxic memes," which play a critical role in shaping human minds.[31] Dennett had developed similar ideas earlier. In *Darwin's*

---

27. Richard Swinburne, *The Existence of God*, 2nd ed. (Oxford: Clarendon Press, 2004). At a more popular level, see Alister E. McGrath, *Surprised by Meaning: Science, Faith, and How We Make Sense of Things* (Louisville, KY: Westminster John Knox Press, 2011).

28. For the origins of this idea, see McGrath, *Dawkins' God: Genes, Memes and the Meaning of Life*, 119–37.

29. Joseph Poulshock, "Universal Darwinism and the Potential of Memetics," *Quarterly Review of Biology* 77 (2002): 174–75.

30. Dawkins, *The Selfish Gene*, 212–13.

31. Dennett, *Breaking the Spell*, 328–33. Dennett's approach here is simply assertive, not evidence-based.

Dangerous Idea (1995), he asserted that, far from being "godlike creators of ideas" who can manipulate, judge, and control them from an independent "Olympian standpoint," human beings are who they are, and think what they think, on account of "infestations of memes."[32] The idea of a human mind which somehow transcends both its genetic and memetic creators is nothing more than an outmoded myth.[33] For this reason, the human mind is particularly prone to being manipulated by these "new replicators." In *Breaking the Spell*, Dennett sets out a naturalist account of religion, based largely on an appeal to the meme. The analysis raises some awkward questions. Are *all* beliefs spread by what Dennett terms "toxic memes"? Or just the ones that anti-religious critics don't like? Is there a meme for atheism? Dennett's "Simple Taxonomy of Memes" certainly suggests so.[34] If so, the "meme" offers a reductive explanation for any belief system, whether religious or anti-religious.

Yet the empirical evidence for memes is somewhat underwhelming, putting Dennett in the somewhat difficult position of having to resort to the use of aggressive rhetoric to distract attention away from the weak evidential foundations of his approach.[35] His atheist apologetic at this point rests on the assumption that belief in God is demonstrably the outcome of memetic influence. Yet neither the notion of the meme, nor its alleged influence on religious beliefs, is scientifically proven; indeed, it has not even been stated in a form capable of scientific verification or falsification. Dennett, like other memeticists, has no answer to the question of why a "toxic" or "maladaptive" meme such as religion seems to be much more contagious than "adaptive memes" such as science.[36]

Dawkins argues both that scientific belief *undermines* belief in God; it also *explains it away* as an unintended outcome of human evolution. Believing in God is an "accidental by-product" of the evolutionary process. Religion arises from a "misfiring of something useful."[37] Yet if Darwinian evolution is a random and purposelessness process, as Dawkins insists it must be, how can anyone speak about it having "accidental" or "unintended" outcomes? Dawkins argues at several points in his works that the natural world may have the *appearance* of design, but this *appearance* of design or intentionality arises from random developments.[38] However, if Dawkins is right, *all* outcomes of the evolutionary process would have to be "unintended." Or does he really think that evolution is guided by some kind

---

32. Daniel C. Dennett, *Darwin's Dangerous Idea: Evolution and the Meaning of Life* (New York: Simon & Schuster, 1995), 346.

33. Dennett, *Darwin's Dangerous* Idea, 366.

34. Dennett, *Breaking the Spell*, 341–57. Note especially the taxonomy of memes presented on p. 344.

35. For the rather weak case, see Dennett, *Breaking the Spell*, 348–53.

36. Note the points made by Dan Sperber, "An Objection to the Memetic Approach to Culture," in *Darwinizing Culture: The Status of Memetics as a Science*, ed. Robert Aunger (Oxford: Oxford University Press, 2000), 163–73; Kevin N. Laland and Gillian R. Brown, *Sense and Nonsense: Evolutionary Perspectives on Human Behaviour* (Oxford: Oxford University Press, 2002), 209–16.

37. Dawkins, *God Delusion*, 188.

38. See especially Richard Dawkins, *The Blind Watchmaker: Why the Evidence of Evolution Reveals a Universe without Design* (New York: W. W. Norton, 1986).

of metaphorical mind, which steers it in appropriate directions, while permitting occasional digressions and by-ways?

Dawkins and Dennett both offer naturalist accounts of belief in God, holding that the evolutionary process allows us to understand why belief in God should emerge. Their accounts are somewhat different. Yet both raise the same question: is an explanation of an idea equivalent to its dismissal? For example, suppose I could demonstrate that the human capacity and inclination to seek for truth was essentially an outcome of the evolutionary process. Does this invalidate the human quest for truth? The assumption that proposing a reductive explanation for a trait invalidates its legitimacy or application is deeply ingrained within the "New Atheism," and remains one of its more problematic aspects.[39]

SCIENTIFIC EXPLANATION

Yet an objection might be raised here. At least the "New Atheism" is capable of offering explanations. God explains nothing. This criticism is expressed most forcibly in the writings of Christopher Hitchens, whose *God Is Not Great* added to the rhetorical force of the movement in 2008. For Hitchens, God is an explanatory redundancy. God is something that can be explained, but not something that possesses explanatory capacity in itself. Hitchens' view is that God serves no explanatory function, and is thus superfluous to any reasonable account of the world.

Yet Hitchens does not engage with any contemporary accounts of scientific explanation developed within recent works in the philosophy of science. His argument is severely weakened by an absence of serious consideration of what it means to speak of an "explanation" in the natural sciences.[40] In recent years, three particularly significant discussions of explanation have emerged: Paul Humphreys's model of causal explanation[41]; Peter Lipton's account of the nature of explanatory loveliness, which sets a causal approach to explanation within the framework of "inference to the best explanation"[42]; and the account of explanatory unification, initially offered by Michael Friedman and Paul Kitcher, and subsequently

---

39. See the comments in Tom Sjöblom, "Spandrels, Gazelles and Flying Buttresses: Religion as Adaptation or as a By-Product," *Journal of Cognition and Culture* 7 (2007): 293–312; Peter J. Richerson and Lesley Newson, "Is Religion Adaptive? Yes, No, Neutral. But Mostly We Don't Know," in *The Believing Primate: Scientific, Philosophical and Theological Reflections on the Origin of Religion*, ed. Jeffrey Schloss and Michael Murray (Oxford: Oxford University Press, 2009), 100–17.

40. For recent discussions of these issues, especially in the natural sciences, see Philip Clayton, *Explanation from Physics to Theology: An Essay in Rationality and Religion* (New Haven, CT: Yale University Press, 1989); David-Hillel Ruben, *Explaining Explanation* (London: Routledge, 1990); Gerhard Schurz, "Scientific Explanation: A Critical Survey," *Foundations of Science* 1 (1995): 429–65; Lorenzo Magnani, *Abduction, Reason, and Science: Processes of Discovery and Explanation* (New York: Plenum, 2001).

41. Paul Humphreys, *The Chances of Explanation: Causal Explanation in the Social, Medical, and Physical Sciences* (Princeton, NJ: Princeton University Press, 1989); James Woodward, *Making Things Happen: A Theory of Causal Explanation* (Oxford: Oxford University Press, 2003).

42. Lipton, *Inference to the Best Explanation*, 59–61.

developed by Margaret Morrison.[43] In what follows, we shall look at how each of these relates to the debates about God associated with the "New Atheism."

Causal Explanation

In its simplest form, this holds that to explain A is to determine what causes A. This approach has reemerged as significant in the recent past in relation to the debate about God, in that the realization that the universe had an origin raises the question of whether it can be said to have been "caused."[44] The notion of a static or eternal universe was not seen as demanding a theistic explanation.[45] Theistic explanatory accounts of the origins of the universe hold that the appeal to God as the cause of the universe avoids the potential incoherence implicit in suggesting that the universe simply happened. This is a contested question; it is, however, important to note how the idea of God as a causative explanation has reentered serious debate.

Inference to the Best Explanation

As we noted earlier, the debate here concerns the identification of the best framework for accounting for observed phenomena, without a demand to prove that this is correct. The approach in question sets out a set of criteria—which remain contested in terms of both their identity and priority—by which a set of possible explanations can be assessed. A given explanation is not "proved" to be correct; it is merely shown to be the best presently available.[46] Theistic arguments increasingly suggest that God can be proposed as the best explanation of themes on which the sciences ultimately depend—such as the regularity of nature.

Unitive Explanation

This approach takes several forms. Its basic feature is the demonstration of connections between theories that were initially assumed to have no fundamental connection. To "explain" things is to show how they fit into a bigger picture. The capacity of a theory to "group" such observations—which may include other

43. See Michael Friedman, "Explanation and Scientific Understanding," *Journal of Philosophy* 71 (1974): 5–19; Paul Kitcher, "Explanatory Unification and the Causal Structure of the World," in *Scientific Explanation*, ed. Philip Kitcher and Wesley Salmon (Minneapolis: University of Minnesota Press, 1989), 410–505; Margaret Morrison, *Unifying Scientific Theories: Physical Concepts and Mathematical Structures* (Cambridge: Cambridge University Press, 2000), 192–206.

44. Rem B. Edwards, *What Caused the Big Bang?* (Amsterdam: Rodopi, 2001).

45. See, for example, Albert the Great's arguments against Aristotle on this point in the Middle Ages. Steven Snyder, "Albert the Great: Creation and the Eternity of the World," in *Philosophy and the God of Abraham*, ed. R. James Long (Toronto: Pontifical Institute of Biblical Studies, 1991), 191–202.

46. For the difficulties this raises, see Laurie Calhoun, "The Underdetermination of Theory by Data, 'Inference to the Best Explanation,' and the Impotence of Argumentation," *Philosophical Forum* 27 (1996): 146–60.

theories—is seen as indicative of its reliability. Christian apologists such as G. K. Chesterton and C. S. Lewis developed theistic arguments based on the ability of Christianity to demonstrate a fundamental unity within the natural world, which can be seen as anticipating some aspects of this approach.[47]

The implications for this for the debate about warranted religious belief is clear. In an important recent discussion of this issue, Alvin Plantinga argues that a theistic framework—supremely, that offered by the Christian faith—offers us a conceptual framework which safeguards the reliability (within limits) of human reason.[48] The kind of naturalism advocated by Dawkins, he suggests, is obliged to regard the reliability of human reason simply as a piece of unintended good luck. The Christian doctrine of creation, in marked contrast, holds that God created a natural order governed by immutable laws, and created humans in his image, providing us with faculties that allow us to discover that order by using perception and reason. For Plantinga, this way of thinking led inexorably to the rise of the natural sciences. It is no accident, he remarks, that the "scientific revolution" took place in Christian Europe.

Plantinga is particularly critical of the form of naturalism developed by Dennett. If human beings are products of an unguided process of Darwinian evolution, what grounds do we have for believing that our cognitive faculties are reliable? How can we believe any theories they may lead us to develop? Plantinga takes Dennett to task for a radical lack of consistency. If indeed Darwinism does undermine religion and ethics, it also undermines human rationality—and hence any outcomes of human reason, including Dennett's own naturalist philosophy.

CONCLUSION

So what is the overall relationship of the "New Atheism" to the philosophy of science? The movement is keen to present itself as a bastion of "reason and science," a bulwark of rationalism in the face of rising irrationality within Western society. There are clear echoes here of the agendas of the "science wars" which played such a significant role in American academic culture in the 1990s[49]; this time, however, the enemy of science is not portrayed as the academic left, but as religion. The persistence of religion tends to be interpreted, not as reflecting any fundamental weakness with atheism itself, but as a consequence of a resurgence of irrational ways of thinking. For Dawkins, science is the most noble form of rationality; religion the most irritating form of superstition.

It is difficult to sustain this position in the face of the intense criticism that it has been subjected to in the last five years, some of which have been noted in this

---

47. William Oddie, *Chesterton and the Romance of Orthodoxy: The Making of GKC, 1874–1908* (Oxford: Oxford University Press, 2008); Alister E, McGrath, *The Intellectual World of C. S. Lewis* (Malden, MA: Wiley-Blackwell, 2013), 105–46.

48. Alvin Plantinga, *Science, Religion, and Naturalism: Where the Conflict Really Lies* (New York: Oxford University Press, 2011).

49. Keith M. Ashman and Philip S. Barringer, ed., *After the Science Wars* (London: Routledge, 2001); James R. Brown, *Who Rules in Science? An Opinionated Guide to the Wars* (Cambridge, MA: Harvard University Press, 2001).

essay. The "New Atheism" has made a limited contribution to serious philosophical debate, given its overriding desire to present a simplified, rhetorically effective case for atheism, which causes it to take logical short cuts, misrepresent their opponents, and present occasionally crass accounts of complex philosophical, theological, and scientific debates. There is no doubt that this approach resonates with at least a section of American culture, which prefers precise statements based on empirical grounds.[50] Yet the real discussion continues, attracting little media attention. As media interest in the New Atheism has waned, however, there are encouraging signs of a renewal of interest with the classic questions of philosophical theology.

Perhaps this is just as well. There are serious debates here about the nature of human rationality, the place of science in our society, the intellectual and imaginative dimensions of religion, and the manner in which competing viewpoints can be accommodated and managed in a liberal democracy. The "New Atheism" has raised public interest in the debate about God, yet regrettably seems to have made no significant contributions to the issues underlying it. This is, however, hardly a matter for concern for the wider atheist community, which has already distanced itself from this splinter movement. The important thing is that others continue these discussions, realizing that exploring these questions properly remains integral to our identity of human beings. We must be grateful to Richard Dawkins and his colleagues for renewing public interest in the fundamental questions of the philosophy of religion; yet we must look elsewhere for serious discussion of these themes.

---

50. For the development of such attitudes in its social context, see James Turner, *Without God, Without Creed: The Origins of Unbelief in America* (Baltimore, MD: Johns Hopkins University Press, 1985), 132–40.

MIDWEST STUDIES IN PHILOSOPHY 1976–2013

Vol. I	Studies in the History of Philosophy	February 1976
Vol. II	Studies in the Philosophy of Language *Rev. Ed.*, Contemporary Perspectives in the Philosophy of Language	February 1977
Vol. III	Studies in Ethical Theory	February 1978
Vol. IV	Studies in Metaphysics	February 1979
Vol. V	Studies in Epistemology	February 1980
Vol. VI	Foundations of Analytic Philosophy	1981
Vol. VII	Social and Political Philosophy	1982
Vol. VIII	Contemporary Perspectives on the History of Philosophy	1983
Vol. IX	Causation and Causal Theories	1984
Vol. X	Studies in the Philosophy of Mind	1985
Vol. XI	Studies in Essentialism	1986
Vol. XII	Realism and Anti-Realism	1987
Vol. XIII	Ethical Theory: Character and Virtue	1988
Vol. XIV	Contemporary Perspectives in the Philosophy of Language II	1989
Vol. XV	The Philosophy of the Human Sciences	1990
Vol. XVI	Philosophy and the Arts	1991
Vol. XVII	The Wittgenstein Legacy	1992
Vol. XVIII	Philosophy of Science	1993
Vol. XIX	Philosophical Naturalism	1994
Vol. XX	Moral Concepts	1995
Vol. XXI	Philosophy of Religion	1996
Vol. XXII	Philosophy of the Emotions	1997
Vol. XXIII	New Directions in Philosophy	1998
Vol. XXIV	Life and Death: Metaphysics and Ethics	1999
Vol. XXV	Figurative Language	2001
Vol. XXVI	Renaissance and Early Modern Philosophy	2002
Vol. XXVII	Meaning in the Arts	2003
Vol. XXVIII	The American Philosophers	2004
Vol. XXIX	Free Will and Moral Responsibility	2005
Vol. XXX	Shared Intentions and Collective Responsibility	2006
Vol. XXXI	Philosophy and the Empirical	2007
Vol. XXXII	Truth and its Deformities	2008
Vol. XXXIII	Philosophy and Poetry	2009
Vol. XXXIV	Film and the Emotions	2010
Vol. XXXV	Early Modern Philosophy Reconsidered	2011
Vol. XXXVI	The Concept of Evil	2012
Vol. XXXVII	The New Atheism and Its Critics	2013

Volumes XXIII onwards are available through Wiley Periodicals, Inc. All previous volumes may be available through University of Notre Dame Press.

Contributors

Edward Feser, Department of Philosophy, Pasadena City College
Richard Fumerton, Department of Philosophy, University of Iowa
Gary Gutting, Department of Philosophy, University of Notre Dame
Jonathan L. Kvanvig, Department of Philosophy, Baylor University
Alister E. McGrath, Professor of Theology, Religion, and Education, King's College, London
A.W. Moore, Department of Philosophy, St. Hugh's College, Oxford
Massimo Pigliucci, Philosophy Program, The Graduate Center, City University of New York
Michael Ruse, Department of Philosophy, Florida State University
David Shatz, Department of Philosophy, Yeshiva University
Kenneth A. Taylor, Department of Philosophy, Stanford University
Gregg Ten Elshof, Department of Philosophy, Biola University
Andrew Winer, Department of Creative Writing, University of California, Riverside

Peter A. French is the Lincoln Chair in Ethics and Professor of Philosophy at Arizona State University. He was the founding Director of the Lincoln Center for Applied Ethics from 2000 to 2013. Before that he was the Cole Chair in Ethics, Director of the Ethics Center, and Chair of the Department of Philosophy of the University of South Florida. He was the Lennox Distinguished Professor and Chair of Philosophy at Trinity University, and served as Exxon Distinguished Research Professor in the Center for the Study of Values at the University of Delaware. During his distinguished 48-year career in academia he has also been a professor of philosophy at the University of Minnesota, Dalhousie University, Nova Scotia, and Northern Arizona University. Dr. French earned a BA from Gettysburg College, an MA from the University of Southern California, and a Ph.D. from the University of Miami, and did post-doctoral work at Oxford University. He was awarded a Doctor of Humane Letters (L.H.D.) degree for his work in philosophy and ethics from Gettysburg College in 2006.
Dr. French has an international reputation in ethical and legal theory and in collective and corporate responsibility and criminal liability. He is the author of twenty books including *War and Moral Dissonance; The Virtues of Vengeance; Cowboy Metaphysics; Ethics and College Sports; Corporate Ethics; Responsibility Matters; Collective and Corporate Responsibility; Ethics in Government; The Scope of Morality; Corporations in the Moral Community; The Spectrum of*

Responsibility; Corrigible Corporations and Unruly Laws; and *War and Border Crossings: Ethics When Cultures Clash*. He is a founding editor with Howard Wettstein of *Midwest Studies in Philosophy*, a leading annual book series in analytic philosophy. As a single author, co-author, and editor he has contributed 61 books to the philosophical literature.

Dr. French has lectured at locations around the world. Some of his works have been translated into Chinese, Japanese, German, Italian, French, Serbian, and Spanish. Dr. French also was the editor of the *Journal of Social Philosophy* for 16 years and general editor of the *Issues in Contemporary Ethics* series. He has published scores of articles in the major philosophical and legal journals and reviews, many of which have been anthologized. In 2002 Dr. French was appointed to the Board of Officers of the American Philosophical Association. In 2008 the APA's *Newsletter on Philosophy and Law* dedicated an issue to him.

Howard K. Wettstein is Professor of Philosophy at the University of California, Riverside. He holds a M.A. and Ph.D. from the City University of New York and a B.A. from Yeshiva College. In 2013 his book, *The Significance of Religious Experience*, was published by Oxford University Press. Earlier books include *Has Semantics Rested On a Mistake? and Other Essays* (Stanford University Press, 1991) and *The Magic Prism: An Essay in the Philosophy of Language* (Oxford University Press, 2004). He has edited or co-edited several volumes, including *Themes From Kaplan* and *Diasporas and Exiles: Varieties of Jewish Identity*. He is currently writing a new book on the philosophy of religion.